OFFSETTED

Cooking Sections

OFFSETTED

Cooking Sections

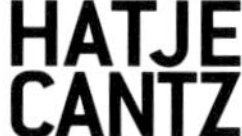

HATJE CANTZ

The trees featured in the exhibition have grown on the unceded
territories of the Canarsie, LenapeHoking, Shinnecock,
Lekawe, Merrick, Munsee Lenape, Wappinger, Matinecock,
Nissaquogue, Setauket, and many others whose memories
and ancestral rights have been erased by the violence of
settler colonialism.

Contents

Preface

Irene Sunwoo

In a windowless room, an offset forest grows. Bathed eerily (and inexplicably) in yellow light, a meandering network of steel poles supports an assortment of tree fragments, cuffed and bolted into place. A heaving palm frond with delicately browned extremities towers overhead. Giant tree slabs stand upright, anthropomorphic obstructions with their grainy guts gloriously exposed. A whole Christmas tree is suspended mid-air, quietly shedding its needles in post-holiday resignation. A spidery expanse of roots juts out low to the ground, tendrils nakedly unfurling in a soilless spectacle not intended for human eyes. Yet this prosthetic forest has been designed precisely for intense scrutiny, its eccentric choreography of tree gestures making visible an invasive global financial system that stealthily mobilizes the environment.

With the immersive installation *Offsetted*, Cooking Sections nods knowingly to a long tradition of collecting and displaying tree matter, a tradition that developed in step with the history of extractive practices. In 17th-century Europe, the xylotheque emerged as a type of cabinet of curiosities: carved to resemble books, wood samples from native and exotic trees opened to hollow interiors stuffed with data, notes, and fragments relevant to the species of each "volume." Less precious, though more enduring, the xylarium continues to provide institutional space for the classification and study of wood specimens, advancing industry, and interdisciplinary scientific research. Both the xylotheque and the xylarium attend to a hybrid delight that is intellectual and sensory as much as it is deeply rooted in colonialist imaginations. Bits of organic material are accumulated, measured and documented, ordered and archived, but also pinched between fingers, probed, rubbed, smelled, and scrutinized by expectant minds eager and empowered to envision other worlds—distant, uncharted, abundant. Such enchantment recalls what Susan Stewart in her analysis of the miniature describes as "the daydream of the microscope"—that is, "of life inside life, of significance multiplied infinitely *within* significance."[1]

The deracinated tree morsels on display in *Offsetted*, however, derail such daydreams. Or rather, they uncover the evolution and implementation of parallel fantasies—namely, the myriad ways that trees have been instrumentalized in urban contexts. Hyperlocal and historical specificity abound in this offset forest, which comprises arboreal odds and ends from sites across the five boroughs of New York City, the original concrete jungle. From the marshes of Staten Island to parks in the Bronx and Brooklyn, from the sidewalks of Queens and Manhattan to the highways, airports, and bridges at the city's edges: each specimen on display has a companion micro-narrative that elucidates its origin. A pin oak branch from the former site of Seneca Village, a settlement of Black residents who were evicted in the 1850s to make way for Central Park. A sprig of gingko from a tree on the site of the Seagram building—vital evidence of the post-war zoning provision that granted architects and developers additional floor space in return for public plazas. A clipping from a magnolia tree in the Bedford-Stuyvesant neighbourhood of Brooklyn, which the local community pushed to have designated a living landmark in the late 1960s to stave off plans for redevelopment. Tree cores from various locations throughout Queens, a 2005 harvest of biological data that facilitated the design of software for translating the environmental "benefits" of trees, such as carbon dioxide reduction and energy conservation, into dollars. If the xylotheque and the xylarium position the materiality of tree matter as both industrial resource and fetish, the fragments in *Offsetted* bring into focus the cultivation of the immaterial value of trees. It is a shape-shifting operation in which the disciplines of the built environment unequivocally play a central role. For this process is, as Cooking Sections' offset forest reminds us, inextricable from the historical and ongoing development of New York City and, invariably, of all cities.

Yet the project also opens up a broader global perspective on the monetization of the environment. It points not only to the transactional capacity of individual trees but also to the potential, and indeed very real, transmutation of the environment at all scales—forests, mountains, rivers—through speculative stewardship: that is, from ecosystems of interconnected life to agents conscripted into a system of property and industrial entanglements. "Challenging the imposed obligation on trees to perform as speculative assets and environmental mitigators," Cooking Sections thus seeks to (re)establish "the right of trees *not* to serve as carbon offsets, allowing them to *just be trees*." In *Offsetted*, this philosophical through line dismantles opaque and limited notions of sustainability and carbon offsetting tactics that ultimately preserve the rights of capital. At a moment even when tree-stuffed balconies, roofs, courtyards, and sidewalks blur the line between virtue and excess, and as environmental collapse becomes ever more unambiguous and palpable, the offset forest charges architects, urbanists, and designers to radically reimagine the built environment, from fragment to whole.

1   S. Stewart, *On Longing: Narratives of the Miniature, the Gigantic, the Souvenir, and the Collection* (Durham, NC: Duke University Press, 1992), p. 54.

Ground Proof:
Trees as Evidence of Inhabitation

Paulo Tavares

What strikes me about *Offsetted* is that this is a botanical garden, right in the gallery. The trees are testimonies to stories that call forth a different understanding of trees and of nature itself, that call for trees to be recognized as rights-bearing entities. I think that is very profound and interesting to see. And, to my mind, it raises two questions. First, what kind of jurisprudence of the rights of nature, or what I would call non-human rights, is being demanded? One of the first and most important books for that jurisprudence is *Should Trees have Standing?* by Christopher Stone,[1] which discusses whether trees should be allowed to enter court, whether trees have the right to speak in court, whether they have rights. That raises the second question: Who are the advocates of trees? Who can speak on their behalf? Space, the environment, the city, is a right. And if we understand space, the city, the environment as a right, spatial practitioners are somehow the advocates of such rights. We need to find interesting ways of visualizing and telling those histories, so that those rights can be upheld.

My practice is very much oriented around spatial practice as advocacy. In 2016, my practice was invited by a group of indigenous people in Brazil, the Xavante, who were displaced from their land by the military government in 1966 so that the government could build large-scale agribusiness. They were removed by the Brazilian Air Force to a new site 500 km away from their traditional territory. They filed a lawsuit against the government for reparations, and they asked us if we could provide evidence, if we could help them show that they had been living on that land for hundreds of years.

We started to investigate certain types of archives made by the state itself that documented the process of conquest of their land. At that time, that process was portrayed as a civilizing mission. It was portrayed as a process of modernization, and featured in different illustrated magazines as state propaganda, celebrating how Brazil was conquering its interior.

We began with images of the villages of this group, the Xavante, in the very state archives that were documenting the process of the state arriving on their land, because that was the only sort of archival register of the ancient villages. These documents were seen as documents of civilization, but they are documents of barbarism. They were seen as documents of modernity, but they are documents of colonialism. We began using those documents as evidence of that process of violence, in violation of these people. We did a sort of "image archaeology" to rebuild settlements that do not exist anymore because they have been displaced or destroyed by the government. We reconstructed them using different archaeological methods based on images. The villages themselves have an arc-like shape, and you see a kind of consistent pattern, a consistent urban-architectural pattern.

As part of this image archaeology, we looked at a series of recently declassified satellite images produced by the USA in the 1960s, 1970s, and 1980s as part of a secret programme during the Cold War to map the whole Earth. We wanted to find evidence of those villages in the images. They are images of the Earth, but they are also historical documents—and we were able to identify several shapes that were very similar to the arc-shaped villages. We found several footprints of those villages in those images, meaning that they were so robust, they were so ancient, that they had inscribed themselves on the Earth. The footprint of the images was very similar to the footprints we had found in the image archaeology that we had done with the photographs from the conquest of the territory.

What was most striking when looking at a contemporary image of the village is how that patch of trees follows the architecture of the village. This area is now a soy farm that has been occupied by white settlers, who destroyed practically everything that remained of the forest. But, for some reason, the landowner left those trees intact, maybe because they are so old, they are so robust, they are so productive, that even the landowner decided it was worth keeping them—and they follow the shape of the village. They are the remains of the village architecture. We travelled frequently to meet and work with the elders. The elders are the survivors of the genocide, and they have a very sophisticated understanding of the landscape and of the local botany. Even if the landscape has changed a lot, the elders can guide you because they have a deep memory of the territory and can do what we call the "ground proof."

If you look at the contemporary images, you can see that there is a patch of forest that grew within the very same footprint as the village. This is the major political cultural centre of these people from when they used to live on this land. You can see the cemetery, and you can also see a botanic formation around the encampment. By comparing with the arc shape in the satellite image, you see that some trees have grown in the same layout as the architectural layout of the village. There are a bunch of trees or botanic formations that follow the footprint: those trees are the ruins of the village, the remains of the village, the cultural product of the village.

The city is a space saturated with urbanity, with layers upon layers of ruins—ruins that remain alive because we inherited the historical fabric. We need to understand the trees in the Xavante village as architecture. We need to understand those trees as a cultural product, we need to understand those trees as an architectural monument. The Xavante are one of the few indigenous people that have managed to exert their right to return to their land. But when the Brazilian government legalized the Xavante's land, they ignored the cultural, political, and theological centre of the territory where those archaeological sites are located. A big part of the Xavante's territory, a big part of their history continues to be expropriated. We are writing a petition to the Institute of Historic and Artistic heritage of Brazil, and UNESCO, so those trees can be recognized as archaeology, so those trees can be recognized as an architectural monument, so those trees can be recognized as ruins. As ruins, they need to be protected.

This also relates to the question that *Offsetted* is posing: How can we challenge the idea that we have of nature? With trees as one of the most symbolic elements of nature, how can we question the notion of nature that we inherited from Western epistemology, which sees nature only as an object or as a commodity, or as a resource detached from the human? How can we find devices and mediums of advocacy in order to intervene, not only in the law, but also in the archive of architectural history itself, and open up a different space to decolonize the way in which we understand architecture? The petition to protect the rights of trees connects to the idea that we need to see nature in a totally different light.

1   C. D. Stone, *Should Trees Have Standing?: Law, Morality, and the Environment,* 3rd edition
     (New York: Oxford University Press, 2010).

Offsetted

Cooking Sections

TREES HAVE NO VALUE

Once referred to as "America's greenest mayor," Michael Bloomberg launched MillionTreesNYC (MTNYC) in 2007.[1] This project, initiated as the subprime mortgage crisis began to garner public attention, ventured to protect citizens from the effects of air pollution and climate change. Aiming to add 1 million trees to the city canopy, MTNYC was at the time considered the largest urban afforestation effort in the world. Highlighting the benefits of improved air quality, more shade, and less energy consumption, the majority of the trees were planted in low-income neighbourhoods with little tree cover and high rates of asthma. The aspiration was to increase the city's "urban resilience" in times of devalued real estate assets and ecological collapse. The project was accompanied by an extensive community-based survey that invited people to document trees in their neighbourhoods, involving the community in the process. Volunteers contributed 12,000 hours of their own time, to inventory the city's trees. With that help, every single tree in the city was assigned an economic value based on its "environmental services" (i.e. the services the trees provide to humans). It is difficult to argue against afforestation, but why is the economic value of every single tree so relevant? Who benefits from that data?

Today, financial quantification has become a dominant theory and practice in conservation. The New York Street Tree Map (NYSTM), released online in early 2017 by the Department of Parks and Recreation, is deeply embedded in the financial quantification of trees and reveals a less than totally benevolent agenda behind urban greening. Despite the publicly stated goal of maintenance and care for the trees in the city, the argument for the NYSTM is to "provide tools for developers."[2] The 689,227 listings provide much more information than the species, trunk diameter, and exact address of each plant.[3] Utilizing the Tree Carbon Calculator (TCC), a federally approved spreadsheet developed by the Center for Urban Forest Research, the yearly capacity of stormwater interception, energy conservation, air pollutant removal, and carbon dioxide reduction defines each tree in the database. This information allows the TCC to accurately calculate the annual financial benefits provided by each tree, benefits that developers or industrialists can buy to "neutralize" the detrimental effect of their own activities.[4] The extraction of value from trees does not imply the subtraction of physical matter (sap, bark, leaves, roots, or oil extracts), but centres rather in keeping all that materiality intact and in place.

Brooklyn relies on 177,873 trees worth US$27,460,003.44. Queens has 237,027, which together are worth US$39,516,844.93 per year in environmental benefits. Throughout the five boroughs of New York City, all mapped trees annually provide US$102,768,094.84. Marked with a fully articulated and mathematically sound price tag, trees can become objects of transaction and "start" to offset the environmental damage of development. Planting trees is thus part of an emerging and carefully engineered government of financial flows: the cartography of street trees offers a dataset for the calculation of these "environmental services." With the help of software, these services can then be turned into "financial gains."

NYC trees are branded as an "urban forest." But more than just greening the city, they are an "offset forest:" the city's trees have acquired the mission to exonerate environmental destruction. This circulation of greening capital to mitigate architectural development is indebted to George H. W. Bush's No Net Loss policy, passed in 1989. According to No Net Loss, any development that destroys natural habitats (especially wetlands, streams, and vernal pools) has to be recouped by the restoration of an "equivalent" landscape elsewhere.[5] The net amount of biodiversity is meant to remain "the same" in terms of surface, quality, or quantity. Like the trading of air rights to build higher developments, for each acre of lost wetland, for instance, at least one acre should be created or restored. As we documented in our project *Speculations on Disappearance* (2016), the possibility of disappearance has itself become crucial to this form of speculation, where rare ecologies and unstable habitats become especially valuable—or profitable—as an environmental asset.[6] Following this logic, the first wetland mitigation scheme in New York was set up in Saw Mill Creek, Staten Island, in 2017, and is still available to offset wetland destruction elsewhere. Similarly, in the case of New York street trees, the "environmental services" they provide can be sold off by the city to compensate for environmental destruction elsewhere. What is conserved is not just trees that improve air quality in the city, but also real estate capital flows.

This one-for-one logic becomes even more perverse when the idea of preservation gets thrown into the mix. That is, a developer can destroy a forest for the construction of a condominium on site A and pay the owner of an equivalent number of trees on site B to merely preserve them—rather than plant new ones. Air pollution can be legitimized as long as it is traded for the planting and maintenance of trees that absorb the equivalent amount of carbon dioxide. The US government has recently

updated its social cost of carbon to US$51 dollars a ton, which refers to
the total social and environmental benefits that accrue from avoiding the
emission of one ton of carbon dioxide, or, alternatively, the damage done
by releasing that ton of carbon dioxide.[7] Once these equivalences are set,
trading can easily commence. Offsetting becomes a financial practice that
swaps destruction *here* with reconstruction or preservation *there*.

In the same decade that saw the advent of No Net Loss, concepts
of "biodiversity" and "sustainable development" also began to appear
in the literature and practice of financial ecology. In the 1980s, biologists shifted from providing facts about the natural world (already social
constructions themselves) to speaking of nature's "values."[8] This subjec-
tive valuation of nature was readily manipulable by different economic
interests. There are many ways of making a valuation, but unlike the
concept of wilderness, the moment "natural variety" appeared—natural
variety being that different species contribute differently to the ecological balance of a habitat—the gradients of environmental specificity easily
became something that can be compared, exchanged, lost, gained, depleted,
restored, quantified, and scientized. Metaphors such as the "balance of
nature" came to disguise poor understandings of ecology.[9]

Environmentality—the complex control over human–environment
relations—has inflamed contemporary power struggles between polluting
and cleansing sites in the global North and South, which have only worsened since the first carbon offsetting schemes were formalized in the 1997
Kyoto Protocol.[10] Air pollution in the global North was accepted as a
lesser evil of modernization if compensated by "sustainable" afforestation
programmes in the global South. Rich nations became entitled to pollute
as long as impoverished nations protected their forests, or expropriated
land to green the planet. This logic reinstated abusive colonial power
dynamics through a pseudo-environmentalist discourse. In one
of the first post-Kyoto offsetting projects, US-based Applied Energy Services promised to plant millions of trees on the highland hills of western
Guatemala in exchange for permission to construct a large, coal-burning
power station in Connecticut.[11] This "participatory" planting project,
branded as *Mi Bosque*, was calculated to absorb as much carbon dioxide as would be produced by the power station over its lifetime. It was
meant to sequester between 15.5 and 16.3 million tons of carbon over
40 years, but, in reality, only 270,000 tons of carbon were offset by the
forest over the first ten years.[12] Attempts to neutralize carbon footprints
through corporate social responsibility only exacerbate the still-colonial
relationships between rich and poor, between high carbon emitting
nations' right to pollute and enjoy and low carbon emitting nations'
obligation to cleanse and labour.[13]

From No Net Loss to bioassets, what is emerging appears to be a new
green space race. Nations and companies are competing to appropriate

the last fragments of "untapped" forest that can provide the greatest
density of "environmental services." Eco-utilities and forest bonds boost
the neoliberal valuation of space as companies and governments determine how to classify and demarcate it. The main challenge for this form
of speculation, however, is how and whether to make offset calculations
standard and universal. In order to securitize ecology, the definition of
the "value" of each tree is crucial. For that, standard measurements and
quantifications of forests' properties are necessary. However, transnational agreement on valuing units has yet to become a reality, which in
any case would not solve the ethics of pricing nature to protect it.

Pierre Bourdieu argues that there are three forms of capital—
economic, social, and cultural—and that value can be translated from
one category to the other by means of economic conversions.[14] Ernst
Friedrich Schumacher further articulated this morphology when, after
the 1973 oil crisis and the accessibility of fossil fuels was threatened for
Western powers, he posited the idea of *natural capital*.[15] Then at the
end of the 20th century, Paul Hawken and Amory and Hunter Lovins
expanded natural capital into the notion of *natural capitalism*, showing
how to make sense of nature by making money, and arguing that environmental sensitivity is necessary to shareholders for business reasons.[16]
Natural capitalism did not refer to capitalism as a *natural* phenomenon,
as was misunderstood at the time, but as something embedded in the
trading of nature. Natural capitalism implies that the environment is full
of assets waiting for human stewards to make the most of them.

In New York, citizens are invited to participate in a stewardship
scheme for "tree care activities." Popular city-wide, these activities are
meant to enhance relations between humans and trees, provide outdoor
leisure, and support communities' mental health through gardening. Tree
carers do not make such commendable efforts for profit, and yet their
dedication is being cashed in on by others, most probably without them
even knowing. Under the values of stewardship—the act of taking care of
something—the environment is seen as a socially significant space providing resources and/or services in and of itself. At the same time, these
social values generate financial value that is traded behind closed doors.[17]
The rise of the principles of stewardship in the past decades reflects the
essence of a neoliberal economy: protecting the environment in order
to extract value from it.[18] The problem here is not that people need to
care more for the environment. As Maria Puig de la Bellacasa argues, the
problem is in recognizing what it means and how to care.[19] Advocacy for
trees for the city is focused on controlling the object of care, rather than
caring about why trees need to be there. This is parallel to the so-called
"Cousteauization" of the oceans: a popular movement to cultivate public
interest in the ocean's biota, through figures like Captain Jacques Cous-
teau, in order to generate financial support for further marine research

and governmental and/or corporate stewardship of marine resources. In this way, neoliberal environmental conservation can extract even more value by "protecting" nature in order to further boost its speculative value, be it real estate potential or prospective natural resources.[20] This perverse logic of profiteering from environmental protection is what Bram Büscher and Robert Fletcher frame as "accumulation by conservation."[21]

The double agenda of calculating the carbon footprint for each tree, and the services it provides, exposes how every tree in New York is connected to a very specific architectural site of destruction. Trees might be purifying the air on-site, but the financial value of each tree does not stay in front of citizens' houses. Quite the opposite. Tree planting in low-income areas is just another wave of what David Gissen refers to as "environmental gentrification," in reference to a park improvement process initiated in NYC during the 1970s, which enhanced urban nature at the cost of pricing people out of their homes and neighbourhoods.[22] With offsetting as a means of environmental mitigation, architecture has acquired the agency to destroy, displace, and replicate natural landscapes miles away from their original location. It is thus the responsibility of architects and realtors to de-quantify the "value" of trees instead of profiteering from them and what they offset. Neither energy-efficient glazing nor LEED certificates will insulate humanity from the effects of the climate crisis; instead, architects must be responsible towards the sites they are asked to build in, engaging with the consequences of damage before externalizing or offsetting it. It is time to imagine new forms of architecture and environmental care that include more-than-human worlds.

NATURE'S NEW TERMS

According to the United Nations Framework Convention on Climate Change, deforestation is the conversion of forest to non-forest.[23] Although logical, the difference between the two is not so clear-cut, especially as forests are usually imagined to be merely a large group of trees, and non-forests to be a lack thereof. Industrial monoculture plantations with their cloned trees thus fall into the category of "forest."[24] Sweden, for instance, is one of the most forested countries in Europe, with 70 per cent tree-cover, while only 8.7 per cent of that area is *urskog* (ancient woodland, the ur-forest).[25] The rest is just a plantation. True forests do not need to be polyculture, multigenerational, and not preclude the co-existence of humans and more-than-humans in space. And yet, forests are also continually constructed, especially by humans. Paulo Tavares describes the "cultural forest," where every tree is a sign, a trace of different forms of inhabitation and interaction between humans and more-than-humans (enriched anthropogenic soils, earthen mounds, raised agricultural fields, cultivated forest islands, concentrated clusters of palm species) that keep the forest alive.[26]

In Europe, during the Middle Ages, "forest" was a juridical term for land placed off limits, untouchable, reserved for the king's sole pleasure and recreation. Once a region had been "afforested," or declared a forest, the populace could neither cultivate nor exploit it.[27] Today, ambivalent carbon offset plantations return to these exclusive roots of the forest. Worse, plantations are understood as the solution to deforestation, despite their role in accelerating it.[28] Afforestation projects by Scandinavian and Dutch banks in Mozambique expose how monocrop trees displace local villagers and exhaust their agricultural soil—all so "green-investing" companies can become carbon neutral through net zero emissions schemes.[29]

Global outcry is pushing back against these false equations. Work on the ground by different scholars and activists, such as Kristen Lyons and David Ssemwogerere, has been crucial in exposing these postcolonial relations and in actually changing policy—for instance, in persuading the Swedish Energy Agency to divest from carbon offset plantations in Uganda in 2020.[30] With environmental offsets, loss is accepted as unavoidable collateral damage to urbanization and progress. Yet this loss is described in terms of the least of all possible evils by changing "yes loss" into "no net loss."[31] Equivalent to net zero, the no net loss policy legitimizes the acceptance of loss; it takes for granted that nature can be quantified, and that loss can be *nettified*. In other words, the logic of compensation has urbanized damage. Under fallacies such as "making space for nature"—the British government slogan to open up the carbon offset market—the assigning of value to natural landscapes before they are urbanized is what makes it possible to destroy, offset, and, arguably, restore the damage.[32] It is assumed that all development inevitably results in ecological damage, and that new "nature sites" need to be created or improved to mitigate that damage.

In the field of law, "damage" is understood as the monetary value of what was lost or withheld, but also that which is given to repair a cost—financial compensation for someone who has suffered an injury or has been harmed by someone else's wrongful act, as well as an acknowledgement of responsibility. Spatial offsets, however, are directly entangled with the offsetting, and obfuscation, of responsibility. As María Gutiérrez remarks, even if spatial offsetting was environmentally sensitive, it is not clear yet who is accountable if, for instance, the mitigation forest catches fire or succumbs to a disease, releasing all the "stored carbon" back into the atmosphere.[33] Environmental mitigation and holding trees accountable as a solution is still quite nebulous.

While accountability remains vague, the language for describing all of the possible environmental investments has become more specific—a new lexicon has arisen in the world of ecological reparation and natural capital. Global financial institutions—like the European Investment Bank, World Bank, Environment Bank, International Monetary Fund, Asian Development Bank, and a litany of other national banks and pension funds—all require a new vocabulary to manage their environmental assets. Nature's new terms describe speculative forms of investment, including carbon credits, carbon sinks, carbon offsets, carbon trade-offs, carbon footprints, carbon taxes, carbon funds and blue carbon. Such modes of financial exchange have, in turn, created new forms of violence: green grabbing, blue grabbing, accumulation by conservation, accumulation by decarbonization, accumulation by encroachment, accumulation by displacement, or the making of conservation refugees. Even the UN has a glossary of terms and units to quantify/mitigate climate catastrophe through the carbon market.[34]

Despite trying to address the problems of the Capitalocene, the search for net zero or negative emissions often increases the risk of people being the ones offsetted by green investments. Net zero is not zero; it is the illusion of taking action while doing little to change business as usual.[35] A majority of polluting governments and corporations use the phrase to evade responsibility, shift burdens, disguise climate inaction, and, in some cases, even to scale up fossil fuel extraction, burning, and emissions.[36] Natural capital has contributed to an imagination of nature as something dependent on complex equations, confusing eco-liberal greenwashing with serious efforts at rewilding, afforestation, ecotourism, biodiversity conservation, and environmental stewardship. However, the cynical imposition of greenness can backfire. In the USA, residents in cities from New York to Detroit to Los Angeles have literally uprooted street trees planted without neighbourhood consultation.[37] At a financial level, new forms of investee activism—carbon discrediting, carbon divestment, and climate-related asset stranding—are creating new tools to oppose the carbon market.[38]

With growing demands to respond to the climate emergency, economic transactions between nature and the built environment are being constantly renegotiated. The New York City Street Tree Map has become a global reference for other cities that want to map, quantify, and trade the environmental services that each specimen can deliver, including Chicago, Washington DC, San Francisco, Los Angeles, and even London and Melbourne. As governments and institutions embrace offsetting for destruction-based conservation efforts, there is an urgent need to change the current paradigm and tackle the sources of pollution and damage rather than mitigating their consequences.

Offsetted continues a body of work exploring neo-imperial/neo-liberal forms of extraction that began with *The Empire Remains Shop* in 2016—where the role of monoculture forestry, species banking, and pension fund investments as post-plantation economies in former colonies were investigated in "Speculations on disappearance," "The forest does not employ me anymore," and "An old world in a former new world."[39] *Offsetted* was first conceived as a lecture, Resilience, at Storefront for Art & Architecture, New York (2017), and a performance for Performa17, Making Room for Action. The *Offsetted* exhibition traced 41 trees in New York that have displaced communities or have been used as protest tools to keep people in place. Curated by Irene Sunwoo, it also included a public discussion on environmental justice and the rights of trees, hosted at e-flux the same year.[40]

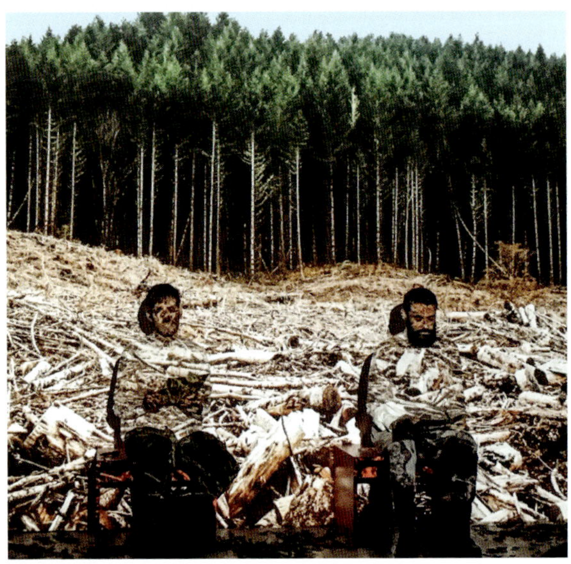

In parallel to the *Offsetted* exhibition in New York, we ran a postgraduate studio at the Royal College of Art, School of Architecture, in London to develop spatial pedagogies that respond to the financialization of the (more and more built) environment. The thematic strands included *Banking Nature: Speculation on Disappearing Spaces* (2016/17), *Financially Built Environments: The Architecture of Carbon Discredits* (2017/18), and *Offsetting the Offshore: On the Illusion, Delusion and Dilution of Waterfronts* (2018/19). This three-year pedagogical framework investigated ways in which speculation on the disappearance of natural spaces is entangled with global financial flows, mitigation of environmental damage, and urban transformation.

Against the continuous erosion of human and more-than-human ecologies, the studio developed counter-financial narratives to explore de-quantified forms of care. Heather Davis remarks how we must learn to accept all kinds of strange life forms, human and non-human, towards which we generate care, compassion, and commitment.[41] In that regard, Davis understands queerness in times of toxicity as the way to provide care and support structures that can allow behavioural plasticity—strengthening the ability of species to respond creatively to a highly changeable and unpredictable world. Along these lines, the studio explored building forms of familial care that could enhance this plasticity; forms that are not bound by biology, forms that generate a sense of responsibility for non-human progeny.

Over its duration, almost 40 students were asked to reimagine inhabitation through such forms of care in spaces affected by deforestation, afforestation, flooding, fracking, carbon emissions trading, drainage, or toxic waste. Research methodologies revolved around mapping contested boundaries, stakeholders, and interscalar relationships to help understand the complex systems in which offsetting mechanisms operate. Following Deborah Bird Rose's analysis of the rich diversity of relationships and agents that make up human lives and lifeworlds, the studio investigated ideas of natural care within the built environment. Aiming to de-centre the human while recognizing its role in the consumption of landscapes, students focused on how other species care. As anthropologist Nicholas Kawa studies in the Amazon, more-than-humans supporting each other are indeed essential in the creation and existence of ecological communities: from seed-dispersing birds, rodents, and winged pollinators to soil microbes and decaying bodies, all contribute humic matter and release nutrients crucial to the forest's perpetuation.[42] In Kristina Lyons's terms, caring for a forest might mean letting the forest cultivate us.[43]

With no other geographic or thematic constraint, students could choose their site of study and develop the graphic language to best unpack the interconnections between human and more-than-human stakeholders at ten different scales, from the microscopic to the planetary. Loopholes and legal tactics were sought as the new tools for spatial practitioners to take advantage of grey areas as spaces of opportunity.[44] The studio also asked students to devise an energy strategy that would bypass the need to mitigate pollution. New proposals included "on-site offsetting," as well as inflatable and gravity-based systems that would allow projects to run off-grid.[45]

Apart from the four pieces included in this book (pages 58, 86, 98, 122), many others helped expand the discussion around offset ecologies and the back-side of technologies that push communities into offsetting schemes.[46] "Carbon reserves" are promoted as a benefit, while also acting as a market trap those same carbon owners cannot escape. This parallels the neoliberal conservation efforts behind the Ishpingo–Tambococha–Tiputini (ITT) protocol, an invention of Ecuador's government to make global actors pay to keep the Yasuni oil reserve in the ground, as Pablo Solón problematizes.[47] By quantifying the potential carbon absorption of the forest on top of the oil field, this protocol nonetheless capitalized on unavoidable exploitation and destruction happening elsewhere.

Climate change is not only about human hubris, Françoise Vergès warns, but is the result of the long history of colonialism and racial capitalism, whereby "Man" can invent a mechanical, technical solution to any problem he encounters, at the expense of racialized and dispossessed peoples.[48] Vergès notes how companies like ArborGen and Futuragene, leaders in genetically engineered eucalyptus, develop "superior growth" trees for the next generation of "profitable forests." Eucalyptus are not to blame for settling faster than other species, but when engineered for even faster growth and planted in higher concentrations, *their* contribution to the depletion of water and biodiversity loss becomes more apparent. And yet, Payment for Environmental Services programmes insist that these and other trees make forest-dependent communities and forest peoples the "big beneficiaries" of carbon neutrality. As Jutta Kill notes, trade in ecosystem services needs destruction to continue: without destruction, there is nothing to offset.[49]

The 41 portraits of New York City trees that structure this book tell the stories of *Offsetted* through the logs, branches, leaves, and cores that were presented in the exhibition. Mixed among them, a series of essays and speculative case studies unpack how environmental mitigation and displacement occur similarly beyond the boundaries of New York City, the leading financial centre in the world. Street trees across the Bronx, Brooklyn, Manhattan, Queens, and Staten Island are just the tip of an iceberg, hinting at the massive speculation on natural capital that is happening worldwide.

Sophisticated politics of planting have contributed to the design of environments hostile to humans and more-than-humans, both in and outside the city, throughout history. The plan to evict formerly enslaved people from the land that would become Central Park echoes in the violence of designating an orchid-protection zone in Calais, France, to discourage asylum seekers from setting up camp.[50] Donald Trump promising accessible green development along the Hudson mirrors the displacement following the construction of one of his golf courses on the "wastelands" of the Scottish coast.[51] Embracing stinky "invasive" trees to reduce heat islands in Manhattan parallels the protection of post-industrial ruins as ecological habitats.[52] Buying out coastal properties to restore the wetlands in Staten Island resonates with the removal of dairy pastures to bring back the wetlands in Aotearoa New Zealand.[53]

Violence does not come without resistance. Communities have fiercely fought for the right of their trees to stay on, be it in their street, city, or forest. From the Chipko movement to Hattie Carthan and UP-ROSE, the different forms of grassroots activism compiled in this book remind us of the importance, and non-monetary value, of trees, as well as of the inventive bottom-up tactics deployed to keep them, and their lovers, standing in place. To appreciate and honour trees for what they are, and not what they are worth, often means just leaving them alone. If we are truly devoted to multi-species cohabitation, we would be better off managing human behaviour than the performance of trees.[54] Allowing trees to care for themselves resists the suggestion of trees or land as idle (non-productive) in favour of idleness as a form of non-quantifiable social productivity.[55] Otherwise, trees—regardless of whether they are in the USA, Bolivia, Scandinavia, Uganda, the UK, or Nigeria—can only ever be seen as ineffective yet uncontrollable, as members of the living dead.[56]

Drawing together larger struggles, this book aims to assemble a new set of epistemologies, questions, and possibilities, to interrupt the property-based legal status of nature, and to spark changes in environmental law.[57] *Offsetted* weaves together cases of environmental justice in New York with resistance to conservation-led displacement in African forests, Latin American plains, European border fens, and wetlands in the South Pacific.

The different cases in this book conclude with a new legal framework on the rights of trees developed in collaboration with environmental rights expert Mari Margil. It expands on the question of how to transform Western legal systems to become *for* the people and *for* nature, as opposed to *against* people and *against* nature.[58] The new public ordinance at the end of this book aspires to do that, moving from the discussion of personhood towards an insistence on naturehood. New York is, in effect, a highly developed experiment in capitalism, and thus it is also just the place where the shift from neoliberal approaches to different forms of tree appreciation may be possible.

London, 2022—a year carbon emissions are expected to reach yet another record high

1   B. Hennelly, The mayor's money: Bloomberg pressed on offshore investments, *WNYC News*, 24 April 2010.

2   New York City Street Tree Map, https://tree-map.nycgovparks.org/tree-map/learn (accessed 17 September 2021).

3   All figures from New York City Street Tree Map, 1 September 2021. For updated stats, see https://tree-map.nycgovparks.org (accessed 17 September 2021).

4   TCC is the only tool approved by the California Climate Action Registry's Urban Forest Project Reporting Protocol for quantifying carbon dioxide sequestration from tree-planting projects.

5   Cooking Sections, Speculations on disappearance, *The Empire Remains Shop* (New York: Columbia Books on Architecture and the City, 2018), p. 93.

6   *Ibid.*, p. 97.

7   I. Lippert, Corporate carbon footprinting as techno-political practice, in *The Carbon Fix: Forest Carbon, Social Justice, and Environmental Governance* (S. Paladino and S. J. Fiske, eds) (New York: Routledge, 2017), p. 120. Value of US social cost of carbon as of March 2021.

8   D. Takacs, *The Idea of Biodiversity: Philosophies of Paradise* (Baltimore, OH: Johns Hopkins University Press, 1996), p. 5.

9   Takacs, *The Idea of Biodiversity*, pp. 27 and 107.

10 A. Agrawal, *Environmentality: Technologies of Government and the Making of Subjects* (Durham, NC: Duke University Press, 2005), pp. 1–2.

11 "History of Carbon Offsetting and Carbon Trading," EBSCOHost, http://connection.ebscohost.com/science/carbon-offsetting/history-carbon-offsetting-and-carbon-trading (accessed 18 June 2017).

12 C. Lang, How a forestry offset project in Guatemala allowed emissions in the US to increase, *REDD Monitor*, 9 October 2009.

13 E. Rosser, Offsetting and the consumption of social responsibility, *Washington University Law Review*, 89 (2011): 28–29.

14 P. Bourdieu, The forms of capital, in *Handbook of Theory and Research for the Sociology of Education* (J. G. Richardson, ed.) (New York: Greenwood, 1986), pp. 241–242.

15 E. F. Schumacher, Introduction, in *Small is Beautiful: A Study of Economics as if People Mattered* (London: Vintage Books, 1993).

16 P. Hawken, A. Lovins, and H. Lovins, *Natural Capitalism: Creating the Next Industrial Revolution* (Boston, MA: Little, Brown & Co, 1999), pp. xvii–xviii.

17 P. E. Steinberg, *The Social Construction of the Ocean* (Cambridge: Cambridge University Press, 2001), p. 176.

18 The emergence of sustainable resource extraction practices occurred in the mid-1990s, with 'sustainable certifications', such as those by the Forest Stewardship Council (1993) and Marine Stewardship Council (1996), which regulate exploitation of natural resources in a more responsible way. Yet the tools and mechanisms by which this is done have been heavily criticized, as the regulators tend to be permissive in order to ensure they will be called back by companies to certify projects and sites in the future.

19 M. Puig de la Bellacasa, *Matters of Care: Speculative Ethics in More Than Human Worlds* (Minneapolis, MI: University of Minnesota Press, 2017), pp. 6–7.

20 Steinberg, *The Social Construction of the Ocean*, p. 178; G. Leddy, Televisuals and environmentalism: The dark side of marine resource protection as global thinking, paper presented at *Annual Meeting of the Association of American Geographers*, Charlotte, NC, 9–13 April 1996.

21 B. Büscher and R. Fletcher, Accumulation by conservation, *New Political Economy*, 20(2) (2015): 1–26.

22 D. Gissen, *Manhattan Atmospheres: Architecture, the Interior Environment, and Urban Crisis* (Minneapolis, MI: University of Minnesota Press, 2014), p. 29

23 The United Nations Framework Convention on Climate Change is an international environmental treaty, negotiated and signed by 154 states at the United Nations Conference on Environment and Development (UNCED), Rio de Janeiro, June 1992. See also the IPCC Special Report *Land Use, Land-Use Change, and Forestry* (IPCC, 2000), and the report *Definitions*

and Methodological Options to Inventory Emissions from Direct Human-induced Degradation of Forests and Devegetation of Other Vegetation Types (IPCC, 2003).

24 Food and Agriculture Organization of the United Nations, Forest, *Comparative framework and Options for Harmonization of Definitions*, http://www.fao.org/3/y4171e/y4171e10.htm (accessed 17 September 2021).

25 Swedish Environmental Protection Agency, https://www.skogssverige.se/en (accessed 17 September 2021).

26 P. Tavares, *An Architectural Botany* (2018–ongoing). Collaboration with ethnobotanist William Balée reading the Ka'apor heritage in the Amazon. Paulo Tavares recognizes the rights of nature as a result of structural processes of violence. He has worked to defend Amazonian trees and their people, identifying specimens as integral evidence of indigenous existence. See Paulo Tavares, p.13 in this volume.

27 O. Rackham, *The History of the Countryside* (London: Weidenfeld & Nicolson, 1986).

28 Büscher and Fletcher, Accumulation by conservation, p. 20.

29 "Net zero" describes the idea that by increasing the amount of carbon dioxide absorbed from the atmosphere—most commonly by planting trees—to "compensate" for ongoing emissions, the net total quantity of emissions is reduced to zero, even while continuing to pollute as usual. Cooking Sections, An old new world in a former new world, *The Empire Remains Shop* (New York: Columbia Books on Architecture and the City, 2018), pp. 240–241.

30 K. Lyons and D. Ssemwogerere, Not seeing the forest for the trees: How plantation forestry for carbon offsets in Uganda fails people and climate, p.110 in this volume.

31 J. Sibbing, *Nowhere Near No-Net-Loss* (Reston, VA: National Wildlife Federation), https://www.nwf.org/~/media/PDFs/Wildlife/Nowhere_Near_No-Net-Loss.pdf (accessed 17 September 2021).

32 UK Department for Environment, Food & Rural Affairs, *Making Space for Nature* (London: Defra, 2010).

33 M. Gutiérrez, Forest carbon sinks prior to REDD: A brief history of their role in the clean development mechanism, in *The Carbon Fix: Forest Carbon, Social Justice, and Environmental Governance* (S. Paladino and S. J. Fiske, eds) (New York: Routledge, 2017), p. 62.

34 UNFCCC, *Glossary of Climate Change Acronyms and Terms*, https://unfccc.int/process-and-meetings/the-convention/glossary-of-climate-change-acronyms-and-terms (accessed 17 September 2021).

35 C. Lang, Net zero is not zero, *REDD Monitor*, 28 June 2021.

36 Action Aid, *Corporate Accountability*, 2011, https://www.actionaid.org.uk/sites/default/files/doc_lib/the_real_asda_price.pdf (accessed 17 September 2021); Friends of the Earth International, Global Campaign to Demand Climate Justice; Third World Network, https://twn.my (accessed 17 September 2021); WhatNext?, *'Not Zero: How "Net-Zero" Targets Disguise Climate Inaction*, 2020, https://whatnext.org/research_pubs/not-zero-how-net-zero-targets-disguise-climate-inaction/ (accessed 17 September 2021).

37 B. Mock, Why Detroit residents pushed back against tree-planting, *Bloomberg* News, 11 January 2019.

38 See Carbon Tracker, https://carbontracker.org/reports/absolute-impact-2021 (accessed 17 September 2021); REDD Monitor, https://redd-monitor.org (accessed 17 September 2021).

39 Cooking Sections, *The Empire Remains Shop* (New York: Columbia Books on Architecture and the City, 2018).

40 Parts of this essay were first published in D. Fernández Pascual and A. Schwabe, The offsetted, *e-flux Architecture*, 13 November 2017.

41 H. Davis, Toxic progeny: The plastisphere and other queer futures, *philoSOPHIA*, 5(2) (2015): 231–250.

42 N. C. Kawa, *Amazonia in the Anthropocene* (Austin, TX: University of Texas Press, 2016), p 98.

43 K. M. Lyons, *Vital Decomposition: Soil Practitioners + Life Politics* (Durham, NC: Duke University Press, 2020), p. 70.

44 These included local fishermen's takeover of underwater carbon in the flooded forests

behind the Volta Dam in Ghana (Farouk Kwaning), the creation of water well frontlines as a buffer zone to prevent fracking in the Delaware Rivershed (Stacey Barry), turning the ashes of your ancestors into coral reefs in the south China Sea to claim afterlife sovereignty (Caroline Wing Ying Fok), and replanting and inhabiting mangroves in redundant shrimp ponds in Bali to prevent blue carbon markets to take over customary land (Dika Terra Lin).

45 Projects addressed turning rubbish from New York into compostable energy for New York (Chi-Jen Wang), and bypassing California's energy monopoly through gravitation-based systems (Matteo de Bellis, Rebecca Bradley, Ibiye Camp, Bahnfun Chittmittrapap, Shiqi Deng, Matthew Darmour-Paul, Rhiarna Dhaliwal, and Samuel Evans).

46 These ranged from explorations of the *carbolonial* making of nature reserve boundaries in Kenya (Harry Keene), perpetual carbon markets in London (Giulia Moretti), arbitrary 'safe from fracking' zones (Tanya Kramer), elusive containment in decommissioned nuclear power plants (Charles Redman), or shifting borders to capitalize on valuable animal migrations (Dan Hawkins), to how tech giants have been providing free software and devices to indigenous people in the Amazon (Tatiane Britto).

47 See P. Solón, Buen Vivir in times of chaos, p.152 in this volume.

48 F. Vergès, Racial capitalocene, in *Futures of Black Radicalism* (G. T. Johnson and A. Lubin, eds) (London: Verso, 2017), p. 80.

49 J. Kill, *Trade in Ecosystem Services* (Montevideo: World Rainforest Movement, 2010).

50 H. Rullman, An orchid's natural history of displacement, p.42 in this volume.

51 N. Alexandroff, Handicapping golf: Mobilizing the links, p.58 in this volume.

52 R. Whiteley, Oil critters: Multispecies opportunities in the decommissioning of North Sea Oil platforms, p.86 in this volume.

53 P. Allan, M. Bryant, and H. Smith, Knowing through Harakeke, p.68 in this volume.

54 M. Darmour-Paul, An architecture against wetland mitigation banking, p.122 in this volume.

55 I. Sandeman, Palmed-off, p.98 in this volume.

56 A. Asiyanbi, Forest carbon offsetting or development as usual: Three spaces of a zombie solution, p.134 in this volume.

57 F. D. Scott in conversation with the authors, *Offsetted: On the Rights of Trees*, 22 February 2019, E-flux, New York.

58 M. Margil in conversation with the authors, *Offsetted: On the Rights of Trees*, 22 February 2019, E-flux, New York.

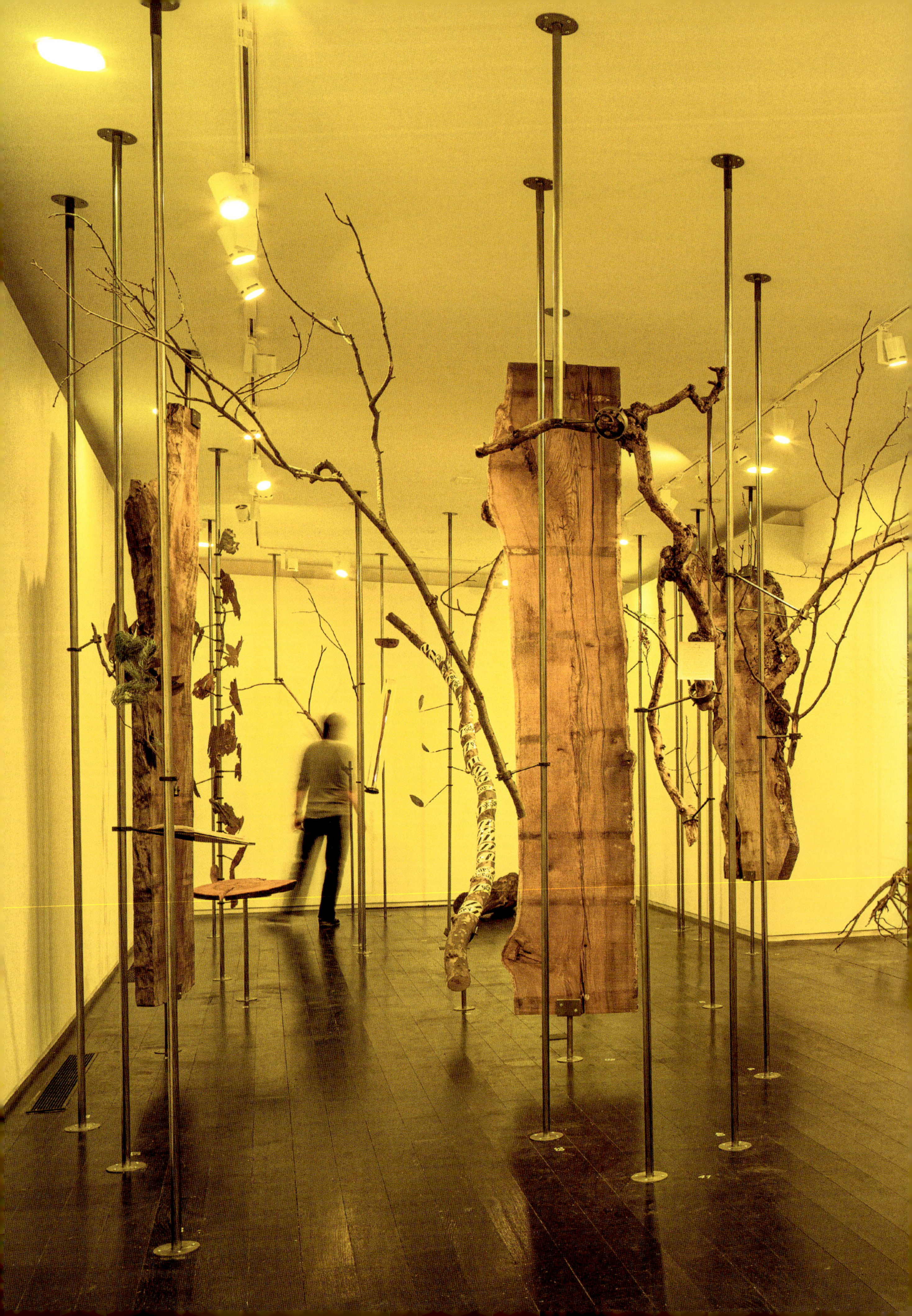

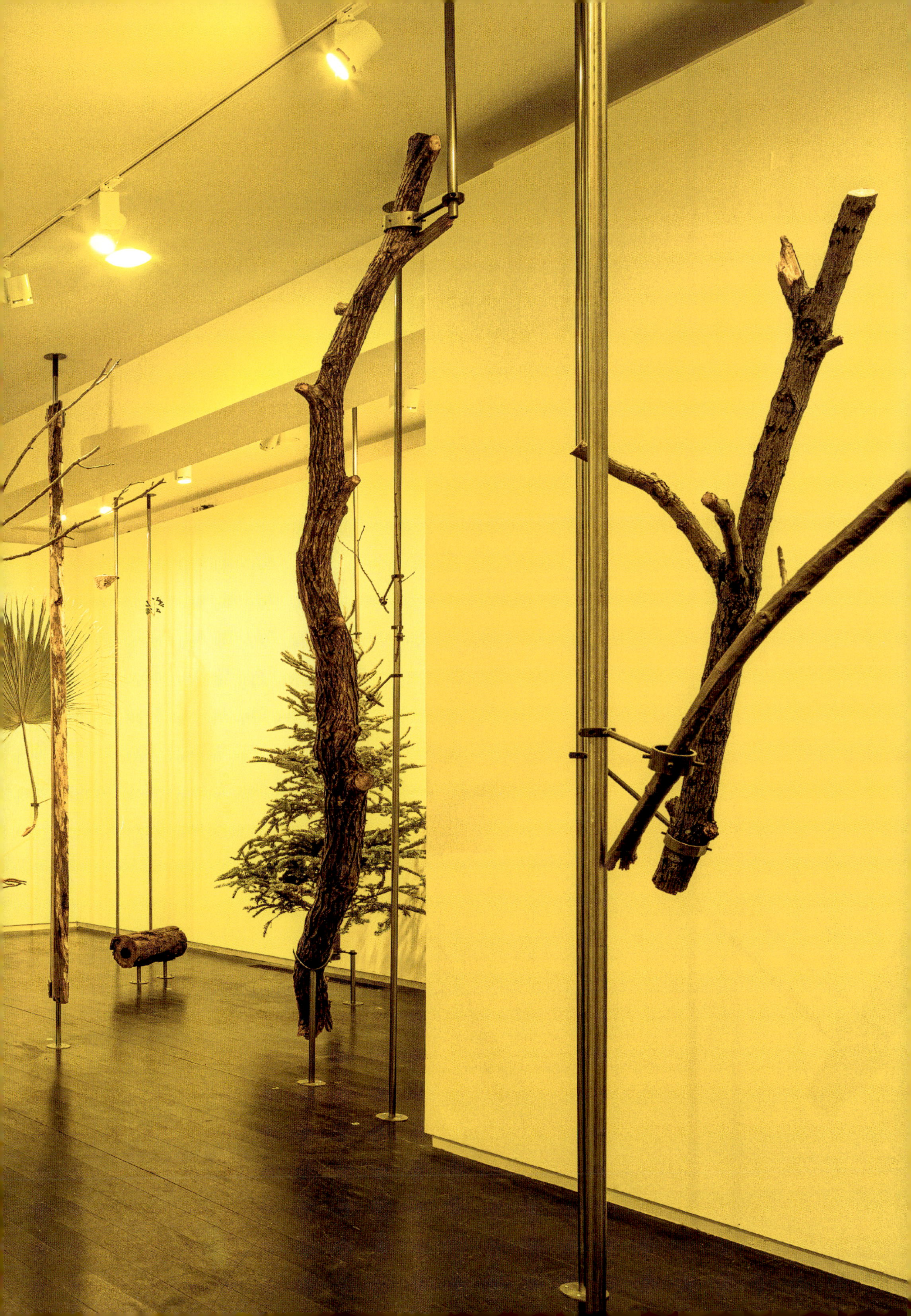

OFFSETTED:
THE RIGHTS OF TREES

A London plane tree at 728 Nostrand Avenue in Brooklyn converts US$13.55 of carbon dioxide annually. In Manhattan, a thornless honey locust at 320 East 42nd Street reduces local energy expenditure by US$194.14. An ailanthus at 95 Astoria Boulevard in Queens absorbs US$46.16 worth of stormwater. In total, 689,227 street trees in New York City provide US$102,768,094.84 in "environmental services" every year.[*] These services correlate to a tree's biological functions, which are translated into dollars—treating trees as instruments to offset human-made ecological degradation. Rather than address the actual source of emissions, wastewater, or energy overexpenditure, the performance of trees is used to legitimize the continuous production of waste and pollutants.

Since the 1980s, environmental preservation efforts have increasingly been justified through economic frameworks. Although "the environment" is an abstract entity of seemingly priceless value, it is nevertheless mined as an economic resource to serve humans, and has been unequivocally transformed into a range of global financial investments. *Offsetted*—an exhibition at the Arthur Ross Architecture Gallery at Columbia University's Graduate School of Architecture, Planning, and Preservation in 2019—examined the emergence of this valuation of nature, questioning the underlying logic and mechanisms of environmental protection. Focusing on New York City, the capital of green finance and one of the most speculatively planted cities, the exhibition assembled histories of individual trees. Through an installation of branches, leaves, cross-sections, and cores from all five boroughs, the active role of trees in "serving the city" shows the evolution of real estate value through its urban environment.

From colonial settlements to community protests against gentrification to recent green renewal projects such as MillionTreesNYC, the tree profiles featured in the exhibition together uncovered the political, spatial, and economic interests behind trees in the city. *Offsetted* revealed the ways that trees have been used to both displace people and make people stay in place. Challenging the imposed obligation of trees to perform as speculative assets and environmental mitigators, we acknowledge the right of trees to not serve as carbon offsets, we acknowledge the right of trees to just be trees.

[*] As of 1 September 2021. For updated stats, visit the NYC Street Tree Map online portal, https://tree-map.nycgovparks.org (accessed 19 September 2021).

PINE TREE RIOTS

In colonial New England, pine trees were at the centre of political and economic disputes between loyalists to the British monarchy and rebels. For English shipbuilders, tall, straight pine trees—referred to as "cloud-kissing pines"—were a valuable resource of the American colonies, providing ideal proportions for the masts of the monarch's naval vessels.[1] By the early 18th century, the increasing scarcity of large pines prompted King George III to legally stake a claim to all 24-inch-thick pines in New England, which from 1711 onwards were reserved for the Royal Navy.[2] As pines of this size dwindled, the ban was modified to trees with 12-inch diameters.[3] To enforce the law, the king's surveyors journeyed through the woods, as well as mills, scoring trees with three slashes in the shape of an arrow to mark them as royal property, and fining anyone in possession of logs of royal size. As punishment, millowners risked the girdling of their remaining pines—the violent act of making a deep cut in the circumference of the tree to kill it.[4] But anti-British activists began to resist. After the seizure of white pine logs in Exeter, New Hampshire, in 1736, for example, residents retaliated by attacking the king's surveyors and sinking their boat. In 1772, during the Weare riot, also in New Hampshire, rebels assaulted authorities with branches and demanded that the royal claim on trees be lifted, while proudly displaying 12-inch pine floorboards in their homes—a domestic symbol of political resistance. These trees embodied the friction between two colonial projects: British efforts to preserve political authority over North American territory, and the aspiration of new settlers to establish their own governance of the lands and forests of dispossessed Native Americans. More than two centuries later, pine trees were, at least symbolically, allowed to return to long-gone forested sites. The Arthur Ross Pinetum, planted in the 1970s in Central Park, consisted of a few dozen precious pine trees that together formed an "evergreen sanctuary." The trees came back, but the indigenous people of these forests were not able to return with them.

1   S. E. Roberts, Pines, profits, and popular politics: Responses to the White Pine Acts in the colonial Connecticut River valley, *The New England Quarterly*, 83(1) (2010): 73–101.

2   Great Britain, An Act for the Preservation of White and Other Pine-Trees Growing in Her Majesties Colonies of New-Hampshire, the Massachusetts-Bay, and Province of Main [sic], Rhode-Island, and Providence-Plantation, the Narragansett Country, or Kings-Province, and Connecticut in New-England, and New-York, and New-Jersey, in America, for the Masting Her Majesties Navy (S.l.: s.n., 1711).

3   J. J. Malone, *Pine Trees and Politics: The Naval Stores and Forest Policy in Colonial New England, 1691–1775* (Seattle, WA: University of Washington Press, 1964).

4   N. E. Scott, *Rioting and the Mob in New Hampshire 1680–1775*, Thesis, Lehigh University, Bethlehem, PA, 1976, p. 54.

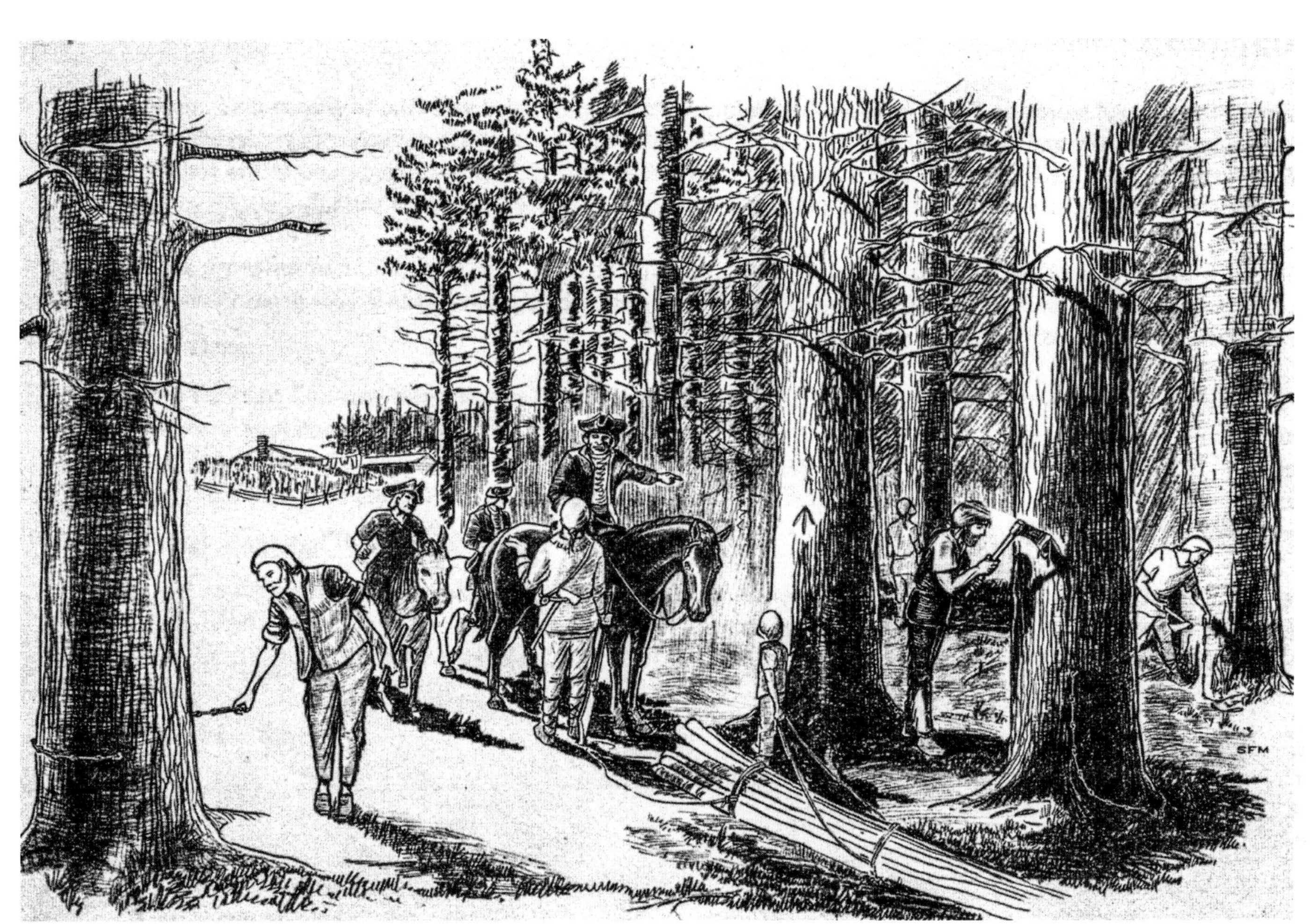

TREE CURRENCY

The exchange value of trees was established almost immediately upon the arrival of British colonists on the eastern shores of North America. Then, as now, the authority to issue money indicated political and economic self-determination, a prerogative reserved for monarchs, princes, and independent states.[1] But without direct access to currency, settlers relied on the bartering of wampum shells, bullets, corn, and beaver pelts for commerce, while timber—vital to the shipbuilding industry—became an important export that closed the loop in the triangular slave trade. In the 1640s, the value of wampum collapsed, and the shell beads were suddenly demonetized.[2] Given the lack of cash flow from England, and that the beheading of Charles I had left the Commonwealth with no king to approve new coinage, Massachusetts opened a local mint and started pressing coins in 1652. After failed proposals for square coins, the first round shillings bore no human image but the imprint of three valuable trees: willow, oak, and pine. Of these three, the pine tree shilling was in production and circulation the longest, reflecting the importance of the tree to the shipping industry and global trade at large. Despite the illegality of an independent monetary system after the restoration of the monarchy, new shillings continued to be produced until 1682, although subversively marked with the date "1652" to evade the newly restored King Charles II's authority over coinage.

1   J. E. Barth, "A Peculiar Stampe of Our Owne:" The Massachusetts Mint and the battle over sovereignty, 1652–1691, *The New England Quarterly*, 87(3) (2014): 490–525.
2   M. Peterson, Big money comes to Boston, *Common Place Journal of Early American Life*, 6(3) (2006).

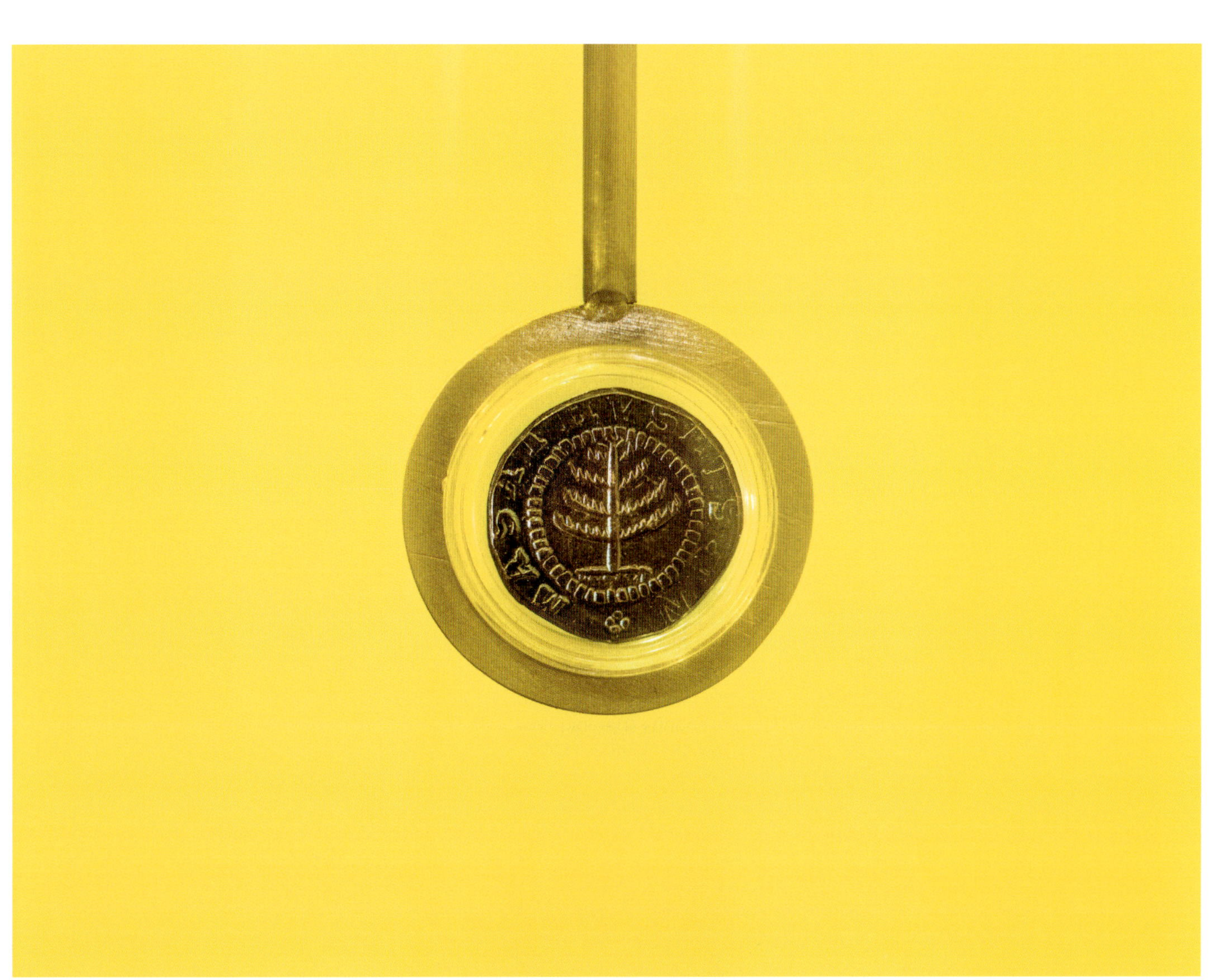

TREES REPLACING PEOPLE

Before the construction of Central Park in 1857, the land stretching from 82nd Street to 88th Street and bounded by Seventh and Eighth Avenues was the site of Seneca Village, a settlement of black residents established nearly three decades earlier. In 1825, Andrew Williams and Epiphany Davis, two formerly enslaved people, purchased the land. The subsequent acquisition of adjacent lots and the construction of houses laid the groundwork for a community that would grow to approximately 250 residents at its peak. The village expanded in the late 1830s after the African American community of York Hill, just to the east, was destroyed by the construction of a holding basin for the new Croton water system. Some of the village landowners built their homes in the village, while others continued to live downtown and either rented out their land or simply used it as an investment.[1] As property owners and residents, some black men living in Seneca Village became legally eligible to vote.[2] Regardless of the opportunities it offered, by the late 1840s racist attitudes had stigmatized the site as a wilderness squatted by unemployed outcasts living in shanties and subsisting on fish and driftwood from the river—only worsened by the fact that a third of the population was made up of migrants of Irish descent.[3] In reality, many Seneca Village residents had jobs as cooks or domestic workers, and had helped create a community that included housing, churches, and at least one school. In the 1850s, plans for the creation of a grand new public park in Manhattan began to take shape. Uptown landowners lobbied for a large, centrally located park, both as a way of inhibiting an influx of poor residents and their associated trades (an early form of zoning), and as a means of removing a large concentration of low-income uptown residents (an early form of urban renewal).[4] Residents of Seneca Village and other communities fought to retain their land and, with it, their voting rights, but all inhabitants of what would become Central Park were evicted and their houses razed. Although many of the Seneca Village residents were believed to be members of the city's African American middle class, the community's stability did not protect it from being destroyed.[5] In 1858, Frederick Law Olmsted and Calvert Vaux began to realize their vision for Central Park, landscaping over the sites of dispossessed communities and introducing a barrier of trees around the new park to isolate it from the city.

1   D. diZerega Wall, N. A. Rothschild, and C. Copeland, Seneca Village and Little Africa: Two African American communities in antebellum New York City, *Historical Archaeology*, 42(1) (2008): 97–107.

2   R. Rosenzweig and E. Blackmar, *The Park and the People: A History of Central Park* (Ithaca, NY: Cornell University Press, 1992), p. 69.

3   Rosenzweig and Blackmar, *The Park and the People*, p. 66.

4   Rosenzweig and Blackmar, *The Park and the People*, p. 63.

5   diZerega *et al.*, Seneca Village and Little Africa, p. 106.

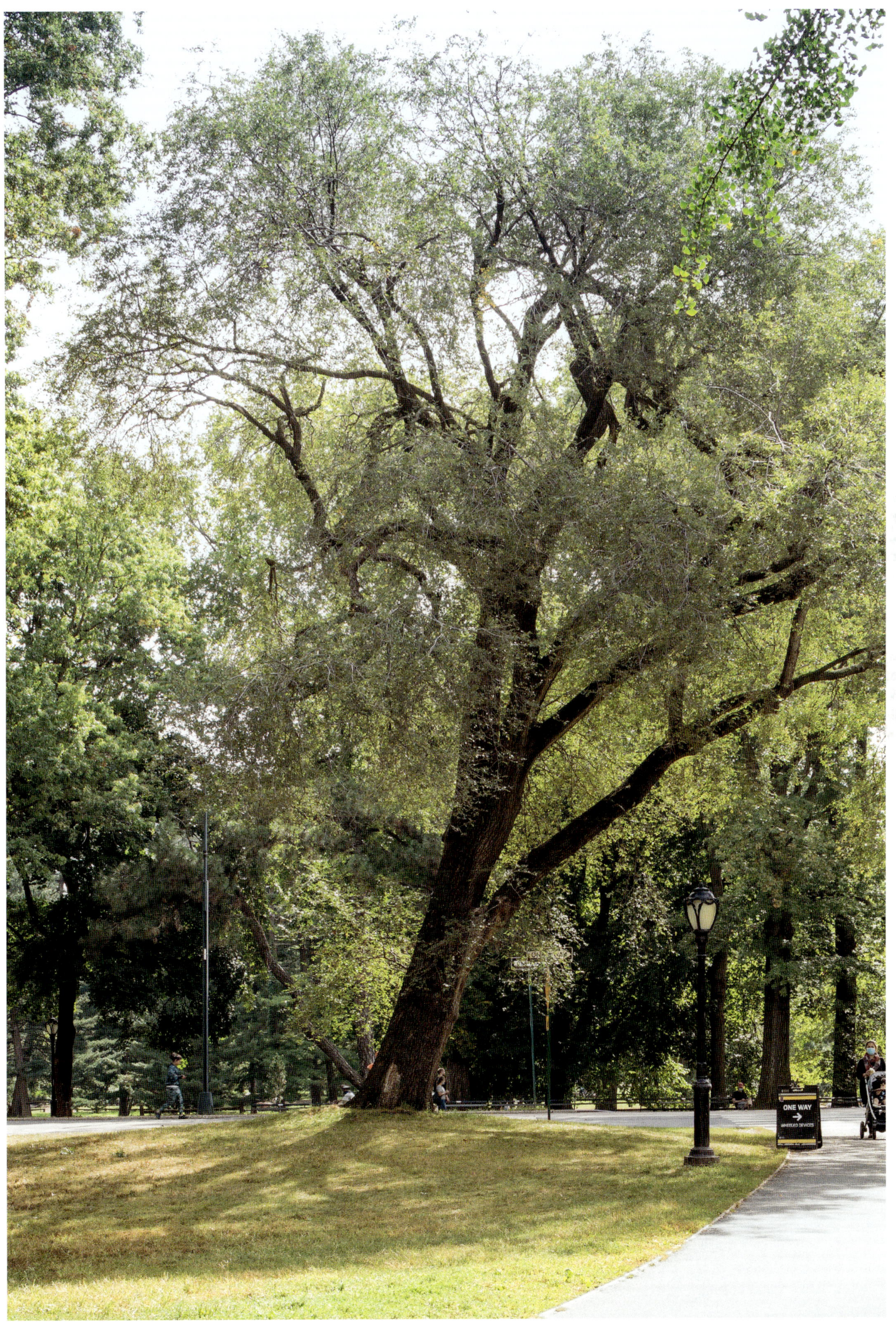
ONE WAY
WHEELED DEVICES

Liparis loeselii:
An Environmental History of Displacement

Hanna Rullmann

In 2012, a planned expansion of the Port of Calais in France—the most important transit connection between the European mainland and the UK—was set to destroy 3.7 hectares of important European natural heritage.[1] As a compensation measure, a nearby 20-hectare site, adjacent to the highway to the port and the chemical factories that surround it, was designated to become a nature reserve. For the preceding 20 years this site, which had been a sand mine in the 1970s and agricultural land in the 1950s and 1960s, had been used as an illegal waste dump. The main species of interest on the site was the fen orchid, *Liparis loeselii*, although it had not been observed there since 2002.[2] In January 2015, however, the location for this nature reserve (called Fort Vert, or Green Fort) became home to the biggest migrant settlement in Calais to date (infamously known as "The Jungle").[3] Migrants, who at the time were located in various places throughout the town of Calais, were forced by authorities to relocate to The Jungle in an effort better to control them. After the camp was violently dismantled at the end of 2016, plans for the nature reserve were reinstated, with adjustments conceived through (financial) collaborations between the UK and French Border Forces and Calais City Council—new additions included moats, sandbanks, and large lakes aimed at preventing access and settlement by migrants.[4]

Liparis loeselii—a rare species listed as endangered by the Convention on International Trade in Endangered Species of Wild Fauna and Flora (CITES) and the European Environmental Agency—is a small, yellow-flowered orchid that grows in fens and humid dune slacks.[5] Its recovery is one of the main objectives of the biodiversity restoration efforts at Fort Vert. [Fig. 1]

Framed by an attempt to "re-nature" (from the French *renaturer*) the site, the fen orchid became synonymous with the landscape's historical "natural" state, in contrast to the migrants' presence, which was perceived as damaging and a disturbance.[6] However, it is precisely these things, disturbance and human activity, that create a favourable habitat and help the fen orchid to thrive. In *The Mushroom at the End of the World*, Anna Lowenhaupt Tsing untangles the existence of the matsutake mushroom as it comes to life in the midst of human disturbance, as a departure point, evoking possibilities for multispecies entanglements that arise from capitalist practices.[7] Tsing draws attention to the "overlapping world-making activities" of human and not-human beings, exemplifying how cultural and natural histories are created through the meeting of species.[8] I will follow the fen orchid across its own histories of encounter with humans and other species, materialized through (in)formal labour, logistical infrastructures, displacement, nationalisms, and migration. In particular, I will trace the politics and sometimes discriminatory practices involved in establishing these encounters, and interrogate the space (or rather lack of space) given to narratives of human activity in natural histories, environmental policies, and classifications.

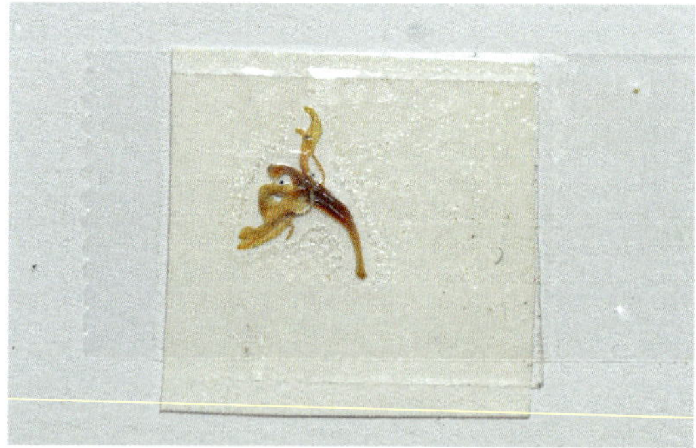

Fig. 1 Dried specimen of Liparis loeselii, Centre for National Conservation, Bailleul, France, April 2019

Just as Fort Vert conservationists aimed to restore the landscape to what it was like 10,000 years ago, classical restoration ecology imagines a fixed nature prior to human interference. Instead, I look at the specific histories of two of the fen orchid's habitats—the fenland in the UK and the dune slacks in Calais, France—and the human and non-human entanglements that find a place in their management (through conservation policies) and perception. Given the orchid's histories of encounter as generative of ever-changing, entangled, and cyclical landscapes, these two habitats double as records of a complex of stories and political relations.

FENLAND: CYCLES OF RESIDUE, DISTURBANCE, AND REJUVENATION

The earliest known record of the *Liparis loeselii* (originally named *Ophrys loeselii*) dates back to a specimen collected in fens near the town of Aldreth, UK, in 1678.[9] Since then, the area has been drained and cultivated, and only the surrounding street names (Fen Side, Church Fen Drove) recall what the landscape must have looked like. The fen orchid has been in serious decline for more than 200 years due to loss of habitat in most of its geographic range (Europe and North America). [Figs 2 and 3]

In June 2018, I visited one of the three remaining fen orchid populations in Norfolk, UK, guided by local conservationist Tim Pankhurst. Pankhurst, a fen orchid specialist, gave me a tour of the reserve, navigating along a footpath marked by little white flags to ensure visitors don't fall into one of the fen's many hidden water holes. In fact, the fen that we were walking through had been open water some 150 years ago, as is the case for all the fens that still host fen orchids in the UK. This is evidence that the orchid thrives in dynamic habitats with nutrient-poor water and soil, and that it doesn't like to be overshadowed. These days, this cycle of renewal is artificially managed by conservationists, for example through cutting regimes and removing trees, but historically management has long been intertwined with traditional economic use of the fen. [Fig. 4]

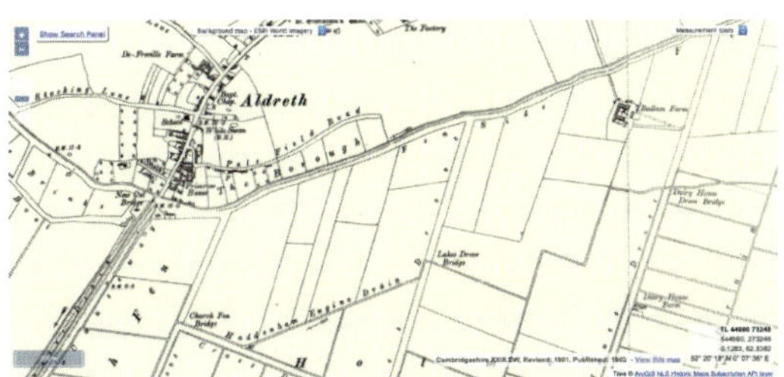

Fig. 2 Location near Aldreth, Cambridgeshire, UK, where the first specimen of *Liparis loeselii* was collected (note the place names "Fen Side" and "Church Fen Bridge," 1901)

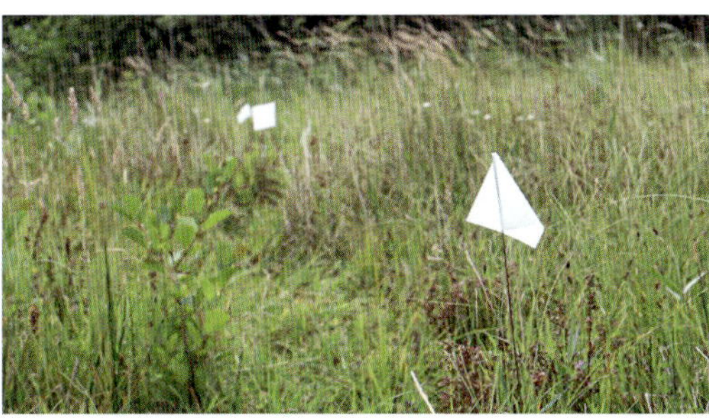

Fig. 4 The fens in Norfolk, UK, May 2018

As Pankhurst explained to me, there were three main reasons for human activity in the fens: sedges (reed-like vegetation), litter (dried and decomposing grasses), and peat (an accumulation of decaying vegetation over several thousands of years).[10] Sedges were mainly cut and used for roof thatching, whereas litter served as fodder and bedding for horses in towns. A detailed account of vegetation patterns in Wicken Fen, near Cambridge, from 1929 describes how "fenmen" practised these various activities in their respective plots of fen over centuries.[11] The different intervals between cutting, accessibility of certain areas, and, more generally, the "necessities and whims of each individual owner" make for a "patchy" distribution of vegetation, which, even though it is often seen as "natural," is subject to particular agricultural histories.[12] As one such plot is described:

> This is "common" land on which cutting is allowed to begin on the third Monday in July each year. The amount cut varies with the local requirement, but areas near the main drove are always used first. *Cladium* increases in abundance towards the other end.[13] [Fig. 5]

The other main use of land in the fens was the digging of peat, which can be used as fuel. The practice of digging peat (also known as "cutting turf") dates back thousands of years and has had a significant impact on landscapes in the northern hemisphere. For example, a lake area in the UK known as The Broads, long believed to be a natural formation, was discovered to have been artificially formed by the cutting of large deposits of peat many centuries ago.[14] [Fig. 6]

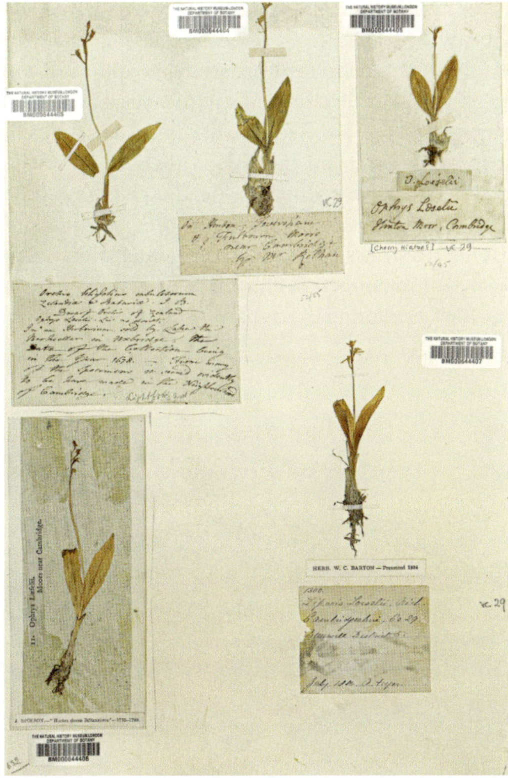

Fig. 3 Several specimens of *Liparis loeselii*, the oldest of which (from 1678) is in the collection of the Natural History Museum in London

Not only did the cutting of peat, sedges, and litter clear out vegetation and create patches of open water, the activity itself—people and animals walking through—generates conditions conducive to the germination of species like the marshwort, a ground-covering creeping plant that suppresses the growth of reed, therefore reducing competition for the *Liparis loeselii*.[15] Although peat harvesting still happens in some places (mainly Canada, Ireland, and India), peat, sedges, and litter became largely obsolete once horses ceased to be the primary mode of transportation and people started using coal for fuel. For centuries peat harvesting interrupted the fen's natural succession from open water, to fen, to woodland. As localized peat digging created pools of open water over and over again, the fen had to recolonize these patches, providing the particular young habitat that the orchid thrives in—it germinates in moss that grows in the early stages of a fen. Once these traditional forms of labour ceased, shrubs and trees gradually moved in, while other fens were drained and turned into farmland. Neither of these developments are favourable to the *Liparis loeselii*: overgrowth by shrubs, dense reed vegetation, stabilized water tables, and drainage have caused the loss of its habitat and thus its decline.

UNITY OF MANAGEMENT: PARCELS AND FIELDS

The patchiness of the fen orchid's habitat points to its entanglements with centuries of formal and informal labour: harvesting cycles, germination through human and animal movement, management of water tables, and communal land use. The development of the orchid through encounters with other species and residues—such as moss, marshwort, litter, peat, and sedge, and the people that extract, cut, and germinate them—reveals a natural history rooted in disturbance. However, concepts such as "patchiness" and "disturbance" find little resonance in the European environmental vocabulary. One of the main pillars of European environmental management is the EC Habitats Directive, which classifies every type of landscape in Europe, gives each a name and code, and indicates which habitats are rare and in need of conservation. This system, according to Pankhurst, throws up a number of contradictions: rather than accounting for gradation or transitional vegetation, it finds its base in the history of land use in Europe, where "land tends to be parcelled up in recognisable units with a consistent management approach within a parcel, a field."[16] Patchy and variable vegetation formed through particular localized conditions and types of management finds no place in these typologies. In addition, "protection" focuses primarily on the conservation of a habitat or species as a self-contained unit, rather than the relational processes that allow them to thrive. Associations with human activity in particular are absent from these conservation narratives, suggesting that they are apolitical. [Fig. 7]

152   *The "Sedge" and "Litter" of Wicken Fen*

metre (say an average of 2); there are many isolated clumps 1·5 to 2 m. high, perhaps 10 to 20 bushes in each square of 20 metre sides. The S.W. end has big clumps 2·5 m. high. *Salix repens* var. *fusca* occurs 60 or more to the 20 metre square. *Scabiosa succisa, Angelica silvestris, Thalictrum flavum, Cirsium anglicum, Hydrocotyle vulgaris, Valeriana dioica* and *Ulmaria palustris* are all

I LITTER.   II LITTER.

III MIXED SEDGE.   IV MIXED SEDGE.

(M) Molinia coerulea ·Cc Cladium Mariscus × Carex panicea ·P Phragmites communis ·J Juncus obtusiflorus ·H Hydrocotyle vulgaris ·Va Valeriana dioica ·S.s. Scabiosa succisa ·R.f. Rhamnus frangula ·S.f. Salix repens var. fusca ·Th Thalictrum flavum ⚡ Mosses. ·R. Peucedanum palustre ·Eu Eupatorium cannabinum ·A Angelica silvestris ·Ci Cirsium anglicum ·U Ulmaria palustris ( ) indicates the seedling stage.

FIG. 2.

Fig. 5 Hand-drawn maps of the patchy vegetation of litter and sedges in Wicken Fen, Cambridge, UK, 1929

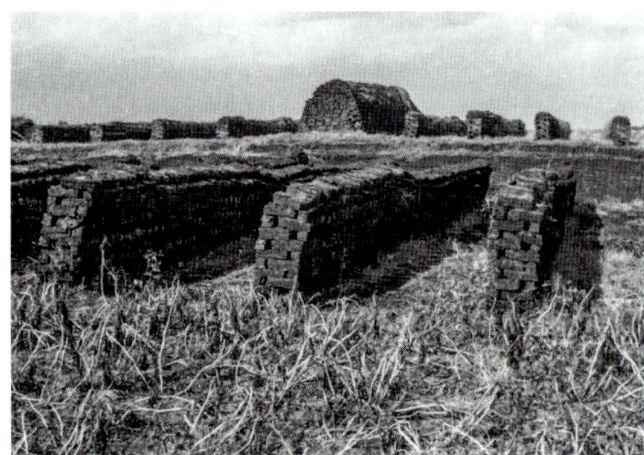

Fig. 6 Peat drying in a field in Nieuw-Schoonebeek, The Netherlands, 1950

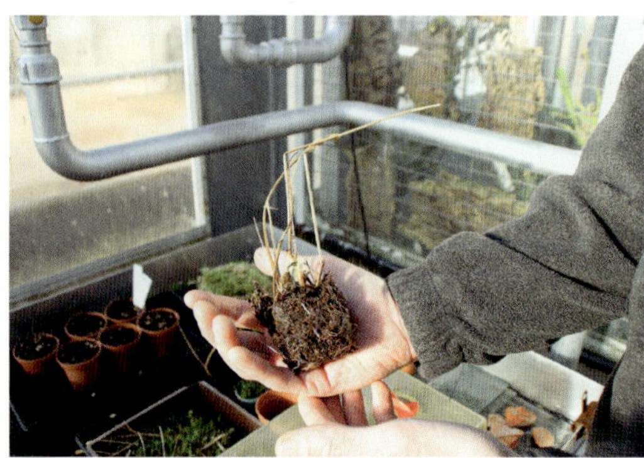

Fig. 7 Reintroduction programme for *Liparis loeselii* at the Botanical Institute, Cambridge University, November 2017

The second variety of *Liparis loeselii*, which grows in a habitat called "humid dune slack" (code 2190 in the EC Habitats Directive), is equally dependent on cycles of regeneration and also prefers nutrient-poor soils. When looking at aerial photographs of the Fort Vert nature reserve in Calais, the area in which the fen orchid was first observed in 1997 was used as a sand mine when the nearby port and highways were first built. The excavation of sand, and by proxy the removal of shrubs and other vegetation, most likely created the ideal conditions for *Liparis loeselii* to emerge. Informal activities such as quad-bike riding, fly tipping, and fishing could also have contributed to processes of germination and additional clearing of vegetation.[17] [Fig. 8]

When plans for the Fort Vert nature reserve were taking shape just after the destruction of the migrant settlement in 2017, they were centred around the idea of "re-naturing," using centuries-old maps to discover the site's original "natural" state.[18] One of the techniques explored to restore historical habitats was the stripping of 20 cm of topsoil to bring 60- to 70-year-old seeds to the surface. In that sense, the type of restoration ecology implemented here seems to consider history as a linear series of progressive moments, one of which is chosen to return to. It implies the existence of a before and after disturbance or human interference—a natural and an unnatural state.[19] Rather than understanding natural histories as an accumulation of multi-directional processes, in which multispecies entanglements with infrastructure, agriculture, and so on crucially generate life, a narrative is elected that excludes human presence in general, and the presence of migrants in particular.[20] An illustration of this is the fact that the reserve, once established, was closed to the public (bar one observation post on the eastern sandbank). This exclusion of human activity reinforces the imaginary situation of the "natural" landscape as separate from the cultural. In this particular case, such a representation plays right into the hands of European nation states that not only aim to justify the expulsion of migrants but also to obscure the political and physical violence of this act and of the nature reserve's function as border-security infrastructure.[21] Moreover, it builds upon ecofascist tropes that perceive migration as threatening to European nature, and that place value on all that is considered native (as opposed to invasive) and pristine. In the division of what is natural and what is unnatural, racialized migrants are what comes after, set outside of natural spaces. The discriminatory practices involved in the framing of who or what is a threat, who or what needs to be protected, etc., are, in fact, integral to the making of nature.

The questions of who or what forms a threat and who or what needs to be protected are determined through systems such as the EC Habitats Directive, CITES endangered species lists, and Natura 2000.[22] Based on the value attributed to certain features, these systems establish hierarchies between species and habitats. That means hierarchies of protection as well as hierarchies of threat. The things that are valued—such as rarity, nativeness, wildness, and vulnerability—reject (human) disturbance, invasiveness, and common-ness.[23] As we look at the fen orchid in the context of a border zone, but also in the context of its "key species" role in national restoration plans and protection schemes, I want to interrogate the logic of these hierarchies, and recount how what is valued in nature is echoed by what is valued in the nation state. [Fig. 9]

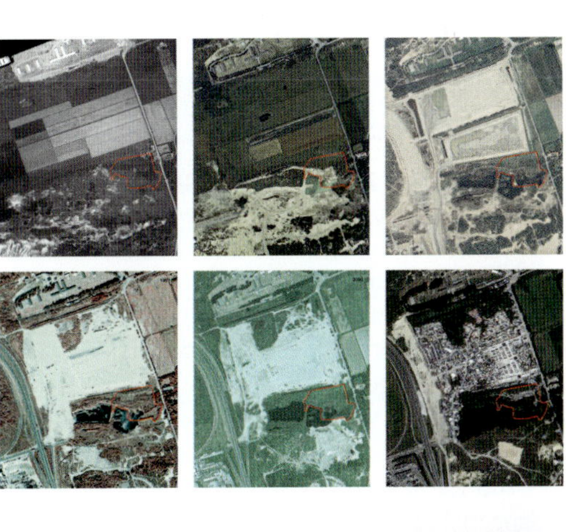

Fig. 8 Aerial photographs of Fort Vert, from 1965 to 2016. The area where the fen orchid was observed in 1997 is marked in red

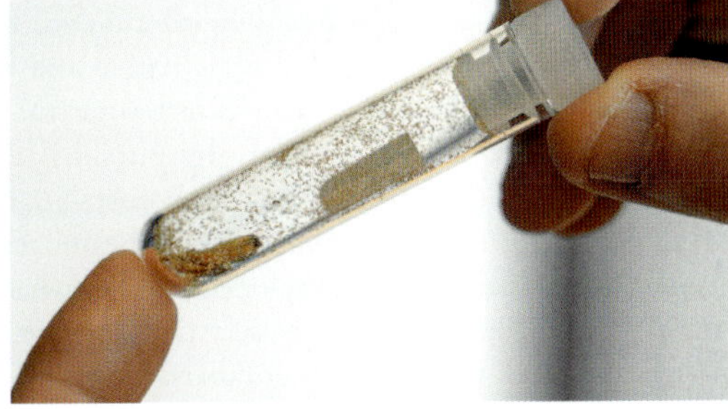

Fig. 9 Seeds of *Liparis loeselii* at the Centre for National Conservation, Bailleul, France, April 2019

Rarity, in particular, is one of the most important qualities when nominating a species or habitat for environmental protection. This may seem obvious, as rare things in all categories are generally perceived to be precious, but when examined more closely it indicates a sometimes skewed set of relations. To explain the logic of rarity, Tim Pankhurst pointed me to a subcommunity of the "Tall Herb Fen" (in the typology "Alkaline Fens," code 7230 in the EC Habitat Directive), which only comes into existence when another type of subcommunity is heavily disrupted. When a new fen forms on top of a disturbed fen, it will mainly grow wood small-reed—a medium height grass with brown flowers, also used as an ornamental plant in gardens—and be generally "species poor," as Pankhurst calls it. However, as this particular disruption does not happen often, the habitat is extremely rare, and therefore automatically attracts greater conservation attention, despite its particular irrelevance in terms of biodiversity.[24]

At the same time, the forces that are considered threatening to endemic species and landscapes, and that make them rare, are almost always perceived as foreign, things that don't belong, and therefore things that must be excluded. What must be preserved, on the other hand, are the native and pristine, contributing to a sense of national belonging. For example, research indicates that it is often nostalgia, the appeal of a shared history, that attracts interest in conservation and restoration efforts.[25] In the framework of nostalgia, certain "key" species in particular play a symbolic role in reinforcing a national identity through natural heritage, no doubt aided by a conservation system that applies protection to individualized species, rather than the relational processes that help them evolve. [Fig. 10]

However, a plant survey conducted by conservationists at Fort Vert in 2017 found non-native and invasive species as a result of the migrant settlement, such as onions and young date palms (most likely the result of food waste).

In a similar vein, in his book *Interspecies Politics*, Rafi Youatt writes about the transboundary conservation of ocelots at the US–Mexico border and asks "What does it mean then, to talk of conservation, ocelots, and thorn scrub at the very place where walls, migration, and detention are also at stake?"[26] Youatt notes that the ocelot—and the fen orchid in the case of Fort Vert—as an endangered species, "intersects with the endangered nation."[27] Exclusionary border practices extend through the nature reserve, serving to protect the native and expel the invasive. Conservation, then, is instrumental in the making of nation states, not only by pursuing the idea of an undisturbed nature and evoking a nostalgia for the pristine, but by exactly establishing the boundaries between what is included and excluded in these habitats and narratives. In fact, it is precisely this concept of the natural that has been instrumentalized by colonial powers to render forests pristine and "empty" and thus legitimize extraction and displacement.[28] Similarly, classification, created to identify, organize, and then extract foreign species follows a logic of isolation and abstraction that clearly still reverberates today. As Youatt writes, nation states are "an ecological process, not just in the sense that they organize resource extraction and consumption, … they are ecological through the interspecies generation

of meanings that form and constrain political life, even in non-resource related contexts."[29]

TOWARDS "INTERSPECIES POLITICS"

In recent years, the UK's peatlands have become an important asset on the carbon market. Peat, as it consists of decayed plant material, essentially "sinks" the carbon dioxide absorbed by plants during their lifetime, making it one of the planet's most effective means of storing carbon. Restoration of peatlands is increasingly financed by the private sector, aiming to offset its own carbon dioxide emissions and become "carbon neutral." The UK's Peatland Code,[30] established to provide a "standard for UK peatland restoration projects wishing to attract private finance," describes how "damaged" peatland emits around 16 million tonnes of carbon a year.[31] "Damage" here is described as degradation that, besides through peat mining, is caused by agriculture, draining, burning, and grazing, which eradicates vegetation and leaves peat vulnerable to further erosion. Erosion is what causes the stored carbon to be released into the air. Restoration is thus aimed at reducing carbon emissions from disturbed peat, by re-wetting and re-vegetating it. Peatlands, as one restoration developer puts it, are then quantified and valued as "tradable carbon stores."[32]

Driven by a thriving carbon market, peat restoration projects mainly focus on maximizing the amount of carbon that can be sequestered, thereby reclassifying traditional activities, such as digging of peat, as environmentally detrimental. Similarly, in Fort Vert, where the main objective is removing migrants, human activities are excluded. In contrast, in the Norfolk fens, these same activities are considered to be essential to the workings of the ecosystem, and are mimicked in order to continually disturb and regenerate the fen, with the aim of increasing biodiversity and restoring endangered habitats. Each of these places puts forward its own history, in which specific technologies and systems, from agricultural tools to communal land accessibility to carbon markets to securitization to classification, determine what can and cannot grow. In examining the fen orchid's historical trajectories in the UK's fens and Calais dunes, their patchiness documents the course of these mechanisms. Histories of nature that include narratives of human disturbance and multispecies encounters can shed light on the political and economic regimes involved in these encounters. This helps us to better understand their "interspecies politics," to look beyond what is visible on the surface, and to seek accountability within distributions of rights, value, access, and protection. [33]

1   Biotope Nord-Littoral, *Calais Port 2015* (Calais, France: Biotope, 2016).

2   *Ibid.*

3   The name "The Jungle," although claimed by the press to have originated from the Pushtun word for forest, has, over the past decade, become a standard and obviously discriminatory term for informal settlements by migrants across Europe, further othering their residents. See A. Hameed, The petrification of the image, *Continent*, 4(4) (2015): 43. According to Help Refugees, just prior to its destruction The Jungle housed over 8,000 people. Residents came from a variety of countries, such as Somalia, Syria, Eritrea, Iraq, Afghanistan, and Ethiopia (Calais "Jungle" cleared of migrants, French prefect says, *BBC News*, 26 October 2016, https://www.bbc.com/news/world-europe-37773848 (accessed 13 September 2021)). Since its destruction, a smaller number of migrants (1,200 in the summer of 2020, see A.-D. Louarn, *Info Migrants*, 26 June 2020, https://www.infomigrants.net/en/post/25590/in-calais-at-least-1-200-migrants-are-on-the-streets-twice-as-many-as-last-summer (accessed 13 September 2021)) have continued to live in temporary camps throughout Calais, dealing with increased police violence and systematic forceful evictions and harassment. See Human Rights Observers, *Annual Report 2019*, https://helprefugees.org/wp-content/uploads/2020/07/HRO-eng-rep2019.pdf (accessed 13 September 2021).

4   For a detailed account of how the Fort Vert nature reserve was conceived to support border security, see H. Rullmann, Fort Vert: Nature conservation as border regime in Calais, *Statewatch*, 24 February 2020, https://www.statewatch.org/analyses/2020/fort-vert-nature-conservation-as-border-regime-in-calais (accessed 13 September 2021).

5   Fens are a type of wetland characterized by reeds, mosses, and peat; humid dune slacks are wet dune valleys with a highly variable water table.

6   As stated by French Minister of Interior, Bruno Le Roux, in March 2017: "I wanted to be in Calais today with the elected officials and the mayor to see that the dismantling [of The Jungle] was a successful operation and that it will now continue with an ambitious project to return this territory back to nature. To ensure that it benefits the environment, and especially to make sure that there will be no new encampments in Calais." Author's own translation, from P. Vandeville, Le Ministre de l'Intérieur ne laissera pas s'installer une nouvelle Jungle à Calais, *Radio 6*, 2 March 2017, http://www.radio6.fr/article-23385-le-ministre-de-interieur-ne-laissera-pas-installer-unenouvelle-jungle-a-calais.html (accessed 13 September 2021).

7   A. Lowenhaupt Tsing, *The Mushroom at the End of the World: On the Possibility of Life in Capitalist Ruins* (Princeton, NJ: Princeton University Press, 2015).

8   Tsing, *The Mushroom at the End of the World*, p. 152.

9   The specimen is in the collection of the Natural History Museum in London, UK. Natural History Museum Data Portal, Specimen BM000644403, https://data.nhm.ac.uk/object/d4c8cb66-33c8-4ea7-ab2e-30954c2549de/1591747200000 (accessed 13 September 2021).

10 Interview with Tim Pankhurst, conservationist, conducted in July 2018, Norfolk, UK.

11 H. Godwin, The "sedge" and "litter" of Wicken Fen. *Journal of Ecology*, 17(1) (1929): 148–160.

12 Godwin, The "sedge" and "litter" of Wicken Fen, p. 159.

13 *Ibid.*, p. 155.

14 This was discovered by botanist Joyce Lambert as recently as the 1950s. The Broads were created by large-scale removal of peat between 1300 and 1500, destined to serve as fuel for the rest of England. The peat would be taken down the river by boat to, for example, London. Lambert found that The Broads were human-made because, among other things, soil samples indicated that the lakes' bottoms were relatively flat and their sides unusually vertical. See *The Norfolk Broads Revealed as Man-made Features: The Discoveries of Dr Joyce M. Lambert*, Norfolk Record Office blog, 13 May 2016, https://norfolkrecordofficeblog.org/2016/05/13/the-norfolk-broads-revealed-as-man-made-features-the-discoveries-of-dr-joyce-m-lambert (accessed 13 September 2021).

15 Interview with Tim Pankhurst, conservationist, conducted in July 2018, Norfolk, UK.

16 *Ibid.*

17 Biotope Nord-Littoral, *Calais Port 2015*.

18 Interview with Alexandre Driencourt, former conservation manager at Eden62, one of the two environmental organizations involved in constructing and managing Fort Vert, as quoted in H. Rullmann and F. Ahmad Khan, *Habitat 2190* (video, 16:34, 2019).

19 In their article on "The changing role of history in restoration ecology," Eric Higgs and his co-authors point out that classical forms of restoration ecology "attempt to return an ecosystem to its historic trajectory," motivated by a conviction that "the integrity of the ecosystem in question is considered to have been greater before modern human disturbance than it is now." More recent forms of restoration ecology, however, "accept multiple potential trajectories for ecosystems" and "[emphasize] process over structure." Still, these practices struggle with addressing new and hybrid ecosystems as a result of, for example, invasive species, unsure of how to place human influences on natural historic trajectories. See E. Higgs, D. A. Falk, A. Guerrini, *et al.*, The changing role of history in restoration ecology, *Frontiers in Ecology and the Environment*, 12(9) (2014): 499–506.

20 As Anna Lowenhaupt Tsing asks, "If history without progress is indeterminate and multidirectional, might assemblages show us its possibilities?" (*The Mushroom at the End of the World*, p. 23).

21 Similar practices have been researched extensively in recent years, for example those at the US–Mexico border (see work by Juanita Sundberg and Jason De Léon) and elsewhere in Europe (see work by Forensic Oceanography https://forensic-architecture.org/category/forensic-oceanography (accessed 13 September 2021)).

22 CITES is the Convention on International Trade in Endangered Species of Wild Fauna and Flora (https://cites.org/eng). Natura 2000 is a network established by the European Commission that catalogues Europe's "core breeding and resting sites for rare and threatened species, and some rare natural habitat types." Most designated nature reserves in Europe are part of the Natura 2000 network (https://ec.europa.eu/environment/nature/natura2000/index_en.htm (accessed 13 September 2021)).

23 In the Habitats Directive, species are marked as "of Community Interest" when they are "endangered, vulnerable, rare, and endemic." European Commission, The Habitats Directive, (2014, https://ec.europa.eu/environment/nature/legislation/habitatsdirective/index_en.htm (accessed 13 September 2021).

24 Interview with Tim Pankhurst, conservationist, conducted in July 2018, Norfolk, UK.

25 Higgs *et al.*, The changing role of history in restoration ecology, p. 501.

26 R. Youatt, *Interspecies Politics: Nature, Border, States* (Ann Arbor, MI: University of Michigan Press, 2020), p. 42.

27 Youatt, *Interspecies Politics*, p. 42.

28 See P. Tavares, In the forest ruins, *e-flux*, 9 December 2016.

29 Youatt, *Interspecies Politics*, p. 4.

30 International Union for the Conservation of Nature (IUCN), *Peatland Code*, Version 1.1, 2017, https://www.iucn-uk-peatland-programme.org/sites/default/files/header-images/PeatlandCode_v1.1_FINAL.pdf (accessed 13 September 2021).

31 A. Mehta, Heathrow looks to peatland restoration in carbon-neutral plan, *Reuters Events*, 22 January 2019, https://www.reutersevents.com/sustainability/heathrow-looks-peatland-restoration-carbon-neutral-plan (accessed 13 September 2021).

32 See Angus Davidson Ltd, *Protecting the Planet with Healthy Peatlands*, https://www.angusdavidsonltd.com/carbon-trading (accessed 13 September 2021).

33 Youatt, *Interspecies Politics*.

THE TREE UNDER WHICH THE LENAPE LOST THEIR LAND

According to legend, in 1626, Peter Minuit, director-general of New Netherland, "purchased" the island of Manhattan from the Lenape people.[1] Some historical accounts indicate that this sale took place under the "Tree of Peace," a tulip tree located in what is today Inwood Hill Park. Formerly known as Shora-Kap-Kok, and once dotted with Lenape settlements and burial grounds, it marked the site of what is arguably New York's most infamous real estate deal. It was also an area where Dutch colonial farmers moved quickly after the establishment of New Amsterdam, displacing the Lenape. The Nagels and Dyckmans, now commemorated in local street names, were the dominant families in the area. They cleared land for orchards, and each owned marshland and forested uplands for woodlots.[2] At the beginning of the 20th century, the unearthing of numerous Lenape artefacts and oyster shell middens near the Tree of Peace led Reginald Pelham Bolton to imagine the area as an "Indian Life Reservation," a human zoo mimicking a Native American encampment, with Delaware or Algonquin tribal members hired to live on site and guide visitors. Later, it became the home of Marie Noemie Boulerease Constantine Kennedy and her son, both of Cherokee descent. They lived in a cottage next to the tree, working as caretakers and also teaching tourists about ceramics. As the tulip tree—at nearly 17 stories tall, the remnant of a once dense forest—began to decay, attempts were made to save it by filling its rotting, hollow parts with cement and wood. As part of the surgery, 500 feet of rods were also added to reinforce the large limbs.[3] A further 1,000 pounds of bone meal and sheep manure were fed into its roots. When Kennedy and another 600 Native American people organized to reclaim the park as reservation land, they were evicted by then Parks Commissioner Robert Moses as part of his 1938 redevelopment plan.[4] That same year, the tulip tree was felled by a hurricane, chopped up, and replaced with a boulder and a memorial plaque. Despite being regarded as Manhattan's last original forest, the tree population in the area had been severely modified over the centuries, especially due to vegetation clearance during the American Revolution, the planting of non-native species, the partial filling of the wetlands with debris from the construction of the A subway line, and the digging of the Harlem Ship Canal. Furthermore, the construction of the Henry Hudson Parkway through Inwood Hill Park led to the felling of hundreds of mature tulip trees, shrubs, and ground-cover plants. In 1985, slopes were reconstructed to reduce erosion, and by 2006 almost 40,000 "native" trees and 34,000 shrubs had been replanted.[5]

1 The fact that there is no written documentation of the transaction, and that a different deed was signed 24 years later between Peter Stuyvesant and three Native Americans, whom Stuyvesant identified as the rightful owners, challenges the legitimacy of an already problematic agreement. National Museum of the American Indian, *America's First Urban Myth?* (blog).

2 S. Horenstein, Inwood Hill and Isham Parks: Geology, geography and history, in *Natural History of New York City's Parks and Great Gull Island* (A. Deutsch et al., eds) (New York: Linnaean Society of New York, 2007), p. 10.

3 Borough of Manhattan, Department of Parks, *Annual Report* (New York: Department of Parks, 1930), pp. 13–14.

4 Y. Wakim Dennis, A. Hirschfelder, and S. Rothenberger Flynn, *Native American Almanac: More Than 50,000 Years of the Cultures and Histories of Indigenous Peoples* (Canton, MI: Visible Ink Press, 2016), p. 1654.

5 J. M. Fitzgerald and R. E. Loeb, Historical ecology of Inwood Hill Park, Manhattan, New York, *Journal of the Torrey Botanical Society*, April–June 2008: 281–293.

SPECIMEN: Tulip (*Liriodendron tulipifera*). Reconstructed tulip tree cavity filling, 1930/2019 LOCATION: Inwood Hill Park, Manhattan

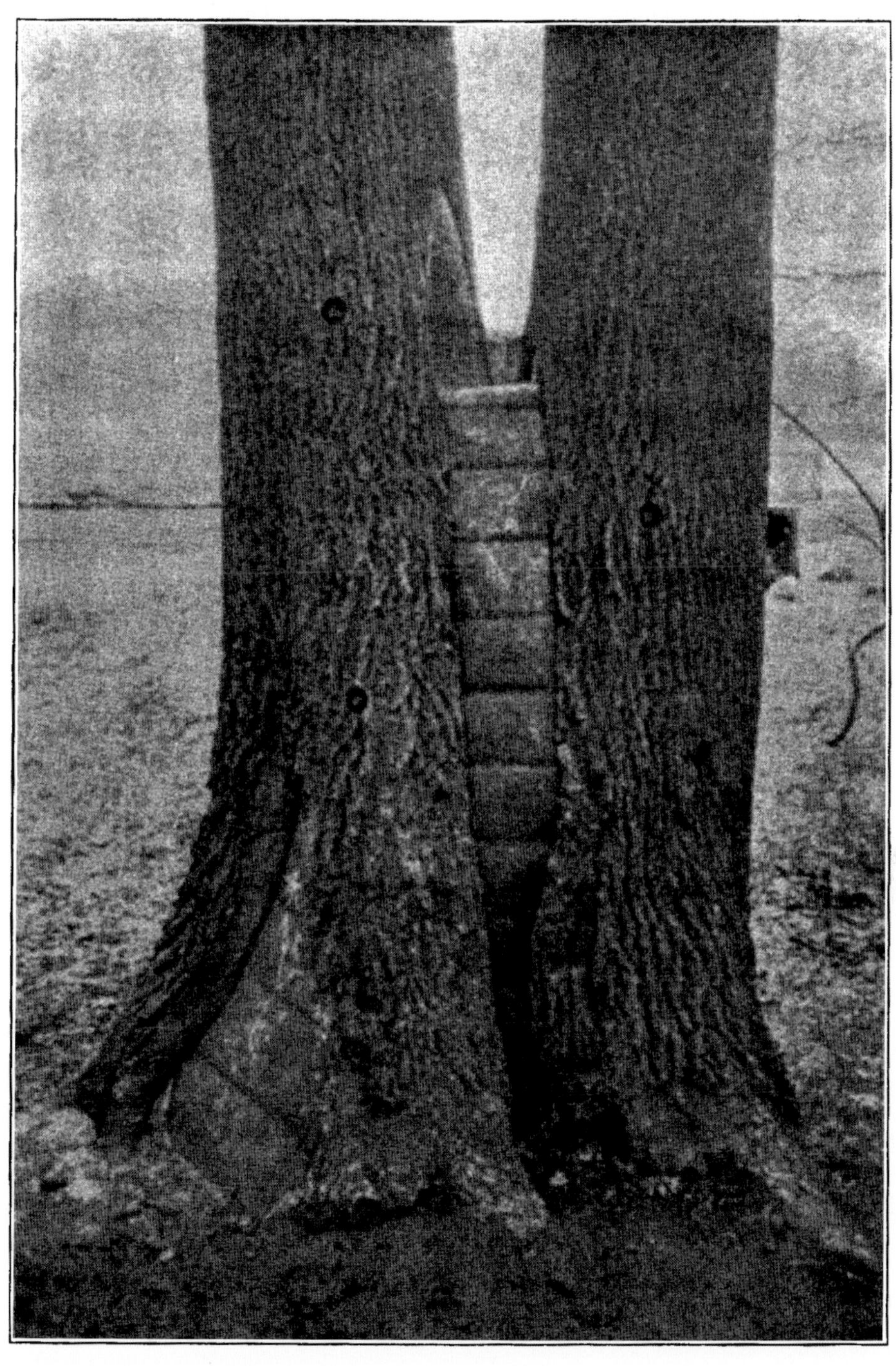

TULIP TREE (LIRIODENDRON TULIPFERA) INWOOD HILL PARK
BASE CAVITY REPAIRED—SEPTEMBER 1930

16

TREES ROOT INTO BURIAL GROUNDS

In 1991, a number of skeletons were unearthed in City Hall Park, revealing an African burial ground dating from the mid-17th to late-18th century, and spanning about five city blocks. On land originally inhabited by the Lenape people, the site had been used by Dutch settlers for grazing and, later, as a parade ground for colonial authority and a stage for the execution of rebels. Excluded from churchyards, nearly 20,000 free and enslaved Africans were buried on the site. Although funerals were banned by the city officials—who feared the gatherings would be used as cover to plan rebellions—some 15,000 burial rituals must have taken place before 1795, when the land was sold. Subdivided into lots and levelled, today the burial ground is still partially submerged under the city. A portion of the burial ground was subsequently transformed into a new civic centre in the early 19th century. Renamed "The Park," it was landscaped and planted with elm, plane, and willow trees, among other species.[1] In the 20th century, the site of the burial ground was redeveloped to house city government buildings. It was during the construction of a new federal office building that the site's history was rediscovered. After 419 graves were found, social pressure halted new construction, and in 1993 the African Burial Ground was designated a New York City Historic District and a National Landmark.

1   M. H. Bogart, Public space and public memory in New York's City Hall Park, *Journal of Urban History*, 25(2) (1999): 235.

LOCATION: Duane Street between Lafayette and Broadway, Manhattan

SPECIMEN: Callery pear (*Pyrus calleryana*). Cross-section of trunk, 2019

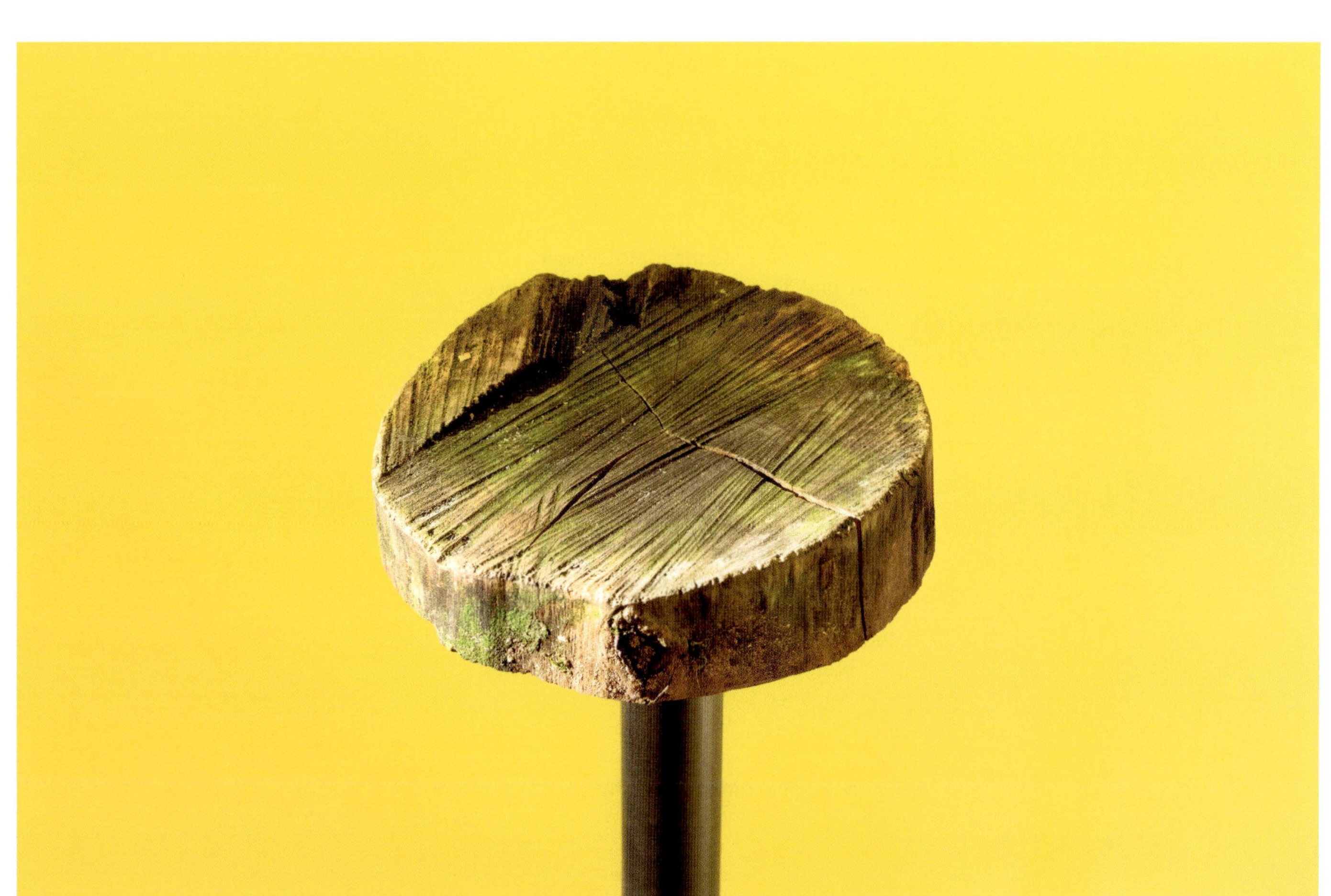

VALUE DISPARITIES ON THE STATE OF TREES

Over the past two decades, the Brooklyn neighbourhood of Fort Greene
has experienced an influx of new, mostly white, middle-class residents,
paralleled by an uptick in demands for improved garbage collection, improved education, and an increased presence of law enforcement.[1] The
new "improvements" were criticized by the long-standing community
for appearing to serve only wealthy newcomers to the neighbourhood.
At the epicentre of the demographic divide is Fort Greene Park, with
public housing on its north side, where gates close at 9 p.m., and with
brownstones on its southern side, where gates close at 1 a.m. Completed in 1850, the park was widely popular. Poet Walt Whitman, once
the editor of the *Brooklyn Eagle*, wrote it would be "a place of recreation" for Brooklynites "where, on hot summer evenings, and Sundays,
they can spend a few grateful hours in the enjoyment of wholesome
rest and fresh air." In that spirit, the city allocated US$5 million to
upgrade the park in 2017, in particular to remove fences and transform
"hardscapes into greenscapes" as part of Mayor Bill de Blasio's *Parks
Without Borders* programme.[2] Part of this plan required the removal
of earth mounds designed by landscape architect Arthur E. Bye in the
1970s, as well as a series of "invasive" trees, in order to make room for
a grand, paved promenade across the park. However, some see these
concrete-paved plazas as a way of carving out commercial space for
vendors in the name of safe wheelchair access. The organization Friends
of Fort Greene Park has been negotiating with the city on the future
design of the park, as discrepancies have arisen concerning the health
of the zelkovas, maples, and plane trees slated to be removed. Large
trees absorb almost 70 times more air pollution each year than small,
newly planted trees, and community activists argue that the removal of
83 mature trees would cause irreparable environmental harm to their
lungs and their neighbourhood. Despite the fact that the infrastructural
upgrade is much needed and welcomed, Fort Greene's residents have
demanded more say in determining how the park should be used and
conserved. The Friends of Fort Greene Park president, Ling Hsu, is ask-
ing the Parks Department to focus on basic maintenance (bathrooms,
grills, drainage, workout equipment, ramps, mature trees) instead of a
grand redesign that would affect the aforementioned trees. In a second
ruling in January 2020, favouring Friends of Fort Greene Park, a judge
questioned the city's destruction of apparently healthy trees and the
impact of young saplings throughout the park.

1 A. Wachs, Bye Bye: Future uncertain for rare public landscape by A. E. Bye in
Brooklyn, *Architects Newspaper*, 26 September 2017.

2 J. Fox, $5 million awarded to Fort Greene Park for improvements, *Bklyner*, 25
May 2016.

SPECIMEN: Zelkova (*Zelkova serrata*). Branch, 2018

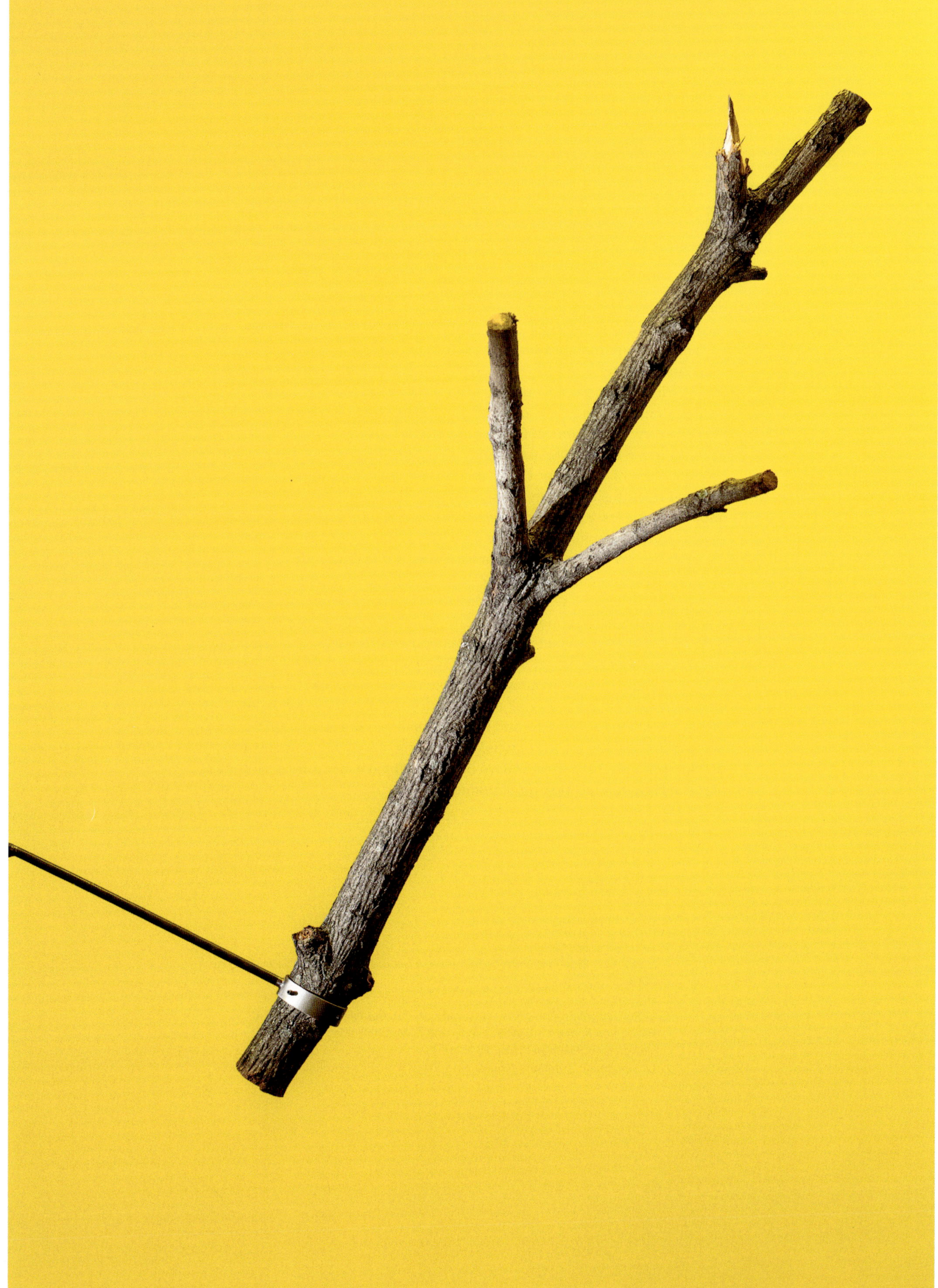

TREES TO NEUTRALIZE RIOTS

In January 1874, Tompkins Square—which had been cleared as an open space for military training in 1866—became a site of dissident political action. In the midst of an economic depression that would endure for several more years, some 10,000 civilians suffering surging food and rent prices and a scarcity of employment opportunities gathered in Tompkins Square to demonstrate.[1] The subsequent confrontation between police and the protesting workers resulted in hundreds of injuries. As depicted in the 1871 Kellogg and Pilat map of Tompkins Square Park, the open field—with three rows of trees around the outer perimeter—was the perfect ground for a public assembly, but also for demonstrations of social unrest. The riot pushed the city to convert the square into a park in 1878, with a labyrinthine layout incorporating natural barriers such as playgrounds, fences, and 450 trees, including a large number of American elms (almost none of which remain today).[2] Aside from providing a recreational space to the bourgeoisie, populating the square in this way was also a disciplinary strategy for neutralizing public gatherings and future protests via a number of obstructions. After many social and demographic changes over the 20th century, in the late 1980s and mid-1990s Tompkins Square Park again became a site of resistance and struggle against the drastic gentrification of the Lower East Side.[3] Encampments on the square became a symbol for urban resistance, providing space for housing and human rights advocacy, queer activism, and demands for action around the AIDS epidemic. By the late 1980s, Tompkins Square Park had become notorious as a refuge for some 300 rough sleepers, triggering what became the larger Tompkins Square Park movement, a grassroots resistance that demanded affordable housing. Frightened by the increasing social upheaval, "regeneration" efforts by the city led to the police riot on 6 August 1988 and subsequent camp eviction in 1991. The securitized redesign of Tompkins Square that followed included widening the pathways to allow police cars to easily drive through and between the trees, as well as the removal of the park bandshell, the scene of many concerts and political rallies in the 1960s, 1970s, and 1980s. While trees were initially planted to serve as obstacles to demonstrations, Tompkins Square has nevertheless become a symbolic place in New York protest movements.

1   Lower East Side Preservation Initiative, *A History of Tompkins Square Park*, 2019.

2   N. Smith, "A Riot is Now in Progress in Tompkins Square Park," 1874, in *Revolting New York: How 400 Years of Riot, Rebellion, Uprising and Revolution Shaped a City* (N. Smith and D. Mitchell, eds.) (Athens, GA: University of Georgia Press, 2018), p. 112.

3   Q. Sakamaki, *Tompkins Square Park* (New York: Powerhouse Books, 2008).

LOCATION: Tompkins Square Park, Manhattan

SPECIMEN: American elm (*Ulmus americana*). Branch, 2018

TOMPKINS SQUARE

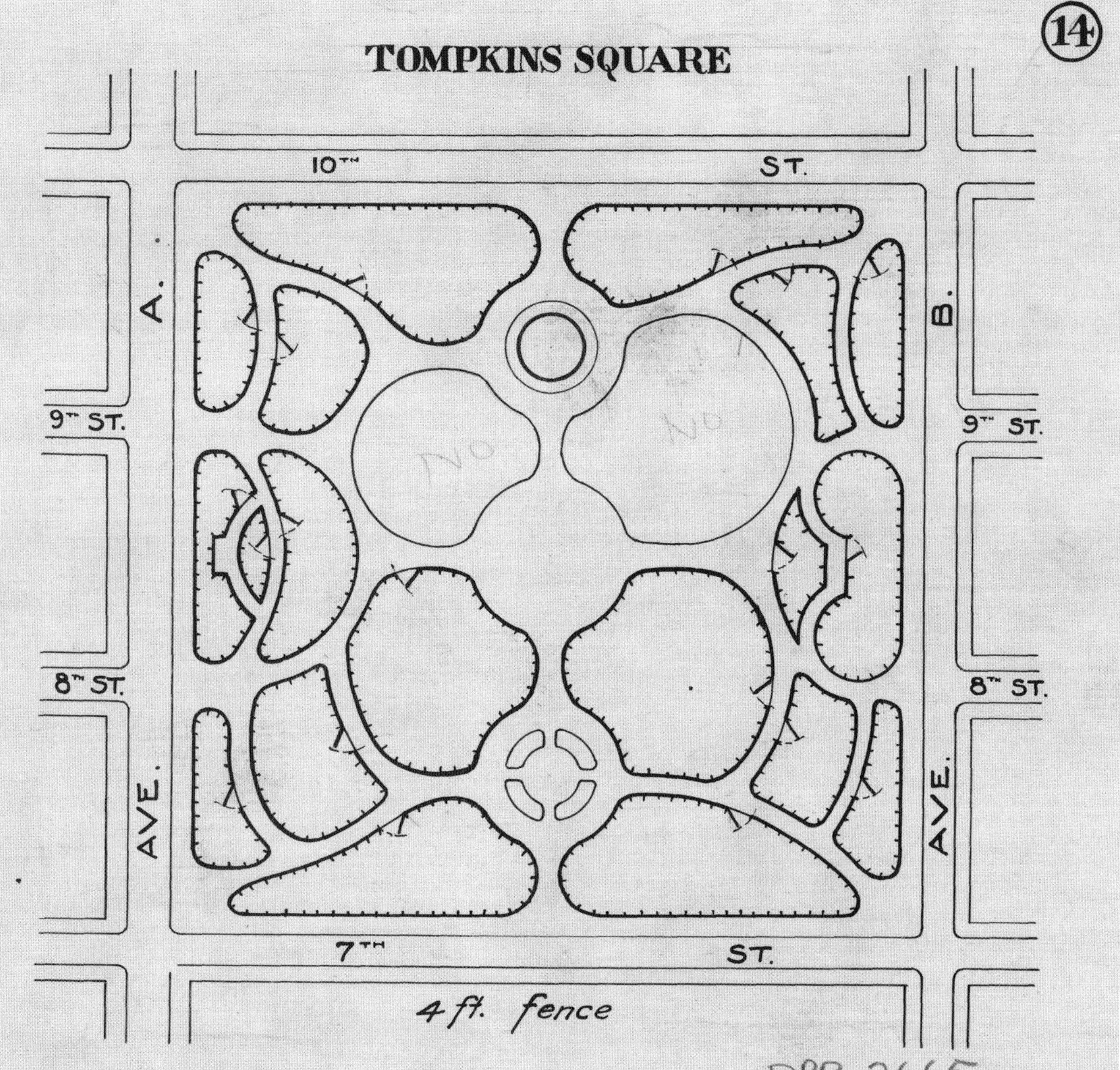

4 ft. fence

DPR-2665

TREES BORN OUT OF ASHES

The area known today as Flushing Meadows–Corona Park was once a tidal landscape inhabited by various Lenape communities, dispossessed of their land in the 17th century by European settlers. By the early 1900s, the site had been envisioned as a new industrial complex, centred on a new port. To create the appropriate conditions for development, the salt marshes were drained and filled with ash. Known as the Corona Ash Dump, the site received waste from industrial coal furnaces, garbage incinerators, and domestic refuse from throughout the city. Although the plans for the new port were abandoned, in part due to the onset of World War I, the dumping of ash continued, creating extremely unhealthy conditions in the neighbouring areas—immortalized as the "valley of ashes" in *The Great Gatsby*. One 100 foot high ash pile was so large that it was christened Mount Corona.[1] In the 1930s, Robert Moses selected the ash dumps, as well as surrounding meadows and an adjacent residential area, for the development of the new "Flushing Meadow Park," which would become the site for New York's 1939 and 1964 World's Fairs and an exemplary case for converting other historic wetlands into city parks. While the park's development led to the displacement of residents and the demolishing of homes, thousands of trees were transplanted to the park to evoke a "natural" landscape—on top of many layers of urban history. But, as the enclosed artificial lakes were deprived of the daily tidal flows that would provide fresh water, oxygen depletion led to high levels of eutrophication. Flushing Creek, the waterway that has been a symbol of environmental racism and community disinvestment for many years in the area, still frequently runs cloudy and sulphurous, full of industrial waste and sewage overflow. Its recent luxury "renewal"—with developers promising "environmental clean-up to a vacant, blighted parcel of land" for the Special Flushing Waterfront District Rezoning—will not protect existing residents from being priced out (p. 140). Such "climate resilience" projects often feature new greenways near disinvested neighbourhoods, a strong predictor of gentrification.[2] Current residents are left to endure the construction of apartments and amenities they cannot afford, and are asked to support the remediation of a park they may not have full access to.[3]

1   Bowery Boys, The Corona Ash Dump: Brooklyn's burden on Queens, a vivid literary inspiration and bleak, rat-filled landscape, *Bowery Boys History*, 9 May 2013.

2   A. Rigolon and J. Németh, Green gentrification or "just green enough:" Do park location, size and function affect whether a place gentrifies or not?, *Urban Studies*, 57 (2019): 402–420.

LOCATION: 111th Street at 50th Avenue, Queens

SPECIMEN: Northern red oak (*Quercus rubra*). Branch, 2018

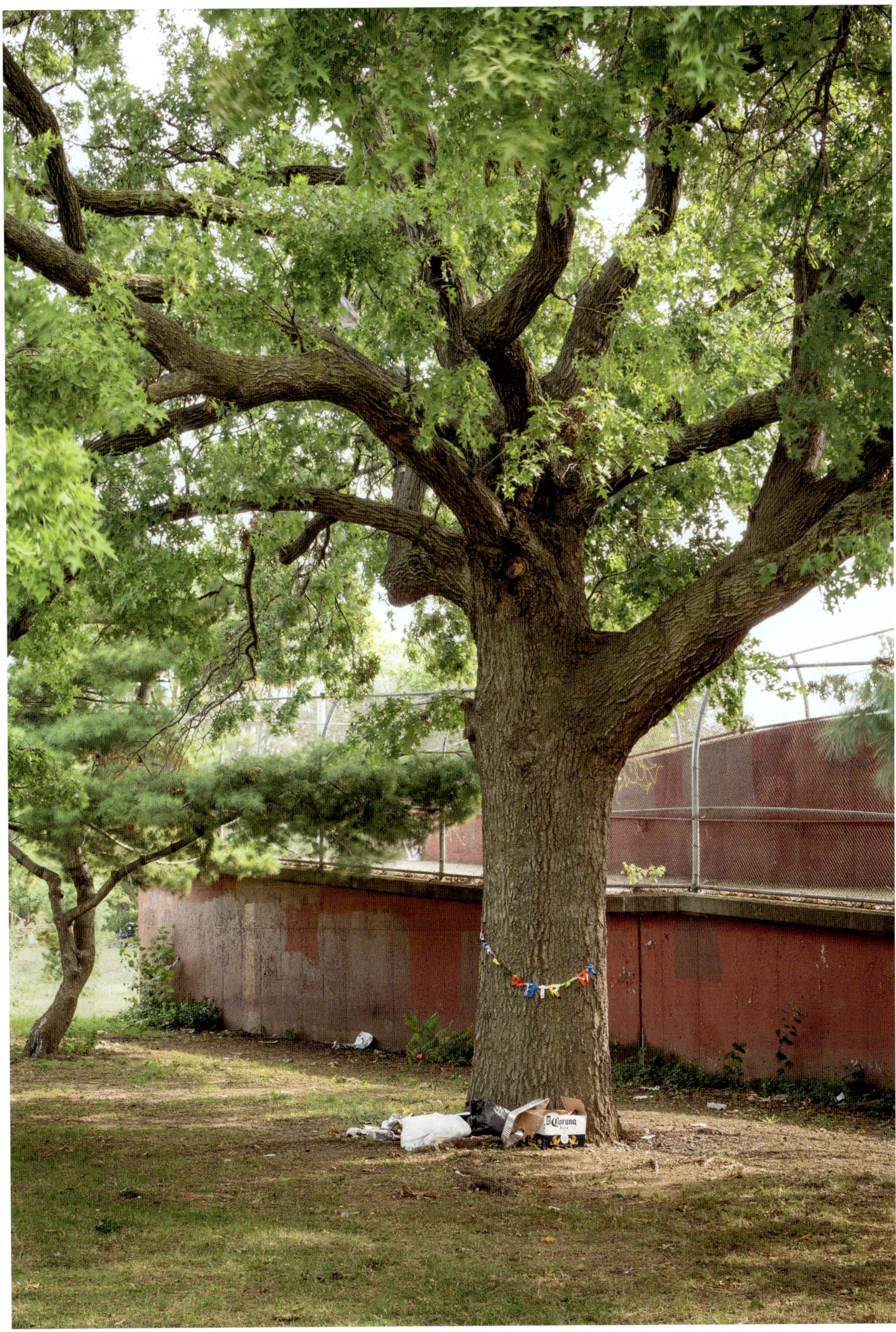

Handicapping Golf:
Mobilizing the Links

Nico Alexandroff

SHIFTING RHIZOME

After he bought the land in 2006, Donald Trump ordered one million sprigs of marram grass for Trump International Golf Links on the Aberdeenshire coast in Scotland. The real estate developer planned to utilize and manipulate the plant's ecosystem services to subsidize a billion-dollar golf resort. Trump planted the marrams for their ability to occupy hostile terrain, to survive in places uninhabitable by other plant species due to high winds, minimal soil nutrients, and the constant spray of saltwater. Marram grass (*Ammophila arenaria*) spreads via rhizomes—horizontal stems just under the surface of the soil. The word "rhizome" originates from the Ancient Greek *rhízōma*, meaning "mass of root." The rhizomes produce a network of roots and shoots, and store proteins and starch so that the plant can survive for years underground. The combination of these factors means that marrams are a "pioneering species" in coastal dune landscapes. Trump's golf course takes advantage of the rhizome network and its stores of nutrients as a way to control the transient and windy landscape known as "links."

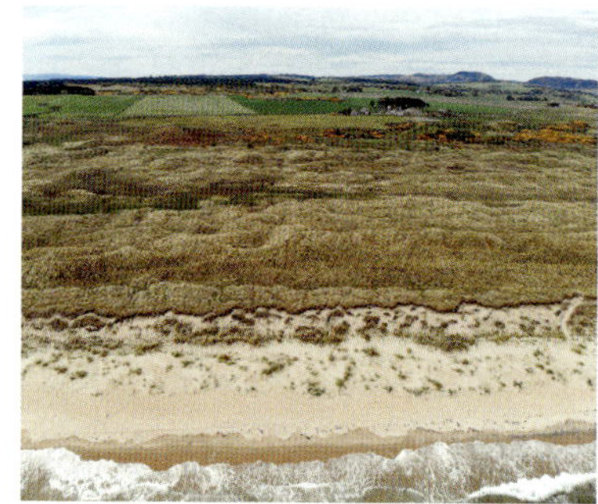

Fig. 1 Coul Links, 50 miles north of Inverness, a convergence for organic and inorganic matter in processes of ecological succession

ON "UNPRODUCTIVE" GROUND

The Scottish term "links" describes coastal grasslands—strips of undulating land that link the seashore and farmland. The sandy soil of links is not suitable for arable farming, and has historically been deemed unproductive. Links have been framed by several golf historians as a wasteland ready to be saved; "just waiting for golf courses

to be built upon it."[1] In the 12th century, King David I of Scotland chose to set aside the links for common use; they would be "treated as public lands, not subject to private ownership and reserved for the recreational use of all Scots, regardless of class."[2] It was here where the game of golf was first played in the 15th century, a way for farmers to pass the time in fallow seasons, hitting stones with sticks, the hardy nomadic sand dunes' erratic disposition making an ideal terrain. This pastime and landscape would later become defined as "links golf."[3]

In today's world, the links are highly valued for golf course developments, due in part to this golfing heritage but also due to the wild and the untameable nature of the dune systems—links golf courses are known to be the most challenging in the world, predominantly as a result of their unruly windscapes.

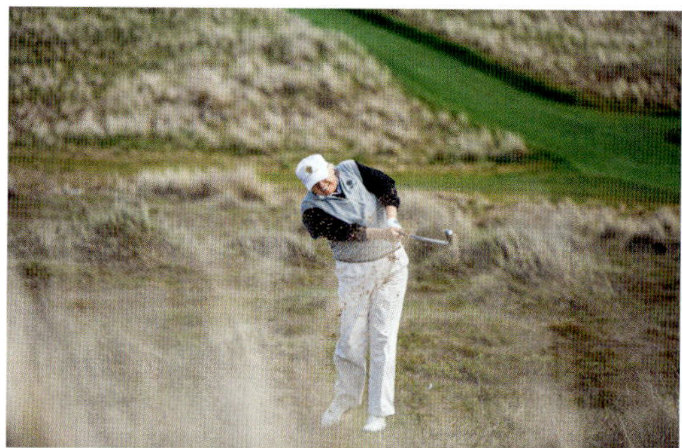

Fig. 2 President Donald Trump photographed at Trump Links International Golf Course in Aberdeen, Scotland

CATCHING THE WIND

It is this same windscape that makes the links so vital to the health of coastlines, being the catalyst for processes of ecological succession—the process of changing ecological structure over time from pioneering species on bare ground to climax communities such as woodlands. The wind is the convergence of gasses at different pressures, and is often at its strongest where the land meets the sea. Dune succession requires the wind for the movement of spores, seeds, sand, and seawater spray.

This liminal zone—the blurry distinction between seashore and farmland—is much more than a threshold, it is an example of a highly concentrated blending of organic and inorganic substances that, when healthy, reveal the full history of ecological succession within the space of a few hundred metres. There are 12 to 15 distinct dune types within this space, transitioning from bare sand with pioneering marrams to dense dune woodland, a stable and self-perpetuating ecology.[4] The links are a landscape in flux, which means there is an eclectic variety of flora and fauna species that depend on the variety of stages of succession. The process of ecological succession is linear, and moves inland according to the amount of nutrient content in the soil—which is itself dependent on the extent of decomposition that has taken place and a site's proximity to the ocean.

COMMODIFYING LINKS

These once "unproductive wastelands" have now been commodified by the golfing industry. Links golf courses are currently one of Scotland's main attractions, and in 2011 Scotland's total golf economy was estimated to generate £1.171 billion in revenue annually.[5] Golfers travel far and wide to experience a sense of wildness when playing the game, a way to escape ordinary life, and most links courses are relatively isolated from large settlements. Today, there are 256 golf links in the UK, with an average course size of about 150 acres, meaning that 38,400 acres (around 155.4 km²) of coastline have been lost to the game of golf. Mobile links untouched by golf are rare.

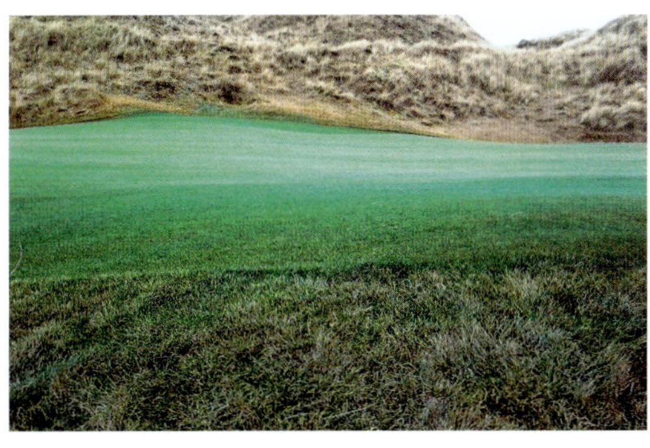

Fig. 3 *The Grass Is Greener On The Other Side Once It's Dyed* by Suzanne Kelly

This form of plundering has endangered fragile ecological processes. Modern golf courses such as Trump International Golf Links could not be further from a wilderness. Suzanne Kelly, a local resident, recounted "huge swathes of the green (and a little patch of sand) had been 'spray-painted' a blue-green colour … Is it possible that the grass is turning yellow in response to the sand and its proximity to the salt spray from the North Sea, making a dose of blue dye necessary for the appearance of health?"[6] Kelly's account speaks to the lack of consideration for the biological order on the site as the metabolic process of the dunescape is inevitably altered. These observations contradict the idea of the "untamed"

that golf courses advertise. Instead, they are meticulously manicured, carefully constructed, landscaped, planted, sometimes painted, and, thus, financialized—they are an exercise in experience design.

Golf has not always required this vast quantity of space. The game has changed drastically since its creation in the 15th century, when wooden golf balls would carry 75 metres;[7] nowadays, the popular Titleist Pro V1 ball can be driven 270 metres.[8] Technological advances in materials and design of the skin of the golf ball mean this distance is constantly increasing as balls become more aerodynamic. Golf equipment is a $2.6 billion industry, and golf balls account for one-third of this.[9] If it wasn't for the Pro V1's 352 dimples, the distance it travels would be halved.[10] Golf has transformed from a game where humans and their golf balls would blend into the existing landscape to a game that is responsible for territorial scales of ecological destruction. The golf ball has terraformed the links, and Trump International Golf Links is a prime example of this levelling.

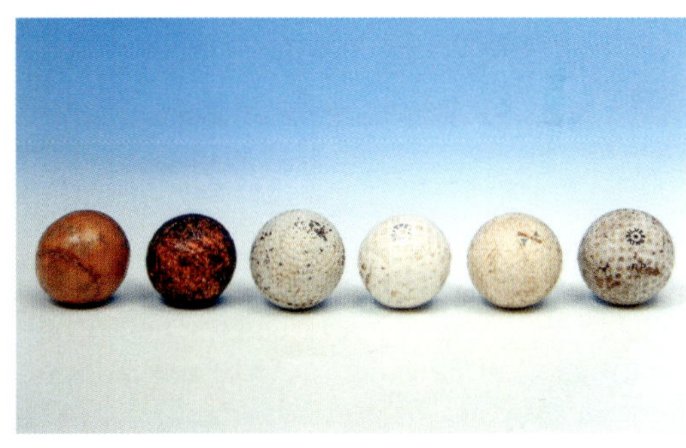

Fig. 4 Development of the golf ball

In 2006, Foveran Links, a dune system in Aberdeenshire, caught the attention of Donald Trump. The real estate developer decided he wanted to build two golf courses, a practice range, 550 "golf homes," a shooting range, a hotel, and a clubhouse, with a budget of one billion dollars and a promise of 6,000 jobs for local people (unsurprisingly, only 150 people have been employed so far).[11] The development sits within a Site of Special Scientific Interest (SSSI) for its dune mobility and biodiversity, and the approval of the golf course by the Scottish Government in 2008 (after it was rejected by Aberdeenshire council) was quite controversial.

The design and construction of Trump International Golf Links showed little to no regard for the existing condition of the dunes. The mobile dune at Foveran Links would once shift 11 metres every year, an essential process for the health of local vegetation that also made it one of the most mobile dune systems in the UK.[12] As well as planting one million sprigs of marram grass to, in Trump's words, "stop the dunes blowing away," the development also bulldozed several 4,000-year-old dunes, and in their place planted bentgrass, perennial ryegrass, and fescue, tightly mown and neatly maintained by a team of "green keepers," who mow the grass from three directions so it

59

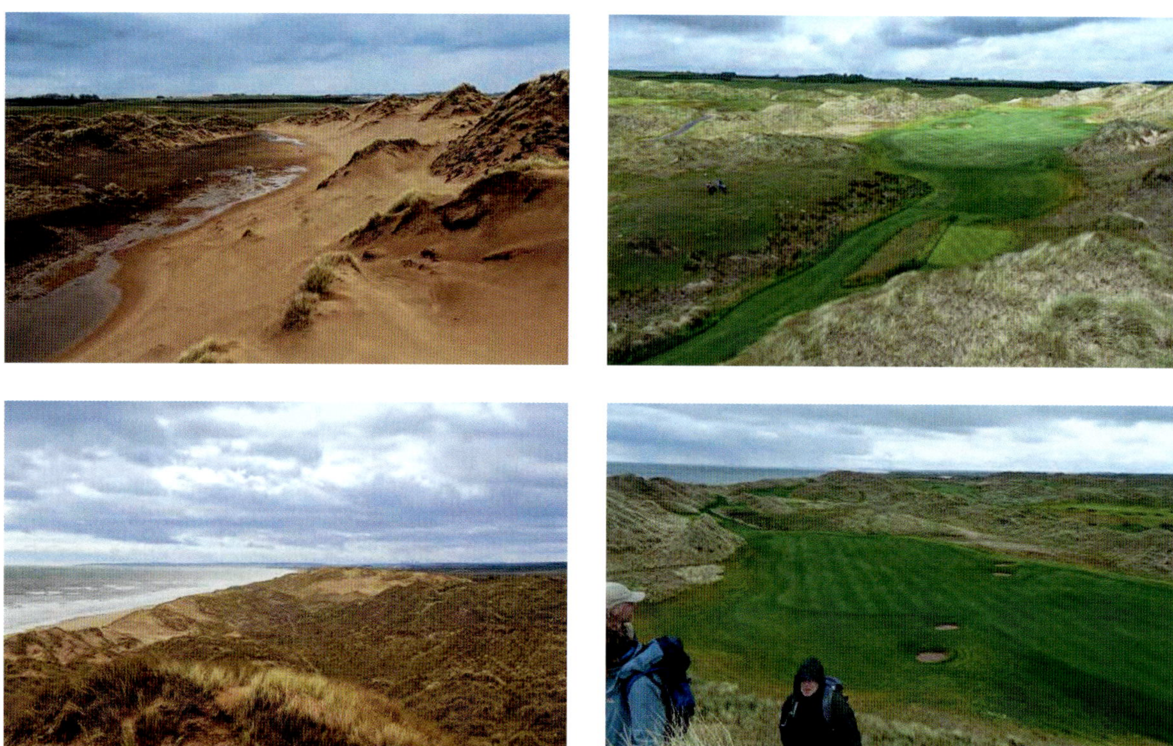

Fig. 5 Before and after construction of the course (2011–2013). *Foveran Links SSSI: NCA Review (Assessment of Geomorphology)*, Scottish Natural Heritage, by Dr Alistair Rennie

grows straight.[13] Trump International Golf Links hotel and clubhouse opened in 2012 and, in June 2019 the Foveran Links lost its status as an SSSI as a result of the golf course. Also in 2019, the 550 "golf homes" were given planning permission, and the construction of the second golf links was approved in 2020.[14]

LANDSCAPES OF EXCLUSIVITY

Donald Trump's golf course reveals a more general trend in the typology—golf courses are microcosms of exclusivity. Keller Easterling refers to such architectures as "spatial products."[15] The American model of a golf course—a model frequently built by Trump—goes hand in hand with housing, hotels, resorts, and clubs. Easterling argues these "spatial products" are land development tools creating intensities of wealth. Local residents near the golf developments are often evicted or bought out of their land to ensure no unsightly vistas for paying customers. These spatial products create a physical barrier between local human and other-than-human residents and their coastline, as the golf courses, golf houses, clubhouse, restaurants, hotels, etc., spread out along the shore to monetize the uninterrupted sea view.

Economic and social exclusivities emerge when the design of golf courses is separated from rightful bioprocesses—that is, when an ecological exclusivity is created. Native plant species are wiped clear, disregarded, and processes of ecological succession are broken when crucial perennial species are dislocated by the monoculture grasses of the fairways and greens (playing area). They are "man"-made landscapes disguised as nature through their "soft" landscaping credentials.[16] But, instead of imagining humans as outside of ecological succession, it is perhaps more productive to imagine them as an alien species imposed on fragile dune ecologies, altering the local equilibrium. This species was then able to copy and repeat its golf course habitat around the world, creating a parallel ecology of wealth intensities. With this perspective, we can now reconsider the game of golf by challenging its ecological exclusivity. By considering the golf ball as an active, holistic element within processes of ecological succession, the golfers—like Trump with the marrams—can be utilized and manipulated to become ecological enablers.

1 M. Campbell, *The Scottish Golf Book* (Champaign, IL: Sports Pub. Inc., 1999), p. 14.

2 J. Williamson, *Born on The Links: A Concise History of Golf* (London: Rowman & Littlefield, 2018), p. 4.

3 Williamson, *Born on The Links*, pp. 4–7.

4 The stages are beach, embryo dune, foredune, mobile dune, fixed dune, grey dune, dune marsh, wet grass flushes, dune scrubland, and broadleaved woodland. Dune slacks are intermittently spread across these stages. They are areas where the wind has been able to blow out until it reaches the water table.

5 KPMG, *The Value of Golf to Scotland's Economy*, Golf Advisory Practice in EMA (Edinburgh: Scottish Golf Union, 2013), pp. 4–5.

6 S. Kelly, The Menie Estate: From SSSIs to bluegrass country, *Aberdeen Voice*, 25 February 2013, https://aberdeenvoice.com/2013/02/the-menie-estate-from-sssis-to-bluegrass-country (accessed 13 September 2021).

7 J. F. Hotchkiss and J. S.t Martin, *500 Years of Golf Balls* (Dubuque, IA: Antique Trader Books, 1997).

8 J. Sherman, Pro V1 vs. Pro V1x tested: How do Titleist premium balls compare?, *Practical Golf*, 2019, https://practical-golf.com/pro-v1-vs-pro-v1x-tested-how-do-titleist-premium-balls-compare (accessed 13 September 2021).

9 B. Alberstadt, Getting a grip on golf's $2.6 billion equipment industry, *National Golf Foundation*, January 2018, https://www.thengfq.com/2018/01/getting-a-grip-on-golfs-2-6-billion-equipment-industry (accessed 13 September 2021).

10 I. Kavas, A brief history of the golf ball, *Golfsupport*, 22 September 2016, https://golfsupport.com/blog/a-brief-history-of-the-golf-ball (accessed 13 September 2021).

11 R. Revesz, Trump fails to create promised jobs and investment in Scotland, locals say, *The Independent*, 7 January 2016, https://www.independent.co.uk/news/people/trump-fails-create-promised-jobs-and-investment-scotland-locals-say-a6801466.html (accessed 13 September 2021).

12 A. Rennie, *Foveran Links SSSI: NCA Review—Earth Sciences, Freedom of Information Request* (Scottish Natural Heritage, 2019) https://www.whatdotheyknow.com/request/603763/response/1446998/attach/3/FOI%20Freedom%20of%20Information%20Request%20Harry%20Jamshidian%20Effect%20of%20Trump%20International%20Golf%20International%20Scotland%20on%20Sand%20Dunes%20at%20Forveran%20Links%20Information%20Released.pdf (accessed 13 September 2021).

13 Tour led by Jonas Hedberg, Golf Operations Manager at Trump International Golf Links.

14 K. Beattie and D. Walker, Trump International to build another golf course in north-east after permission is granted, *Press and Journal*, 17 October 2020, https://www.pressandjournal.co.uk/fp/news/aberdeenshire/2576389/trump-international-to-build-another-golf-course-in-north-east-after-permission-is-granted (accessed 13 September 2021).

15 K. Easterling, *Enduring Innocence* (Cambridge, MA: MIT Press, 2005).

16 A purposeful use of "man" for the sexist industry of golf.

Two Tenement House Acts, one in 1867 and another in 1901, aimed to improve the squalid living conditions of the working class by setting minimum housing standards and adding street trees, among other measures. While trees planted along streets could not directly resolve pressing issues like overcrowding, overwork, and overburdened infrastructure, they were promoted as a substitute for an absent park system. In practice, the Acts facilitated land speculation while appeasing housing improvement demands.[1] Just as the creation of Central Park helped the value of surrounding land to skyrocket, tree-lined streets can increase property value. By the end of the 19th century, a number of organizations dedicated to surveying, planting, and maintaining street trees were established. For example, the Tree Planting Association of New York City, founded in 1897, observed that many of the city's newly planted street trees were already in decline. The Tenement Shade Tree Committee, a subgroup of the Tree Planting Association, created in 1902, aimed to introduce new trees in poor areas of the Lower East Side. While new trees may have benefited tenement dwellers by cleansing the air, water, and earth, in reality poorer neighbourhoods were not the primary beneficiaries of tree-planting efforts. There was, nonetheless, a naturally occurring tree in tenement areas: the ailanthus, known as the "tenement palm" or the "tree of heaven." Imported from China in the 1820s as fodder for moths that would make a silk industry in New York, the ailanthus was too well suited to its new home. Soon after its arrival, New Yorkers began to blame their headaches and allergies on the strong, rancid smell of the trees' flowers in summer, and in 1855 the *New York Times* called not only for a ban on planting new ailanthuses but for a mass uprooting of that "filthy and worthless foreigner."[2] However, ailanthus was one of the few species resistant to the inch worm infestation that devastated the tree canopy, leaving the city without adequate shade in the scorching summer. The ability of ailanthus to thrive in boarded-up lots, rubbish heaps, contaminated soils, and between cracks in the pavement created an enduring stigma around the species, an "invasive" nicknamed the "tree of hell."

1 P. Marcuse, Housing policy and the myth of the benevolent state, in *Critical Perspectives on Housing* (R. Bratt, C. Hartman, and A. Meyerson, eds) (Philadelphia, PA: Temple University Press, 1986), p. 250.

2 M. Nijhuis, A tree persists in Brooklyn, *The Last Word on Nothing*, 5 October 2017; J. Jones, *Urban Forests: A Natural History of Trees in the American Cityscape* (New York: Viking, 2016).

LOCATION: Stanton Street between Clinton Street and Attorney Street, Manhattan

SPECIMEN: Tree of heaven (*Ailanthus altissima*). Branch, 2018

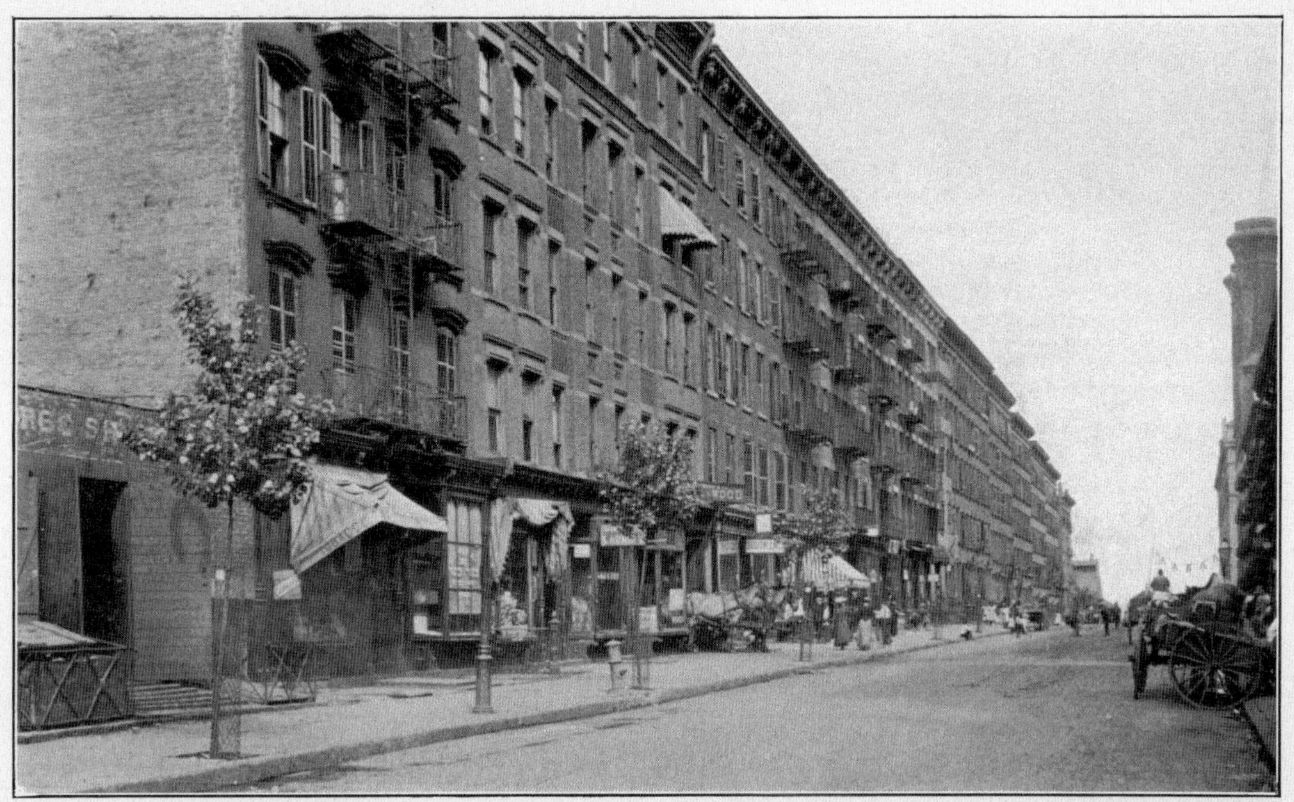

East Thirty-Ninth Street—An Entire Block Planted by the Tenement Shade Tree Committee.

TREE CLEARANCE

With its leprous houses, gambling dens, saloons, brothels, slaughter-houses, and a record-breaking murder rate, Mulberry Bend—a pocket of the Five Points neighbourhood in Lower Manhattan—was the pulse of one of New York's most notorious slums at the end of the 19th century. The area (today bounded by Baxter, Bayard, and Worth Streets in China-town) was named after a grove of mulberry trees. Although mulberry trees were brought from China to the USA to help establish a silk industry (silkworms feed on mulberry leaves), such ventures never flourished, and the mulberries became ornamental street trees. The trees surrounded Collect Pond, a freshwater pond that had been transformed into an open sewer. In 1817, the city drained and filled the pond by digging a canal (which still runs under Canal Street). While Jacob Riis' depiction of Mulberry Bend in his book *How the Other Half Lives* raised awareness about the conditions of the neighbourhood, his reformist ambition came up against his own racism towards Mulberry Bend's tenement dwellers, whom he characterized as "shiftless, destructive and stupid" and openly blamed for the neighbourhood's decline.[1] Mulberry Bend was eventually razed and replaced with Calvert Vaux's Mulberry Bend Park (renamed Columbus Park to commemorate an Italian figure, and a genocide). Its design was inspired by Italian landscapes, in a weak attempt to reach out to the local community. Riis insisted that poverty could be eradicated (displaced) through slum clearance—praising the replacement of ramshackle houses with new trees, flowers, and grasses.[2] Where the homeless residents of the Bend went is unclear. Some were reported to have sought shelter in the heated basement of the neo-Italian pavilion that had replaced their homes in the severe winter of 1903. As in other 19th-century European and North American cities, the primary aim of the slum clearance of Mulberry Bend was not to improve social and political inequalities, but to enhance the economic efficiency of urban space for capital investment in its surroundings.[3] All the mulberry trees along Mulberry Street by the former Mulberry Bend are long gone; only the street remains in place.

LOCATION: Horatio Street at Hudson Street, Manhattan

SPECIMEN: Mulberry (*Morus nigra*). Branch, 2018

1   J. Riis, *How the Other Half Lives* (New York: Charles Scribner's Sons, 1890), cited in M. Page, *The Creative Destruction of Manhattan 1900–1940* (Chicago, IL: University of Chicago Press, 1999), p. 79.

2   Page, *The Creative Destruction of Manhattan*, p. 82.

3   M. Gandy, *Concrete and Clay: Reworking Nature in New York City* (Cambridge, MA: MIT Press, 2002), p. 37.

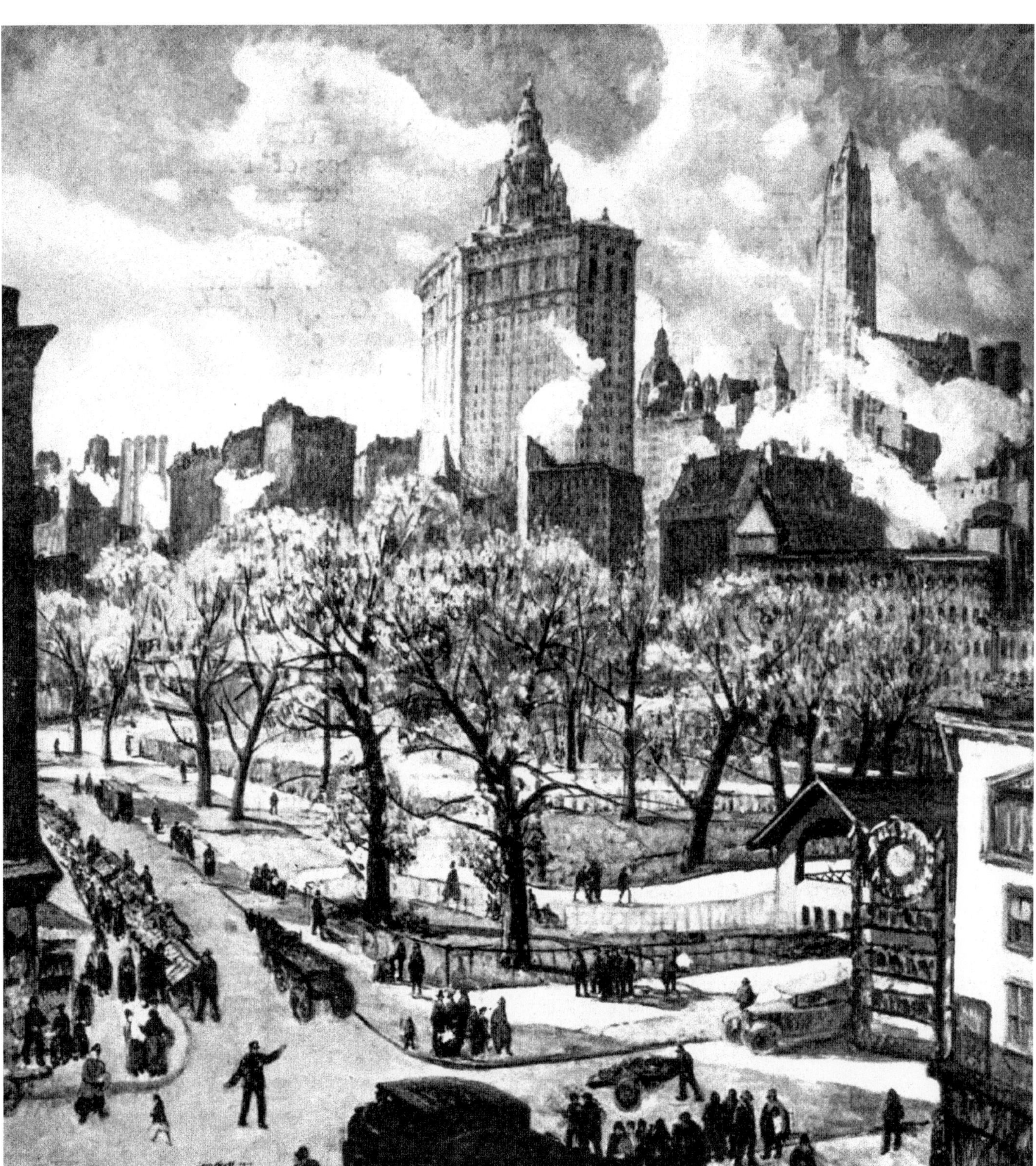

TREE KIN

Donar's Oak—located in what is now Hesse, Germany—was a tree venerated by pagans until the eighth century, when Anglo-Saxon missionary Saint Boniface removed it to build a church in its place. Scholars have speculated that this act inspired the modern custom of cutting Christmas trees, a tradition that may derive from Christian rejection of tree-worshipping cultures.[1] Ironically, Christmas trees today have acquired a ritual value that seems to compete with the religious significance that they are meant to commemorate. In New York City, pines, spruces, and firs from as far as Virginia and Alaska flood the streets in advance of Christmas. Many trees also come from Vermont, the "Green Mountain State," which was already suffering from intensive clearcutting by the end of the 19th century, and where today 3,650 acres across 70 plantations are solely dedicated to Christmas tree production. These monoculture plantations are heavily dependent on pesticides and other biosecurity-enhancing chemicals, especially as some of the trees are transported to Hawai'i or abroad, which adds to their invisible ecological cost. In addition, competitive bidding on stalls for Christmas tree sales in New York has caused rental fees to spike each year, boosted by the Coniferous Tree Exception in the city's laws, which guarantees the right to sell trees on the street ("Storekeepers and peddlers may sell and display coniferous trees during the month of December"). A stall in SoHo Square cost US$56,005 in rent in 2016, while a stall in Washington Market Park in TriBeCa cost US$31,400 in 2017. One can even track financial booms and busts, as Christmas trees perform like an economic indicator with 6- to 12-year delays—i.e. how long it takes trees to grow to market size. In the happy 1990s, farmers planted too many trees, causing prices to drop to unsustainable minimums in the early 2000s. After the 2008 recession, ailing farmers planted too few trees, which has led to prices skyrocketing in recent years. These new forms of money/tree worship were further disrupted by the 2012 and 2014 droughts and the severe spring floods in 2019. Nonetheless, the recession did awaken New Yorkers' perception of tree value, and they saw a peak in the provision of public mulching sites for their Christmas trees in 2007, from four to over 60. Known as Mulchfest, the city's effort to digest Christmas leftovers has grown to 30,000 sites in recent years. One can enjoy Chipping Saturdays until mid-January, or volunteer to extend trees' afterlife into the city's gardens and parks.

1 R. F. Nash, *The Rights of Nature: A History of Environmental Ethics* (Madison, WI: University of Wisconsin Press, 1989), p. 91; M. Hall, *Plants as Persons: A Philosophical Botany* (New York: SUNY Press, 2011), p. 120.

LOCATION: Harvested in Vermont, discarded in Brooklyn

SPECIMEN: Fraser fir (*Abies fraseri*). Christmas tree, 2018

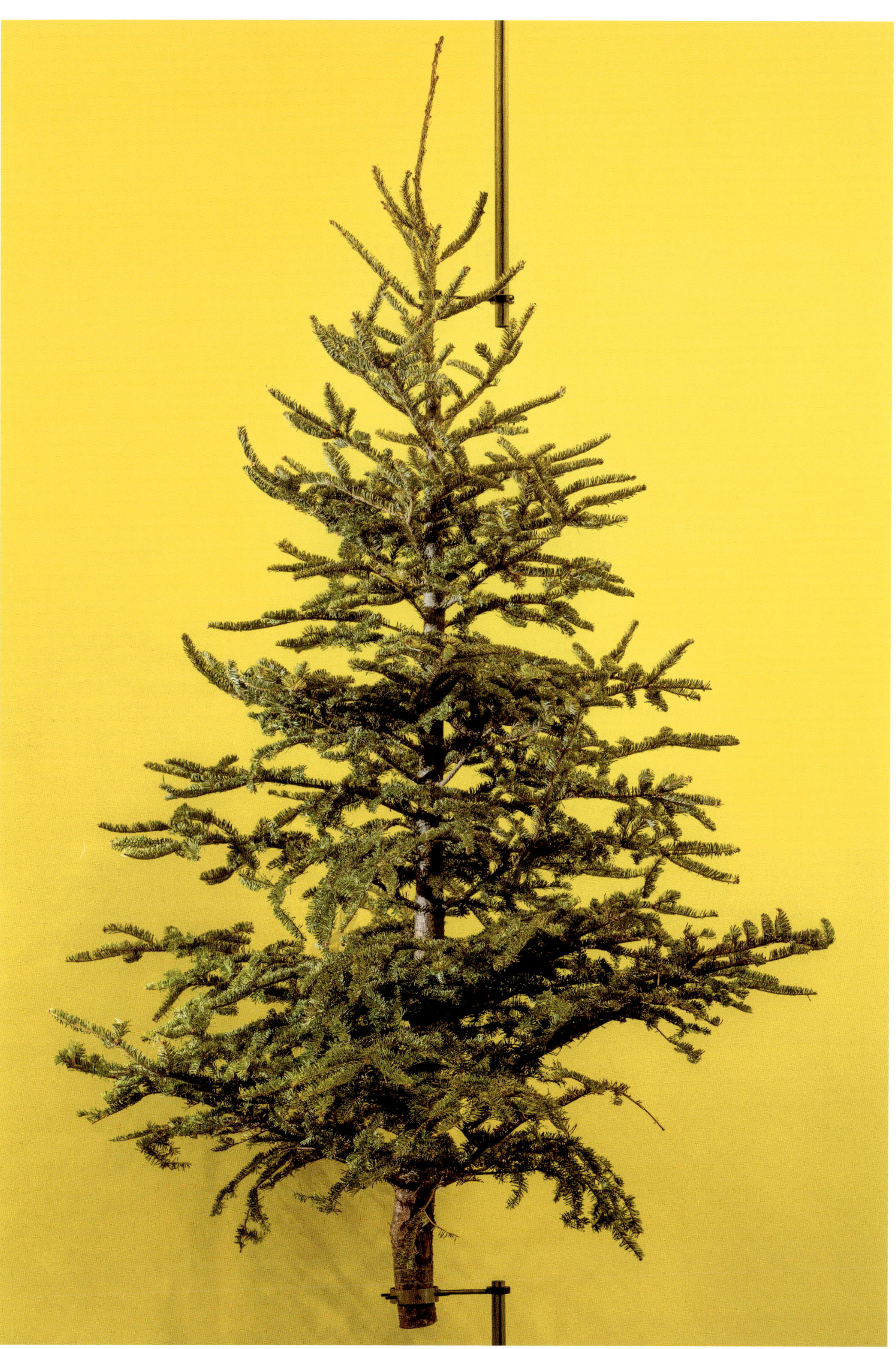

Knowing Through Harakeke

Penelope Allan,
Martin Bryant,
Huhana Smith

THE BIRTH OF HARAKEKE

... each new blade [of harakeke] emerges between two larger blades, a child protected by parents, and the roots of the fans are so intertwined that they stand or fall together as one. [Fig. 1]
    Joan Metge, *New Growth from Old*
    (Victoria University Press, 1995)

According to Māori *whakapapa* (genealogical) narrative, Tāwhirimātea, the *atua* (spiritual entity) of winds, climates, and storms, was distraught when his brother Tānemahuta—the *atua* of humankind and forests—separated their parents Ranginui (sky father) and Papatūānuku (earth mother) from their dark, loving embrace [Fig. 2]. In his despair, Tāwhirimātea tore out his eyes, crushed them into pieces, and threw them into the sky to become Ngā Mata o te Ariki—the "Eyes of the God," now more commonly known as the star constellation Matariki. Although blinded, he continued to battle his sibling Tānemahuta while feeling his way around the sky, bringing winds from different directions.[1] Meanwhile, Tānemahuta coupled with Pākoti to create their offspring, Harakeke.[2] Harakeke (a flax-like plant species, *Phormium tenax*) was born with a fanned form that could withstand any wind that Tāwhirimātea could stir up, and a root system that could soak up and filter water like a sponge.

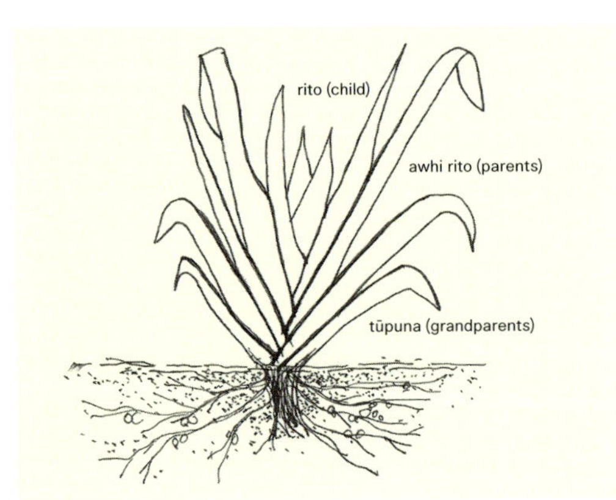

Fig. 1 The fibrous blades and roots of harakeke

How might harakeke, its stories, and its connection with Māori generate another way of knowing in this age of climate crisis?

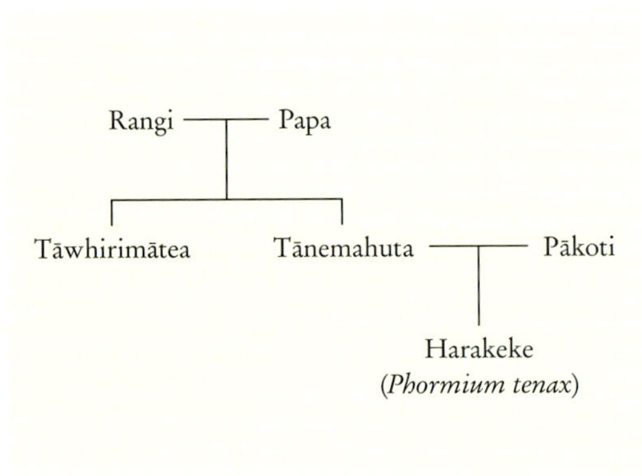

Fig. 2 The *whakapapa* of harakeke, represented here like a family tree

HARAKEKE IS *TAONGA* (TREASURE)

Wai korari is a sweet, syrupy fluid which fills the large reddish-brown flower of the flax stalks ... At low tide the flower is empty, and, as the tide comes in, so the *wai korari* gradually rises in the flower, until at high tide it is full to the brim, and at spring-tide actually flows over in a steady drip. As the tide goes out the wai korari recedes until the flower is dry again, and so on twice a day while the flowers are in full bloom.
    Rod McDonald [*Te Hekenga: Early Days in Horowhenua: Being the Reminiscences of Mr. Rod McDonald*][3]

For Māori who revered it as a whole-plant healer and whole-of-system healer, harakeke is the verdant protector of the lowland waterways and expansive wetland margins [Fig. 3].[4] Its health signifies the wellbeing of *whenua* (land) and *wai māori* (freshwater). Materially it is highly versatile and strong. In everyday practices, Māori fashioned harakeke leaves and their fibre into *kupenga* (fishing nets), *kete* (baskets), and other carrying vessels, *whāriki* (mats), and *taura* (rope), using a mussel shell to soften the *rau* (long leaves) or with a firmer grip to strip off the cuticle and reveal fine *muka* (fibre threads). It was processed by hand to make *kakahu* (Māori cloaks and clothing); weave *tāniko* cloak borders, belts, and sandals; bind lathes for tukutuku panels; form bird snares; or to fashion toggles or interweave feathers or dog skin to the *awe* (collar) of weapons like *taiaha* (fighting staffs).

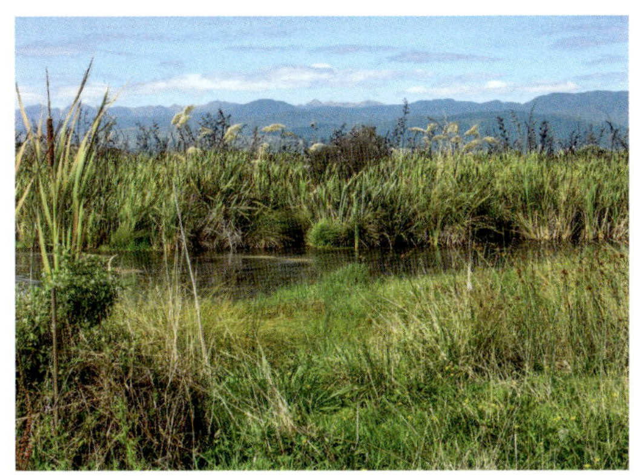

Fig. 3 Dense raupo and harakeke (with black korari flower heads) protecting the Te Hākari dune wetland edge, with the Tararua Ranges behind

Harakeke is also steeped in spiritual and cultural significance. *Tangata* (people) value the plant for its connections to the environmental, spiritual, and astronomical entities of *ngā Atua Māori*. In star lore, stars seen in the predawn sky mark the months, while the rising sun in the eastern sky marks seasonal time. Stellar and solar indicators observed in combination with lunar phases converge to mark Māori understandings of time and the environment. This knowledge, regarded as *taonga tuku iho* (intergenerational treasure, handed on), is the very basis of the dynamic interplay of *whakapapa* within the natural world. Harakeke rich with ancestral legacies is one part of that interrelated environment. Its *whakapapa* connects *whanau* (family) to the *whenua* (land) but also to the stars, the sun and the moon.[5]

VALUING HARAKEKE

Now, you have a treasured item (taonga) that you give to me, without the two of us putting a price on it, and I give it to someone else. Perhaps after a long while, this person remembers that he has this taonga, and that he should give me a return gift, and he does so. This is the *hau* of the *taonga* that was previously given to me. I must pass on that treasure to you. It would not be right for me to keep it for myself. Whether it is a very good *taonga* or a bad one, I must give to you, because that treasure is the *hau* of your *taonga*, and if I hold on to it for myself, I will die. This is the *hau*. That's enough.

Letter from Tamati Ranapiri to Peehi, 23 November 1907[6]

Taonga species like harakeke are important to the health of the land. They create a deep sense of ancestral belonging, and along with this ancestral belonging, a "kin-accountability" that "keeps *taonga* active" within their webs of relationships.[8] This keeps the *taonga* "warm" within the *rohe* (region) through acts of *kaitiakitanga* and the retention of their *korero* (narrative): the knowledge of their history and their *whakapapa*.[9] *Whakapapa* is the essential expression of *whanaungatanga*, where everything in the world—cosmology, peoples, environmental properties and lands, and all entities that exist within it—is understood as interrelated and interdependent.[10] Embodying "environmental ethics, values of respect, sharing, reciprocity and humility," *whakapapa* orders and makes sense of this complex mix of relationships.[11] Within the interrelated world view of *whakapapa*, treasured biodiversity, like *taonga* species, are crucial to the way Māori know their land and waterways (through relational connections) and how they value them.

Western knowledge systems have only recently realized harakeke's ecological importance: as a reservoir for water, as a windbreak, or for its capacity to enhance the productivity of farmland, to improve the condition of water, and to assist in returning resilience to the coastal plains. But for Māori it is more extensive and entangled than that. Harakeke has deep cultural and spiritual significance: not just valued for *what it can do*, it is bound to humans in an intricate web of reciprocal relationships that emphasize the complexity and connectedness of *all* intricate co-existent kin relationships within the natural and cosmological environment.

Western science, on the other hand, favours metrics that place human beings and human needs at the centre of the world. The practice of offsetting, now prevalent across the Western world as a way of justifying extractive practices and clear felling of forests, is just one example of the fruits of this reductive, hierarchical form of knowledge. With little regard for complexity, accountability, or a sense of value independent of human desire, offsetting reduces communities of plants to a simple numerical equation of value, separating them into component parts, then bartering them away. It is easily done, since plants cannot resist. Trapped "in the amber of mathematical models and scientific constructs," offsetting, like its counterpart ecological economics, underappreciates socio-ecosystem complexity because, by default, it subsumes the non-human world into the category of capital.[12]

THREATENING HARAKEKE

By 1914, the area in Kuku under bush was only one quarter what it had been in 1890. Trees were felled and burnt, and the ashes sown with English varieties of grass e.g. cocksfoot, clover. Swamp drainage, an extensive and expensive undertaking, was not carried out in Kuku in the first part of this period. The fact that the swamp zones were owned by a group of impecunious, easy-going Māoris helps to explain this lack of economic development.

John Rodford Wehipeihana, *Sequent Economies in Kuku*[13]

The ancestral lands of Ngāti Tūkorehe (the tribe of Tūkorehe) stretch from the mountains to the sea on the dynamic coastal plain of Horowhenua in the south-west region of Te Ika a Maui (North Island), Aotearoa New Zealand. They extend across aeolian sand dunes to the ocean in the east, and are bordered by the Tararua Ranges in the west. For millions of years, streams and rivers washed soil from the mountains, leaving deep beds of alluvium across the plain, while sea levels rose and fell according to the cycle of advancing and retreating ice ages. Below the surface of the ground, unmapped reservoirs of subterranean fresh water trace the routes of ancient rivers submerged by successive earthquakes.

This porous soil once supported a vast "wet-foot" coastal forest sheltering dune lakes, lagoons, and dune wetlands fringed with harakeke amidst a lush cloak of coastal flora, such as manuka, koromiko, karamū, hukihuki, toetoe, and tī kouka [Fig. 4]. Tragically for us today, very little of these ecologies remain. "Nowhere in New Zealand," says ecologist Geoff Park, "is there still such a forest … and never before has a New Zealand landscape been so ruthlessly cleared."[14] In a matter of 20 years, from the arrival of the first colonial settlers to the advent of refrigeration, the extensive wetlands were drained and the forests felled to create land suitable for dairy and the production of dairy products for Britain.[15]

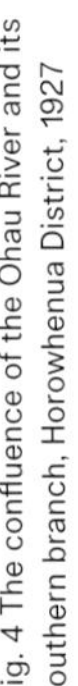

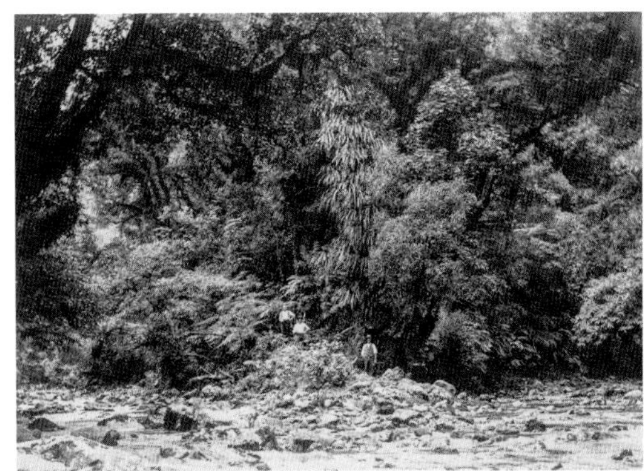

The combined impacts of colonial settlement and expansion—land alienation via colonial legislation, complex shifts in power and governance, and the Crown's refusal to protect the environment from late 19th and 20th century agricultural expansion—forced many *hapū* (collectives of family groups) to move away from their ancestral lands to find work in urban areas. Destabilisation marked the tumultuous period between 1840 and 1870, where major shifts in land tenure created political disturbances over lands and waterways; caused complicated internal struggles amongst *iwi* and *hapū*; and disrupted customary relationships to lands, waters, and knowledge systems. The reverberations continue to impact current generations' customary rights and the roles these generations might play in making better decisions about what remains.

Through these struggles, parts of the Horowhenua coastal plain have remained largely in Māori hands. And yet the land and its Māori "owners" too are suffering. When, from the late 1930s to late 1960s, non-Māori farmers began leasing these Māori wetland and coastal holdings, the clearing and drainage of already fragmented and diminished harakeke–wetland–estuarine ecosystems dramatically accelerated to increase productivity on what was considered "marginal" land for farming.

A typical example is the Tahamata Incorporation of Māori land holders, who care for farmlands dominated by the dynamic Ōhau River, which meanders across the farms' lowlands, between sand dunes, before it drains into the Kuku Ōhau River estuary and empties into the sea. In a feat of engineering hubris, one of the meanders, known locally as the "loop," was cut through in an attempt to force the river to the sea as quickly as possible, seriously threatening the health of the *whenua* (land) and damaging the cultural connections to it. The severed loop languished; the force of the straightened river eroded the low coastal sand dunes that protect this stretch of coastline from the sea; wetlands were drained; and reeds and sedges were cleared. The abundant harakeke, physically and spiritually treasured plant of the lowland ecology, was a casualty to the newly drained ground and its freshly sown, fertilizer-fed pasture grasses. It is difficult to express this loss in Western terms.

A generation later there is severe ecological decline in and destruction of treasured biodiversity. Because limited native vegetation protects the river margins,in a heavy rain, when the river floods, much of the lowlands are covered in water.[16] When flooding coincides with high tides and storms, water can sit on the farmland for days. The remaining wetlands now all have elevated concentrations of nutrients, from phosphate and synthetic fertilizers in their water systems, and are smothered in hornwort, an aquatic weed which lurks beneath the surface of dune and wetland lakes, creating a dysfunctional ecosystem despite attempts at healing.

But there is hope. These volatile shifts have been the catalyst for a cultural and environmental resurgence of *kaitiakitanga* (stewardship) in Kuku led by a small group of passionate *iwi* and *hapū* members who recognize that traditional Western agriculture practices will continue to degrade *whenua*, increase its vulnerability to sea level rise, and accelerate storm-based erosion. Since 1996, they have been gathering information from *kaumatua* (elders), key wild *kai* (food plants and animals) gatherers, and fisherfolk who bring sustenance for the *marae* (communal

Māori meeting place) from *mahinga mataitai* (customary fishing areas). These *kaitiaki* (environmental guardians) have been garnering support from local governments, and drawing deeply on ideas from artists, designers, and scientists to lobby the farm board to shift away from unsustainable, monocultural, Western farming practices to a variety of smaller-scale, local agricultural practices that respect the health of the land and sustain *whenua* by returning *taonga* species, such as *harakeke, manuka,* and *tuna* (eels), to the *whenua*.

One of the most striking things about the resurgence of *kaitiakitanga* in Kuku is that it welcomes all knowledge systems. This works because the collective of scientists, artists, designers, and *iwi* and *hapū*, wherever they are from, are supported by *mātauranga Māori* and underpinned by trust and a deep respect for *whenua*. *Whakapapa* and *korero tuku iho* (narratives handed down that bespeak the land) help to weave them together, braiding the ideas around each other, enriching them, bringing them to light without diminishing them, and encouraging new non-hierarchical forms of order.[17]

THE HARAKEKE PROJECT

Harakeke/flax was valued by both cultures and was cut by Māori as a point of entry into the money economy. The swamps, however, were much more than flax: for Māori they provided a diversity of habitats and a richness of *mahinga kai* (food sources), matched only by the estuaries. For Pākehā, if the economic returns from flax diminished, the swamps could be drained, and the land converted to pasture.[18]

Wood *et al.* (2017), *Environmental and Natural Resource Issues Report*[19]

There is a particular place in a bend of the Kuku Stream near the river where three small disused dairy sheds stand [Fig. 5]. From 2016, this site became the focus of plans to establish a Māori knowledge-based old/new sustainable industry using harakeke plant material that would be regrown on the nearby riverbanks. One of the products of harakeke is *muka*,[20] strong silky fibres traditionally

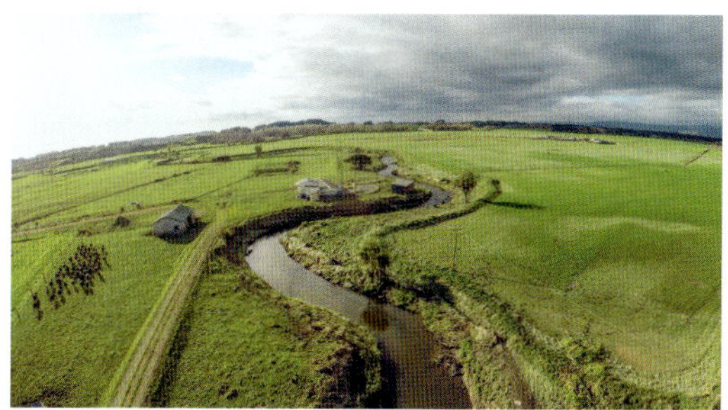

Fig. 5 The dairy sheds on a bend by the Kuku Stream, cleared to increase "productivity," where a new relationship with harakeke promises to rekindle knowledge of the *whenua* and *awa*

stripped by hand using a mussel shell. No one had ever managed to develop a machine that could emulate this action without damaging the long threads or leaving the cellulose cuticles still attached. Rangi Te Kanawa, a long-standing Māori leader in harakeke textile research, has now co-designed such a machine, which replicates the finesse of the hand-stripping process. She has produced spun *muka*, woven in India, to create very strong silken cloth. With Rangi's support, the production of harakeke textiles—its stripping, softening, and spinning—might take place in the three retrofitted sheds.[21]

Repurposing the sheds to house the machinery for processing the harakeke will encourage the revegetation of the Kuku Stream banks with a range of indigenous riparian species protected by a double row of flax for easy harvesting. If successful, this revegetation could extend along the banks in both directions, from the mountains to the sea, to signal the return of *taonga* and the benefits of revitalization for all waterways in the catchment. The return of this harakeke *taonga* will bring multiple benefits to the *whenua*, offering employment opportunities for Māori communities while healing the nutrified and badly polluted water of the Kuku Stream, sustaining lands and waterways and improving farm animal health.[22]

It will also be an intensely symbolic and emotional return: the tripartite fan of the plant has always represented the interdependent and protective relationship nature of *whanau*—with children in the centre, then parents and grandparents as the rau or outer leaves. As these leaves age and die, they evoke the Māori *whakatauki* or the proverb "*Mate atu he tētē kura, ara mai he tētē kura*" ("As one frond dies, another rises to take its place"). In the same way, after 24 years of projects and growth at Kuku, Māori elders are now seeing a surge of youthful energy rising to support and expand their efforts. The project will further offer potential employment opportunities for Māori communities.

HARAKEKE AT THE INTERFACE OF TWO KNOWLEDGE SYSTEMS

The harakeke project is an example of how *whakapapa* and Western science can be interwoven as distinct but complementary knowledge systems, interpreted without any analytical solution-driven agenda to address climate change in a way that is relevant to local communities, and the specifics of place. This kind of expanded thinking offers the potential for sustainable and cultural growth to accompany the economic growth that will enable Māori to uphold *tikanga* (culture and values) and contribute toward *whānau* and community wellbeing.

The current challenge is to acknowledge how Māori spiritual dimensions of *whakapapa*—non-tangible and other similarly difficult aspects to measure—are valued and respected within a Western science framework. As discussed, offsetting and ecological economics seem to be the only two Western science methods for valuing ecosystems. The other alternative is to ignore Western science altogether, but that's not what the harakeke project is about: it is inclusive, not reductive.

In the interests of inclusivity and experimentation, the harakeke project was, in fact, the subject of an ecological–economic evaluation. Although it sought to quantify the qualitative entities, the study was primarily focused on quantitative assessments, mapping the classes of flood-prone land based on 20-year flood frequencies, and describing the breadth of activities taking place in the landscape, from dune restoration to wetland expansion, forestry, and aquaculture.[23] It considered the fiscal benefits of a "no, part, and full" implementation of the plan, and it detailed the harakeke value chain, including manufacturing and employment opportunities and the potential for additional benefits with an appropriate economic strategy. It also listed other environmental benefits, such as water improvement and pollutant reduction, and identified the risks from climate change, market unreliability, and technology.

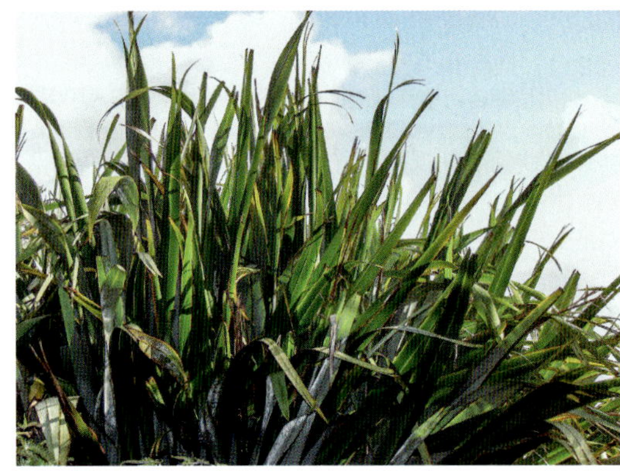

Fig. 6 Harakeke

While the study attempted to balance two world views, its outcomes misrepresent the reality because of the coarseness of the data on which it relied. The plans and assessments were inherently reductive, the 20-year flooding study generalized, and the subtleties of the land flattened by the land-use analysis. Knowledge of the local community and the benefits of Māori knowledge were lost amidst blunt parameters and desktop assumptions.

Although ecological economics is trapped in the amber of its own world view, it still speaks the language of politics, law, and finance to which we are currently bound. If we were to try to maintain such an approach, to enlarge it so that it accommodated and respected many kinds of knowing, one approach might be to undertake better studies with access to real-time and reliable data created by new technologies, and with different, more nuanced methodologies that give value to qualities and relationships that may be invisible or unmeasurable by Western scientific standards.[24] It would also need to be able to argue for the rights of non-human entities to exist in the same way that rivers like the Whanganui in Aotearoa have been granted rights independent of their economic value or what they offer to the world.[25]

WHERE TO?

Even so, the idea of granting rights to a river, while essential and important given current rates of ecological devastation around the world, seems a little impertinent, even hubristic. Granting rights is a dangerously imperialist approach yoked to a very narrow human-centric view of the world. It may be that any solution drawn from the framework of Enlightenment thinking is doomed to yield the same results. Another alternative may be to subvert the framework altogether, by radically rethinking the hegemony of politics, law, and finance from the ground up. Not in order to completely discard the benefits of scientific knowledge, but to leaven it with different ways of knowing that are earth- rather than human-centred, and that focus on connectivity and humility rather than compartmentalization and control.[26] Where *taonga* or treasure is a verb instead of a noun, and something is treasured for what it *is* rather than for what it's *worth*. The Enlightenment world view has brought us to this point of crisis, but Māori knowledge systems, described here through the lens of harakeke, might be able to show us the way out.

1   R. Mātāmua (leading Māori astronomer) (2017) *Matariki and Māori Astronomy with Dr Rangi Mātāmua*, McGuinness Institute, Wellington, New Zealand, 21 July 2017, https://www.mcguinnessinstitute.org/foresightnz/matariki-and-maori-astronomy-with-dr-rangi-matamua (accessed 13 September 2021).

2   G. Gibbs, *Ghosts of Gondwana* (Wellington, New Zealand: Potton Publishing, 2006).

3   Sourced from Rod McDonald's 1929 publication, as quoted in E. Best, *Forest Lore of the Māori* (Wellington, New Zealand: E. C. Keating, Government Printer, 1942).

4   S. M. Smith, *Hei Whenua Ora: Hapū and Iwi Approaches for Reinstating Valued Ecosystems Within Cultural Landscape*, PhD Thesis, Massey University, Palmerston North, New Zealand, 2007, p. iv.

5   This stellar, solar, lunar knowledge, known as *mātauranga Māori*, is based on the ongoing teachings of Professor Rangi Mātāmua, his *Living by the Stars* Facebook lectures and his series of Matariki publications. He has many followers online as he works to privilege indigenous knowledge systems and decolonize the impacts of imperial or universal time. For details see https://www.facebook.com/Livingbythestars (accessed 13 September 2021).

6   Letter from Tamati Ranapiri to Peehi (Elsdon Best), 23 November 1907, p. 2, MS Papers 1187-1127 in the Alexander Turnbull Library, Wellington, trans. Anne Salmond. Quoted in: A. Salmond, Tears of Rangi, *Hau: Journal of Ethnographic Theory*, 4(3) (2014): 285-309.

7   P. Tapsell, *The Art of Taonga* (Wellington, New Zealand: Art History, School of Art History, Classics and Religious Studies, Victoria University of Wellington, 2011).

8   D. Butts, Review of Pukaki: a comet returns, *Te Ara: Journal of Museums Aotearoa*, 28(1) (2003): 50.

9   The role of *taonga* is discussed in depth in Arapata Tamati Hakiwai, *He Mana Taonga, He Mana Tangata: Māori Tonga and the politics of Māori Tribal Identity and Development*, PhD Thesis, Victoria University of Wellington, Wellington, New Zealand, 2014.

10   S. M. Smith, *Hei Whenua Ora: Hapū and Iwi Approaches for Reinstating Valued Ecosystems Within Cultural Landscape*, PhD Thesis, Massey University, Palmerston North, New Zealand, 2007, p. 39.

11   F. Berkes, J. Colding, and C. Folke, Rediscovery of traditional ecological knowledge as adaptive management, *Ecological applications*, 10(5) (2000): 1251-1262.

12   F. Martini, Is there natural capital: A critique of the ecological economics approach, *International Journal of Earth and Environmental Sciences*, 1(123) (2016): IJEES-123, https://doi.org/10.15344/2456-351X/2016/123 (accessed 13 September 2021).

13   J. Rodford Wehipeihana, *Sequent Economies in Kuku: A Study of a Rural Landscape in New Zealand* (Wellington, New Zealand: Victoria University, 1964), p. 33. Note: At that time, the coastal Te Hākari wetland may have appeared "underdeveloped" in terms of farming economic developments. "Impecunious" relates to being "cash poor," so its likely extensive resources were actively used by *hapū* for housing, weaving, medicinal resources, and for sustenance, health, and general wellbeing.

14   G. Park, The lake in the Sand Country, *Nga Uruora/The Groves of Life: Ecology and History in a New Zealand Landscape* (Wellington, New Zealand: Victoria University Press, 1995), p. 166.

15   Park, The lake in the Sand Country.

16   There has been coincidental revitalization of the loop's riparian environment since 2006 while extensive work was underway at the Te Hākari dune wetland across the paddocks. The wetland's planting started in September 2002.

17   A. Salmond, Tears of Rangi: Water, power, and people in New Zealand, *Hau: Journal of Ethnographic Theory*, 4(3) (2014): 285-309.

18   V. Wood, C. Cant, E. Barrett-Whitehead, *et al.*, *Environmental and Natural Resource Issues Report*, report commissioned by the Crown Forestry Rental Trust for the Waitangi Tribunal's Porirua ki Manawatū District Inquiry (Wellington, New Zealand: CFRT, 2017).

19   Wood *et al.*, *Environmental and Natural Resource Issues Report*.

20   Māori have known this since modifying their Pacific skills to a temperate country with different resources.

21   With further support from Massey University and WWF New Zealand, and possible additional funding from the Sustainable Food and Fibres Fund, through the Ministry for Primary Industries (MPI) and Te Pūnaha Hihiko: Vision Mātauranga Capability Fund.

22   Lowland areas of the Kuku Stream have recently been beset by an extremely aggressive freshwater weed, first introduced as an aquarium plant called Senegal tea (*Gymnocoronis spilanthoides*). Suitable habitats include wetlands, streams, and degraded waterways. This plant will completely smother native and even other exotic semi-aquatic plants. It gravely deoxygenates water so that no other life can live in the waterway. A current eradication regimen in the area from central Kuku to the confluence of the Ōhau River is underway (February/March 2021).

23   D. Hardy, A. Spinks, J. Richardson, *et al.*, *Planning for Climate Change Impacts on Māori Coastal Ecosystems and Economies: A Case Study of 5 Māori-owned land blocks in the Horowhenua Coastal Zone* (Palmerston North, New Zealand: Massey University, 2019).

24   For example, new-generation hyperspectral satellite resources are being used alongside airborne hyperspectral imaging to improve the spatial and temporal sampling of water and land resources. The improved monitoring data will be integrated in an overarching Kaupapa Māori approach for improving management practices, and in novel statistical forecasting tools for a better economic decision-making. The data will be used to improve the protection of the future of primary production, while maintaining environmental balance and wellbeing for all.

25   A. Salmond, Tears of Rangi: Water, power, and people in New Zealand. *Hau: Journal of Ethnographic Theory*, 4(3) (2014), 285-309.

26   The Australian Earth Law Alliance (AELA), a not-for-profit organization, advocates for an earth-centred governance that "support(s) rather than undermine(s) the integrity of the earth:" https://www.earthlaws.org.au (accessed 13 September 2021).

After 60,000 New Yorkers were affected by an outbreak of yellow fever in 1798, which killed 2,000 of them, the city chartered the Manhattan Water Company to treat and provide "pure and wholesome" water to lower Manhattan.[1] The project involved laying a network of underground pipes made from segments of roughly hewn pine logs up to 13 feet long, each cored with a 4–5 inch wide passage.[2] Underground bored elm pipes were not uncommon in Europe, and the technique was probably imported. London's wealthy residences used the pipes for waste disposal as early as the 13th century, and all the old London water companies used bored elm pipes for distributing water from the 16th century. Although the Manhattan Water Company never constructed the steam pump and million-gallon reservoir it had originally promised, and the 25 miles of water mains that were laid delivered water unfit for human consumption, the company was a financial success. Its founder, Aaron Burr, used the profits to set up the Bank of Manhattan Company, which later became the Chase Manhattan Bank, and was subsequently subsumed into JPMorgan Chase.[3] The hollow-tree pipe—its cross-section the basis of Chase Bank's octagonal corporate logo—today symbolizes one of the world's largest operators in private investments in public equities (PIPE) market deals.[4] Over two centuries after polluted water devastated the city, a slice of pizza is now often cited by investors to justify the private ownership of aquifers. By claiming that the purity of New York water is what gives the city's pizza its unique flavour, investors argue that the Delaware aquifer, which provides the city's water supply, should be kept under a form of private ownership. By associating "good water" with a "privatized source," the case has become a reference for investors buying out other aquifers across the world. Under the guise of environmental preservation and the prevention of water pollution, neoliberal notions of value are linked to the abuse of collective resources, jeopardizing the livelihood of local communities. Trees and freshwater in New York are treated first as commodities and later as assets to control both space and people. But the financialization of water into a marketable commodity does not end there. Water-stressed regions such as India, the Middle East, and North Africa are now heavily reliant on the import of water-intensive goods to offset food insecurity. The water embedded in these traded commodities, known as "virtual water," is expected to triple by 2100.[5]

1   M. A. Pierce, *Documentary History of American Water-Works*, http://www.waterworkshistory.us (accessed 13 September 2021).

2   To avoid leaks, the segments were fixed together with tapered and flared joints, often bound with reinforcing iron bands once the wood had swelled with water. New York City Department of Design and Construction, Infrastructure Division.

3   M. Gandy, Water and the nascent civic realm, *Concrete and Clay: Reworking Nature in New York City* (Cambridge, MA: MIT Press), pp. 27–28.

4   G. Tett, *Fool's Gold: How the Bold Dream of a Small Tribe at J. P. Morgan was Corrupted by Wall Street Greed and Unleashed a Catastrophe* (New York: Free Press, 2009), p. 82.

5   N. T. Graham, M. I. Hejazi, S. H. Kim, *et al.*, Future changes in the trading of virtual water, *Nature Communications*, 11 (2020): 3632.

LOCATION: Excavated from Peck Slip under Contract HMW 1159 (2011–2013); New York City Department of Design and Construction, Infrastructure Division

SPECIMEN: Species unknown. Wooden water main, 1805

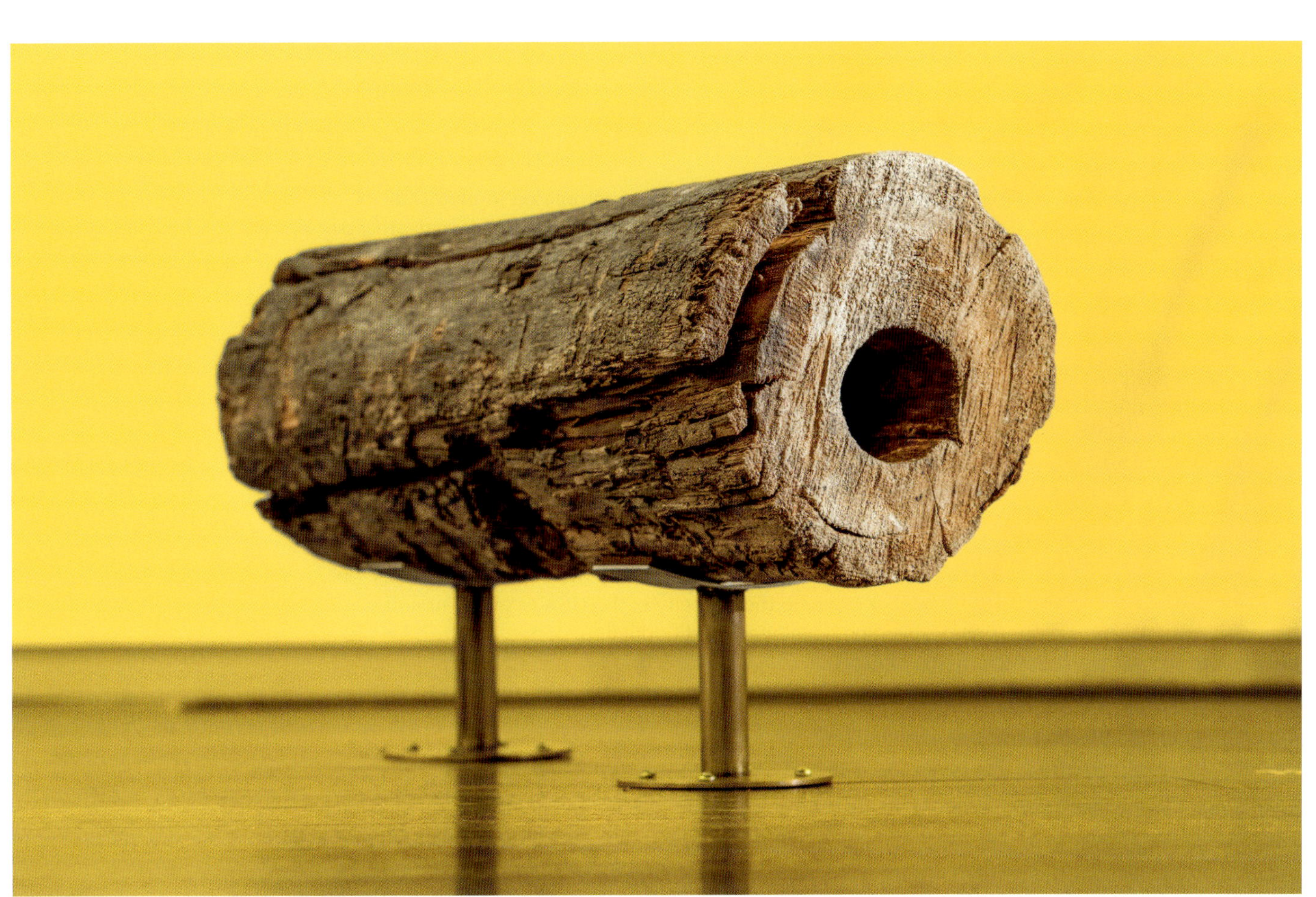

FINANCIALLY BUILT ENVIRONMENT

Mies van der Rohe's Seagram Building, completed in 1958, indelibly shaped corporate modernist architecture in the USA. Its privately owned public plaza was dominated by six weeping beeches, later replaced by gingkos when the original plantings succumbed to air pollution. The curvilinear trees wrapping the sides of the geometric building inspired the corporate production of "urban nature." The granite and marble podium is an example of Mies's urban clearings, Phyllis Lambert writes, which gave rise to a new sense of the urban condition.[1] Several New York architectural firms, such as Kahn & Jacobs, had been urging the then Parks Commissioner Robert Moses to revise the zoning regulations to replace full-site ziggurat towers with large buildings surrounded by open spaces. At that time, there were no direct precedents in midtown Manhattan for this planning scheme. With Seagram's model of public space—a voluntary provision drawn up by the building developer—in 1961 New York became the first city in the USA to offer "incentive zoning," granting developers additional floor space in return for the creation of plazas, arcades, or atria that are accessible to the public. The response was dramatic; there are now more than 500 publicly owned private spaces (POPS) in the city. These spaces include thousands of trees and shrubs, especially since a 1970s regulatory reform required mandatory seating, planting, and trees. Yet just how "public" these spaces are is up for debate. Many POPS restrict public access with fences or barriers, and inhibit use through poor lighting, lack of seating, or obstruction with restaurant tables and chairs. Some even display "For private use only" signs. These contradictory practices have led the city to re-evaluate their design standards for such public spaces, although the planting of trees in POPS remains a token in speculative real estate transactions. For almost three decades, until their 2019 redesign, the POPS logo featured a silhouette of a tree over a grid background—a clear association with Miesian design.

1   P. Lambert, Seagram: Union of building and landscape, *Places*, April 2013.

LOCATION: Seagram Building, 375 Park Avenue, Manhattan

SPECIMEN: Gingko (Ginkgo biloba). Branch, 2018

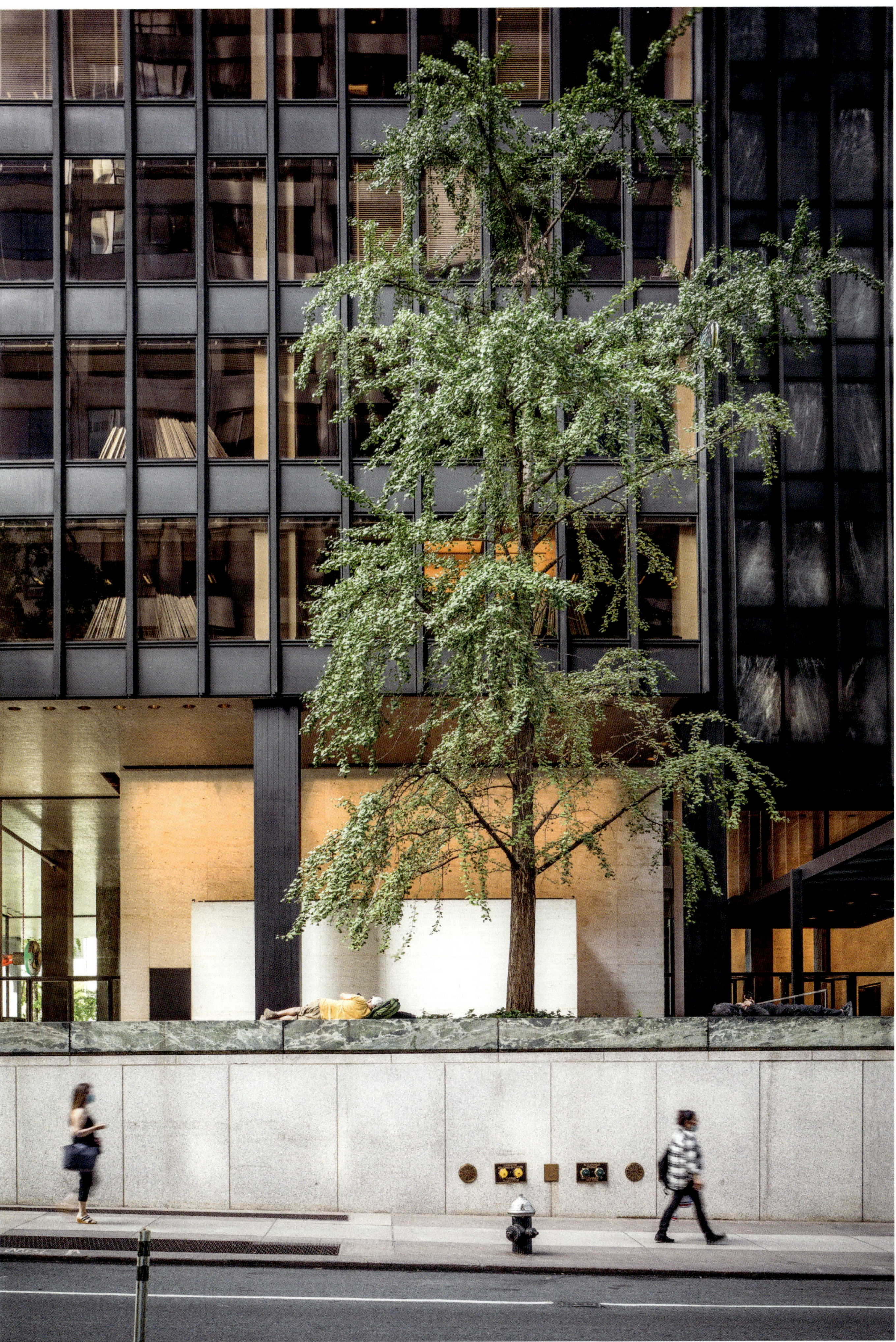

CONDITIONING AIR IN A GREENING REVOLUTION

Offsetting mechanisms can be seen in one of the most iconic corporate atria in New York City: the Ford Foundation Garden designed by Kevin Roche John Dinkeloo and Associates and landscape architect Dan Kiley in 1967 (renovated by Raymond Jungles in 2019). Produced in response to fears of the city's endemic pollution, its protected environment was the first corporate atrium to cultivate indoor trees in New York and introduced a move in Midtown Manhattan towards the planting of climatically stable "nature."[1] The 200,000 cubic foot volume of skylighted, air-conditioned space was designed to help its 40 temperate trees, 1,000 shrubs, and over 22,000 vines and ground-cover plants to survive in the neutral climate of an office interior.[2] The air-conditioning system had to take in the toxic external atmosphere that the corporate garden was aiming to avoid. With almost 5 million automobiles driving through its streets it was not easy to escape the fumes of a city. By 1970, the indoor plants showed the same levels of decay as their outdoor counterparts, and dying trees were frequently replaced.[3] The challenge of growing trees in an enclosed office environment echoed the Ford Foundation's attempts to make soil hyperfertile, whether in its own headquarters or in "developing" countries. As a sponsor of democracy and (car-dependent) city plans worldwide, the foundation's focus shifted during the 1950s from the reconstruction of Europe to the so-called Green Revolution in the global South—efforts that ultimately fostered dependence on US fertilizers and pesticides for farming-based economies.[4] After the 1997 Kyoto Protocol, the Green Revolution slowly shifted from a focus on securing food staples to a focus on carbon offset plantations and blue carbon stocks in order to mitigate environmental guilt in the global North. The Ford Foundation's atrium's vegetation aimed to display how corporations could also care about urban nature, prioritizing floor area for a garden rather than "usable" office space in order to gain a greener reputation. And yet, the legacy of gasoline-fuelled cars is still among and inside us. A typical medium-sized family car—like those created by Ford—creates around 24 tonnes of carbon dioxide during its life cycle. Until zero-emissions vehicles are much more widely available, the nanoparticles in the city and our bodies will keep on being financialized through the planting of new trees.

1 D. Gissen, *Manhattan Atmospheres: Architecture, the Interior Environment, and Urban Crisis* (Minneapolis: University of Minnesota Press, 2014), p. 67.
2 Gissen, *Manhattan Atmospheres*, p. 77.
3 Gissen, *Manhattan Atmospheres*, p. 79.
4 F. D. Scott, *Outlaw Territories: Environments of Insecurity/Architectures of Counterinsurgency* (New York: Zone Books, 2016), pp. 41–44.

LOCATION: Ford Foundation Atrium, 320 East 43rd Street, Manhattan

SPECIMEN: Species unknown. Wedge, 2019

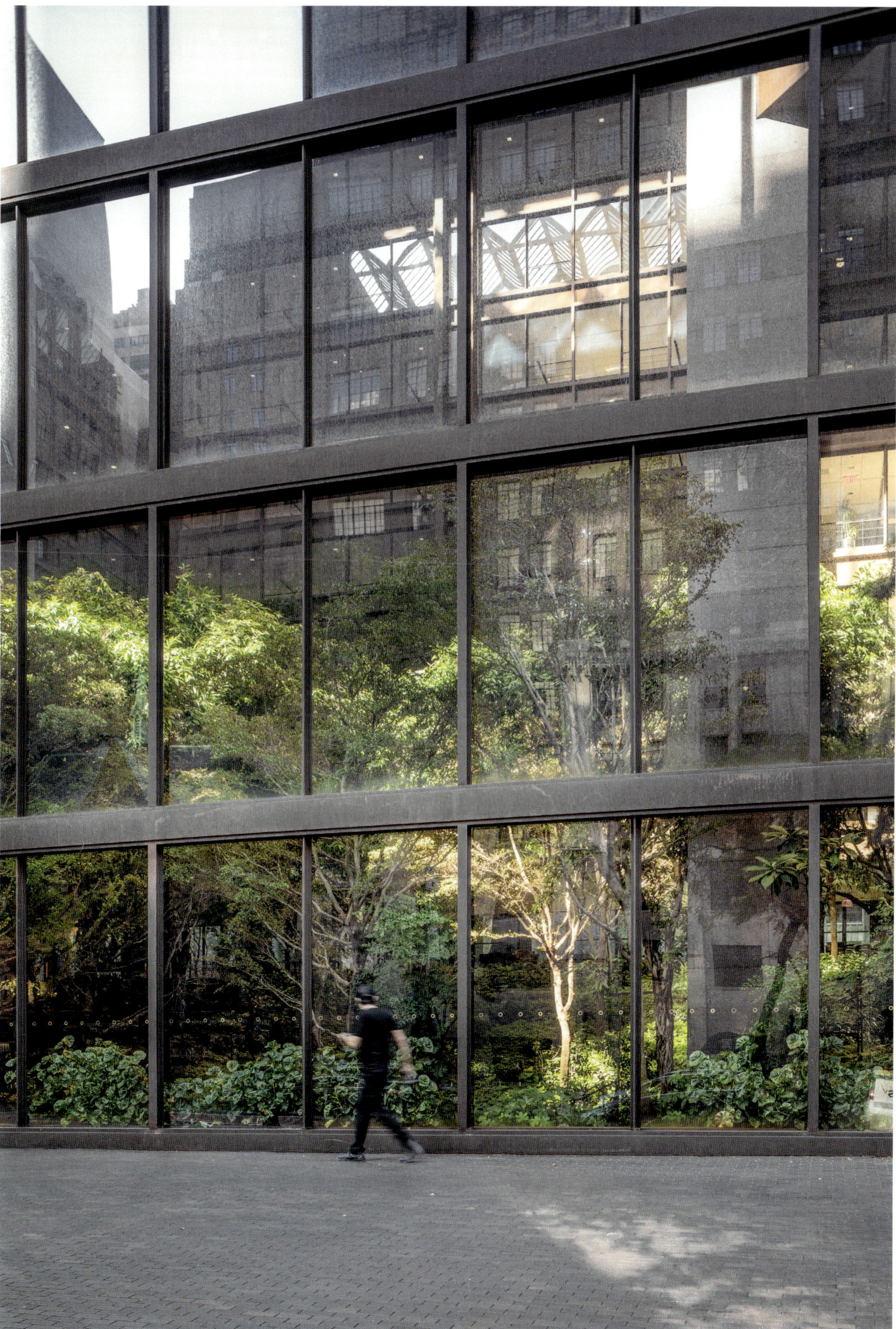

MONEY DOESN'T GROW ON TREES

After the Ford Foundation introduced its corporate garden (p. 78), the atrium spread as an urban spatial typology and continued to evolve with the development of finance in the city. The World Financial Center (WFC), designed by Cesar Pelli and Associates in 1982–88, as well as other atria in Midtown East, began to play a role in a speculative real-estate market in which green amenities served to increase the value of space and command higher rents in New York.[1] The four-tower complex of the WFC contained a winter garden, designed in the late 1980s by Diana Balmori, inside a ten-storey glass-vaulted pavilion, one of the largest in the city. It is home to a grove of 16 40-foot-high palm trees. After 9/11, the palms were removed and new palms from northern Florida were planted at a cost of US$300,000. The new trees were carefully chosen; aesthetic criteria included trunk colour (ruddy red), trunk configuration (straight), trunk taper (smooth and uniform is best), bark configuration (tight), and crown presentation (the top of the tree should be full and leafy).[2] Sixty sun lamps emitting 30,000 watts of illumination (brighter than a typical baseball stadium) were installed to ensure the palms would flourish. In the absence of the shadow cast by the former Twin Towers, the palms, which had previously received sunlight from 2:30 p.m. until dusk, were now exposed to sunlight throughout the day. This obliged the gardeners to readjust nutrients and water accordingly.[3] Meanwhile, in Florida, where the palms were from, officials are prioritizing broadleaf trees over palms to shade and cool their concrete jungle. A 2018 city ordinance in West Palm Beach requires more shade trees in new constructions, with mandatory plantings that are at least 75 per cent broadleaf trees in the parking areas of the soon to be "Oak Beach." In 2013, the palms at the WFC had grown to 60 feet tall—too high to survive in the winter garden. High demand for palms led to a downsizing of the palms, which were replaced by 35-foot-high new ones.

1   D. Gissen, *Manhattan Atmospheres : Architecture, the Interior Environment, and Urban Crisis* (Minneapolis: University of Minnesota Press, 2014), pp. 96–97.

2   G. Collins, Palms return to an island (Manhattan); a major replanting as the Winter Garden prepares to reopen, *The New York Times*, 13 August 2002.

3   Collins, Palms return to an island (Manhattan).

LOCATION: Brookfield Place, formerly the World Financial Center, Vesey Street, Manhattan

SPECIMEN: Mexican fan palm (*Washingtonia robusta*). Frond, 2019

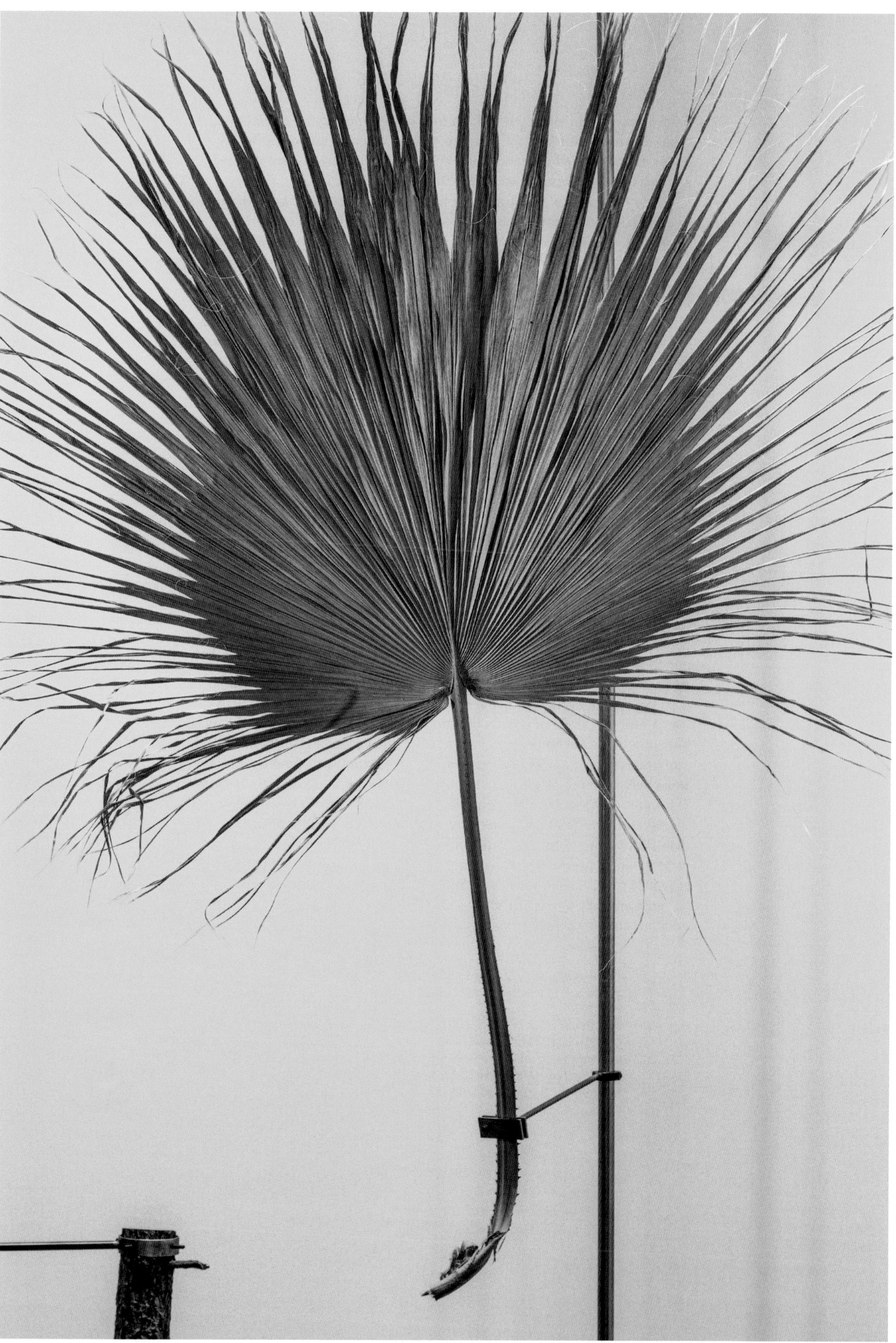

ROOTED CONFLICTS

Sidewalks need to meet the difficult task of negotiating the competing requirements of human feet and tree roots. For a civil engineer, the layer under the concrete or paving stone should be perfectly dry, stable, and without organic matter or root growth.[1] For an arboriculturist, this layer needs to be a porous substrate that retains moisture, sufficiently drained to ensure aeration, soft enough to permit root growth, and receptive to rainfall. This is where root conflicts arise to the surface. The 2003 New York Sidewalk Law transferred liability for sidewalk maintenance, as well as injuries suffered due to tree-root damage, to private landowners.[2] While the city owns the space between the curb and property lines, and therefore oversees tree planting, the home or business owner is responsible for the sidewalk's upkeep and repairs. This dynamic between city and landowner has not been universally popular.[3] When a tree is dead, dying, or in danger of falling, the city removes the tree, but it is not obligated to replace it with a new tree, leaving a hole in the ground where pedestrians can fall. Over the years, multiple lawsuits between the city and citizens have debated whether an accident is due to an unmaintained tree (*Gaifman v. City of New York*, 2014 and *Ramos v. City of New York*, 2011) or other external causes, such as a collapsing tunnel below ground (e.g. *Hidalgo v. City of New York*, 2011). Other cases have pushed the definition of heritage buildings in regard to landmark trees, as in Sean Lennon's US$10 million legal fight in 2017 to allow the 60-foot roots of his ailanthus tree to enter the neighbour's basement. Lennon unsuccessfully appealed, suggesting that the neighbours seek permission from the Landmarks Preservation Commission to remove part of their historic railing so the tree could survive. Debates between city, pedestrians, and landlords often fail to recognize that trees—which did not evolve to grow submerged in concrete and compacted soil—lift or break sidewalks in an attempt to reach the porous and humid substrate essential for their survival. Rather than fighting these lawsuits, the city began to experiment in 2010 with "rain gardens," strips of porous ground along curb sides, although this was not without citizen backlash for narrowing sidewalks. In 2019, New York stopped issuing violations to homeowners for damage caused by street trees, estimating a public investment of US$14 million up to 2022 to fix all sidewalks damaged by city trees. And yet, these roots are key in controversial stormwater absorption calculations that turn trees into commodifiable bioswales. From an engineering perspective, to root well means to reduce runoff costs and needs for drainage infrastructure. But to root well may also mean to increase the overall porosity of the city should we want to avoid unwanted tripping. In the meantime, street trees will keep both inflating and damaging property value.

1   T. B. Randrup, E. G. Mcpherson, and L. R. Costello, A review of tree root conflicts with sidewalks, curbs, and roads, *Urban Ecosystems* 5 (2001): 209–225.
2   NYC Department of Transportation, New York Administrative Code §7-210 – Liability of real property owner for failure to maintain sidewalk in a reasonably safe condition, https://www1.nyc.gov/html/dot/html/infrastructure/19-152.shtml (accessed 13 September 2021).
3   N. Peterson, The sidewalk gray zone, *Deeproot*, 1 August 2016.

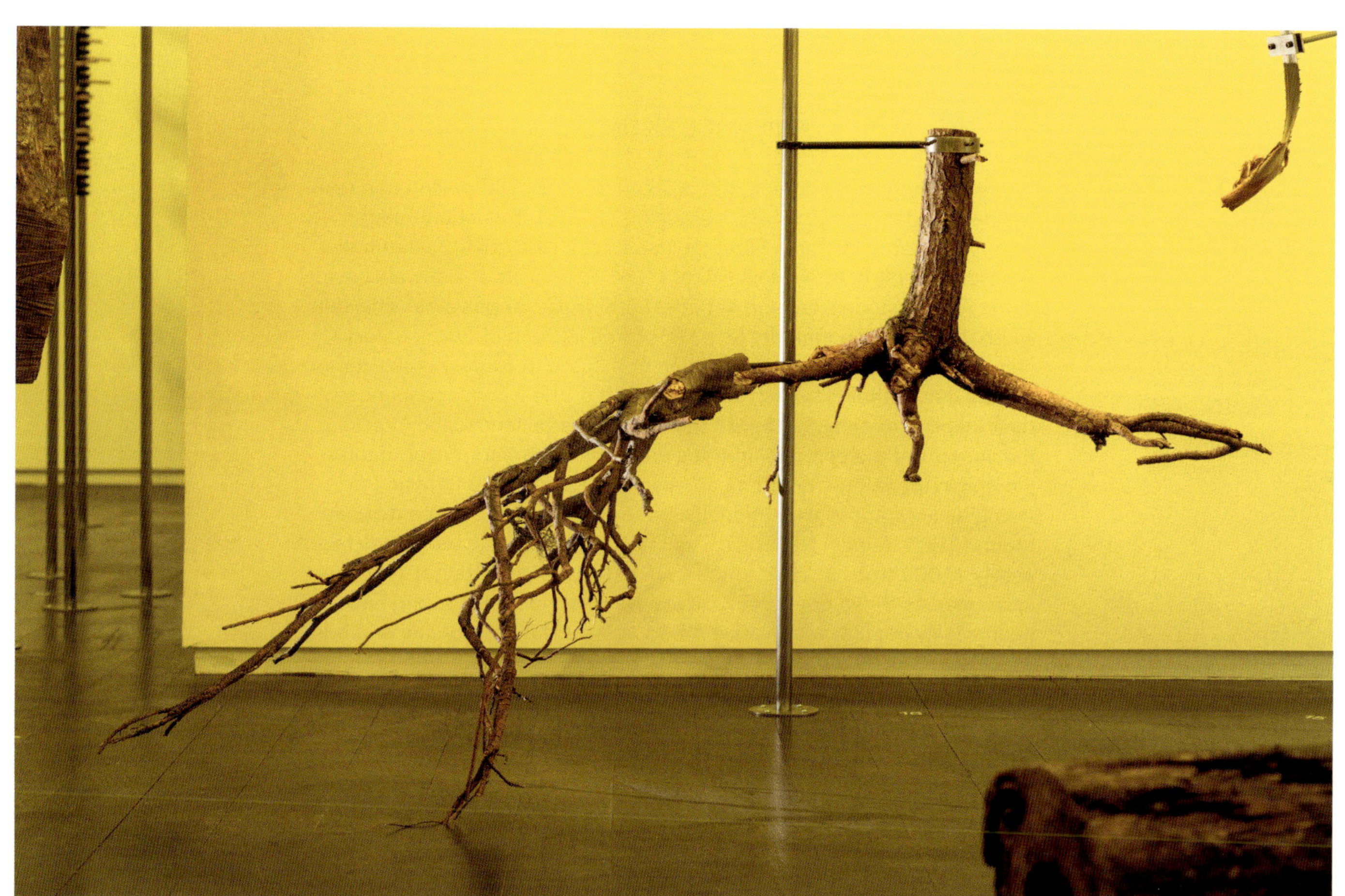

NUISANCE EXTINCTION

A tree's resistance to compacted soil and to watertight paving can result in sidewalk damage as its roots strive for survival. This phenomenon is regularly rated by Parks Forester inspectors, who quantify damage according to different factors, such as the vertical lift of sidewalk paving, damaged flagstones, volume of pedestrian usage, or passable sidewalk width.[1] Despite its popularity as a street tree in the mid-20th century, fast-growing silver maples have been prohibited from New York City streets due to their shallow roots, their soft brittle wood, and, hence, their inability to cohabitate with the city's material landscape.[2] Lacking the support of the companion trees they have in forests, silver maples planted in urban environments are also more vulnerable to falling or losing heavy limbs in exceptional weather events: Storm Irene downed around 1,500 trees in New York City in 2011, while Hurricane Sandy felled nearly 10,000 trees in 2012, some over 120 years old. Drought-resistant silver maples thrive near creeks, waterways, or floodplains, and have been widely popular with Native Americans for their sweet sap and bark, which can be used to treat coughs. US settlers also realized the value of silver maples, as they planted them for fast-growing shade as they colonized the frontier. Despite having one of the highest carbon capture rates—according to the US Forest Service's Center for Urban Forest Research, 25 times more than cherry and plum trees, which ranked last—silver maples are seen as too dangerous to serve the city.

1   NYC Parks, *NYC Tree Valuation Method*, https://www.nycgovparks. org/pagefiles/128/New-York-City-Tree-Valuation-Method-05-04-2018__5b2ad0f011a85.pdf (accessed 13 September 2021).

2   NYC Parks, *Street Tree Planting: Approved Species List*, https://www. nycgovparks.org/trees/street-tree-planting/species-list (accessed 13 September 2021).

LOCATION: Crown Heights, Brooklyn; fell during Hurricane Irene

SPECIMEN: Silver maple (*Acer saccharinum*). Slab reclaimed from fallen tree, 2011

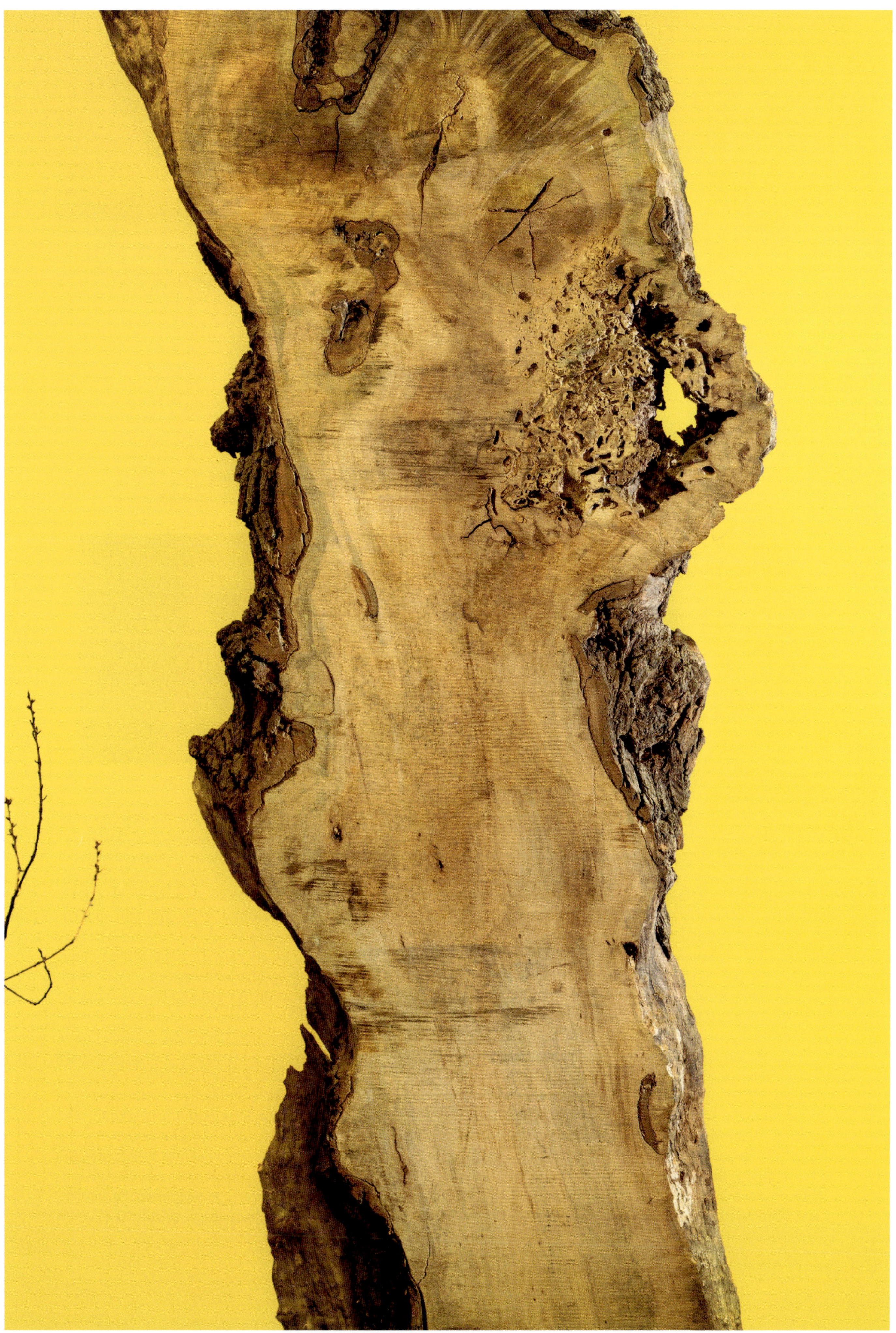

Oil Critters: Multispecies Horizons in the Decommissioning of North Sea Oil Platforms

Rosa Whiteley

CARBON WORLDS

The Anthropocene has come about through a global rearrangement of molecules. Energy has been extracted by displacing materials and dissipating the wastes of this molecular change into the seas, ground, and atmosphere—where new, and often troubling, molecular assemblages accumulate. The oil industry is a dominant force in the fluctuating global metabolism of carbon and other substances associated with oil. These molecules will not return to where they were before, but their rearranged assemblages create opportunities for other worlds to form.

> We must admit that oil … —which, like money, now stands for the whole material universe— creates the very core of our capitalist unconscious.
> Oxana Timofeeva[1]

OIL CRITTERS

The spaces of residue from the material systems of extraction of oil, both in the physical infrastructure and the molecular leakages, create places where other creatures have taken hold—what I call "oil critters." An oil critter is a living being that depends on the infrastructures and logistics of the oil industry and the financial markets that drive it. In often desiccated ocean ecosystems, rigs can provide an ecological haven, where dolphins, seals, and seabirds can visit to feast on critters that inhabit the steel legs of the rigs and reefs can form below the surface. Oil tankers have provided transportation for barnacles, molluscs, and bacteria, which then prosper along oil trade routes. Oil derivatives are swept into the air from synthetically fertilized farms and car exhaust gases, altering the microbiology of the air itself, to the benefit of specific species of bacteria and fungal spores that favour smog-filled air. The oil chemicals in the air also fall to the ground, fertilizing species such as horseweed, nettles, and cow-parsley. These plants then overpower their local counterparts, which succumb to the nitrogen fluxes—changing the vegetal communities of roadside verges. Oil critters are an example of the uncanny and the unexpected; emerging from the financial markets and destructive infrastructures that produce their flourishing environments.

Human-made infrastructures have feral effects.

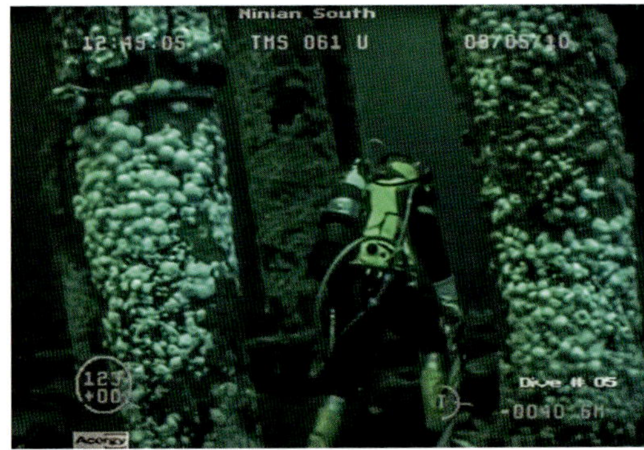

Fig. 1 Visible reef on North Sea oil rig. Screengrab from a video of a saturation diver working on the Ninian south oil rig in the North Sea, 2015

Tracing the multispecies material realities of oil, we might start to see breaks in the neoliberal grid of financial imaginaries. Non-human stories—living and material alike—are so uncertain that they don't fit into the idealized financial model of a material. As a commodity, oil is currently traded as a static and consistent unit, indifferent to all other occurrences of oil. Seen through the lives of oil critters, oil no longer exists as a standardized unit, but as a facilitator of specific multispecies spatial inhabitation and transportation. The methods of exchange of oil as a material catalyses a cascading number of non-human exchanges. For example, the longer a tanker lingers in shallow coastal waters (as happens in order to extend transit time in a declining market), the more time bacteria, molluscs, and barnacles have to attach themselves to the tanker's underbelly and begin their world tour.[2] The exact location of a platform extracting oil from below the seabed determines the sort of environment it creates, depending on the water temperature and currents. Oil critters complicate an economic oversimplification, returning oil to the realities of the material world. "Oil" could be said to be many things: strange, weird and uncanny, living and non-living—too slippery and too forthright to have a singular definition.

THE BLUE MUSSEL

The North Sea oil industry is home to a multitude of accumulations: wealth, neoliberal politics, oil leaks, pipelines, abandoned debris, refineries, heavy metal particulates, and oil-rig graveyards. Growing on and amongst this, kelp, seaweed, clams, lobsters, fish, dolphins, cold water coral, and blue mussels have also accumulated—forming flourishing underwater forests in the form of cold-sea reefs. After centuries of trawling and unsustainable fishing practices, the legs of oil rigs have created some of the only hard aggregate for the development of these ocean habitats.

The blue mussel is an oil critter that is prolific on North Sea oil rigs. Mussels are filter feeders that take advantage of the rig structure in vast quantities. These are reef-building creatures; their continual secretion of hard calcium carbonate for shell growth provides space for new habitats to form.[3] When the oil rig's flaky skin meets the flesh of her bivalve friend, it is protected from the toil of the ocean. As an oil rig ages and degrades, molecules of cadmium, iron, and lead leach into the sea as her steel and paint are corroded in the saltwater. The populations of mussels that live on the rig will filter and absorb these heavy metals and store it within their bodies, where there is a special place for each of her residue metals within their flesh. The rig doesn't end in its steel, its legs, or the end of its drill. The mussel doesn't end in its shell, flesh, or beard. Their boundaries are broken down, dissolved, and blurred. The rig and the mussel ingest and flow through each other, becoming one chimera.

NORTH SEA OIL CRITTERS: BEATRICE THE BLUE MUSSEL

There are currently more than 1,500 oil installations across the North Sea.[4] These installations are only designed to last for 20–40 years, which consequently

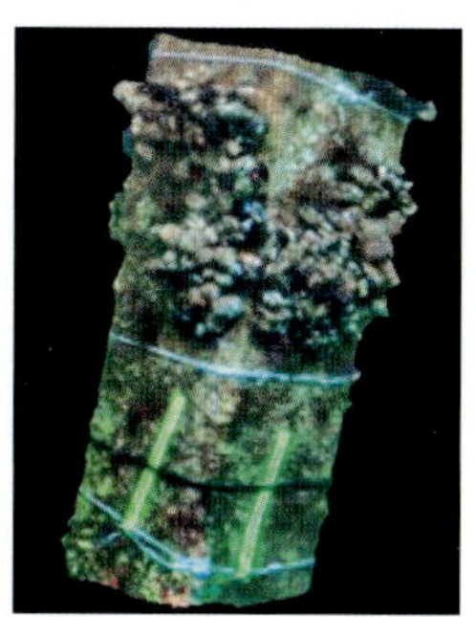
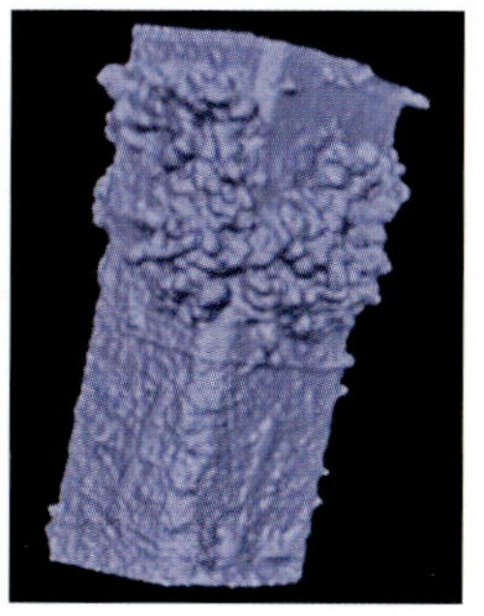

Fig. 2 A 3D scan of mussels on a concrete leg, on an oil rig in the North Sea. Algorithms identify organisms from 2D composite and 3D images, determine marine growth volume, and then biomass

means many oil fields are currently reaching the end of their life-spans. It is expected that over 1.2 million tonnes of topsides and substructures of oil rigs will be removed from the UK continental shelf in the North Sea between 2019 and 2028.[5]

The Beatrice oil field, for example, is a 19,594 tonne fixed steel, subsea, North Sea oil installation. In the decommissioning report submitted to the UK government, the weight of Beatrice's underwater legs was claimed to be potentially 10 per cent marine mass, which, between all the installations, totals 752 tonnes of accumulated reef in the form of seaweeds, corals, and shells.[6] *Beatrice's legs have become an accumulation of blue mussel oil critter.*

The Spoils of Oil searches for material opportunities to reuse and reconfigure North Sea oil infrastructure, through possible afterlives of the three oil rigs in the Beatrice field. The project imagines potential future uses of the redundant material when the industry draws to its inevitable end—either when the oil fields are depleted, or when the subsidies and tax reliefs that prop up the industry are finally deemed unacceptable.[7]

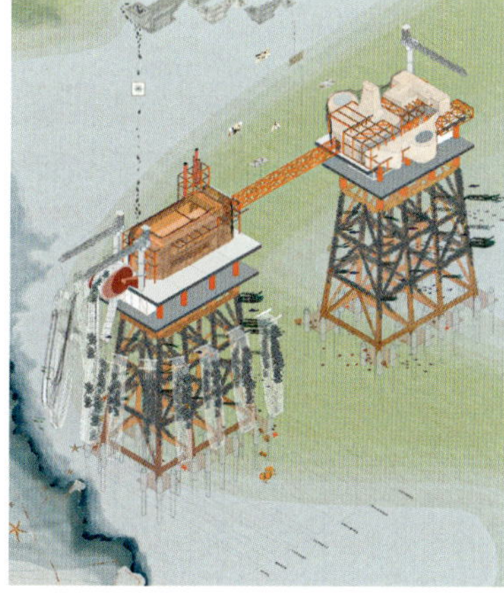

AFTERLIVES OF BEATRICE, THE NORTH SEA OIL RIG

The Spoils of Oil unfolds as fictional and contradicting stories that act to keep Beatrice's reef-growing legs in place. Three stories deliver potential afterlives for each of these rigs, reconfiguring our understanding of offshore space and the future of the post-oil North Sea. *Beheading Beatrice* explores the ceremonial scattering of waste topside material as a way to encourage cold-sea reefs to spread across the North Sea and lay "traps" that discourage industrial trawling. *Got a Crush* investigates material opportunities in the blue mussel shells that grow on Beatrice's legs, using the rig platforms to manufacture mussel-crete, a new building material derived entirely from mussel shells and strengthened by their rig-derived metallic content. In the final story, *In the Bosom of Beatrice*, Beatrice reconfigures her sheet steel into a new draped armour, extending the growing area for the mussels and protecting reef structures hidden beneath the sea surface.

Within these stories, North Sea oil rigs are allowed to remain, in order for new inhabitants to occupy them. Oil critters question the understanding of "oil" as a "commodity," instead bringing the multispecies relationships that form as a consequence of the industry to the foreground. The mussel and rig merge and flow through one another, disassembling the dualities between bivalve and rig, between oil networks and ecological networks, between oil critter and oil commodity. These infrastructures typically proliferate the image of a financialized ocean through a flat and simplified understanding of the material effects of oil. Instead of looking only at the environmental destruction of the oil industry, oil critters demonstrate that the materiality of extraction can collaborate with certain critters to form new environments. The structures and communities involved in oil production exist beyond the whim of a global oil market: oil critters insist on their right to remain, and flourish, in the debris of the oil industry.

Beatrice's blue mussels are an example of a network of critters that remake the worlds we design through our systems. Reimagining the material futures of oil rigs offers a way to consciously and collectively cooperate with the creatures that remake the spaces we produce. This project calls for a multi-species approach to world building, which incorporates the inevitable collaboration that occurs between humans and non-humans within design. Through collective thinking in the decommissioning of structures, new arrivals and species can recuperate habitats that have become damaged by 130 years of industrialized oceans.[8]

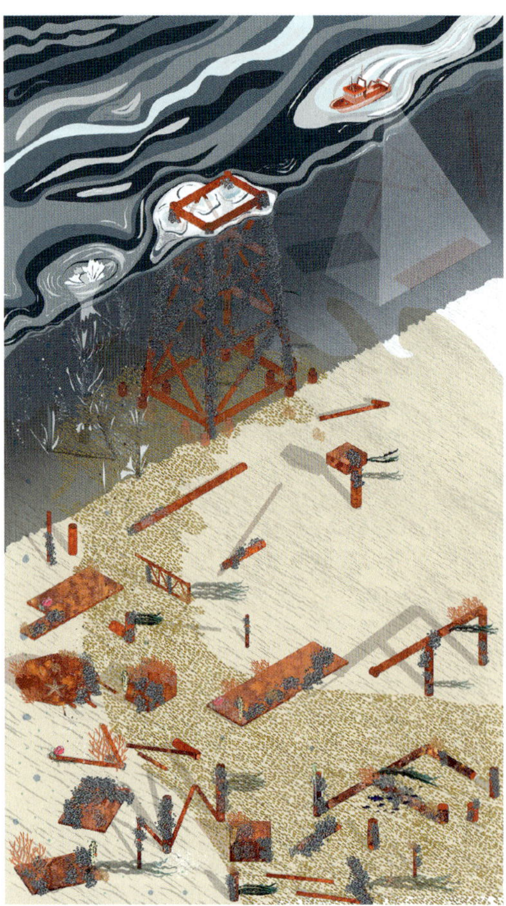

Fig. 4 *Beheading Beatrice*: The scattering of oil rig remains to deter trawlers and develop further reefs, Rosa Whiteley, 2019

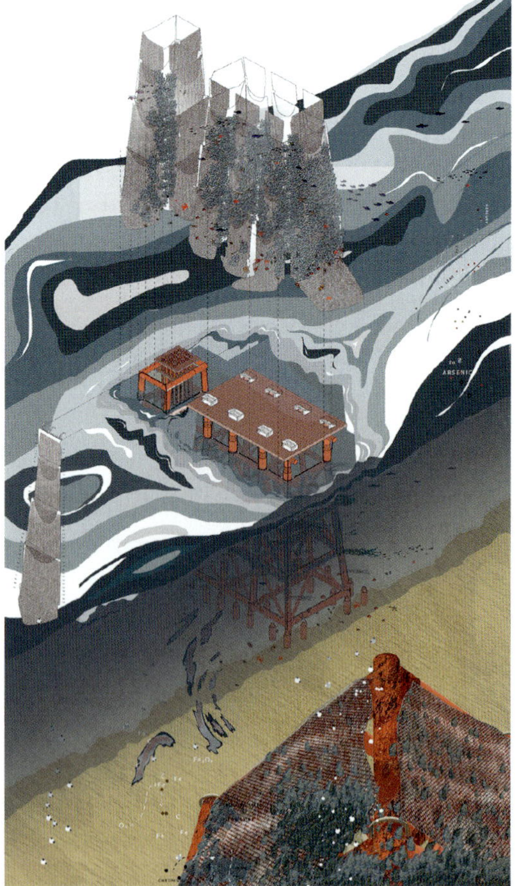

Fig. 5 *In The Bosom Of Beatrice*: Draping oil rigs with chain-mail material to increase the surface-area of the rig, and encourage further reef formation, Rosa Whiteley, 2019

1   O. Timofeeva, Ultra-black: Towards a materialist theory of oil, *e-Flux*, 84 (2017).

2   This occurred, for example, in April 2020, when global oil prices famously went negative for the first time as a result of reduced demand during the Covid-19 pandemic.

3   "Reef building" could be considered as "world building," and an example of the nature with which oil critters build worlds within worlds of human-derived residues.

4   ARUP, *Decommissioning in the North Sea: Demand vs Capacity* (DECOM North Sea/Scottish Enterprise, October 2014).

5   *UKCS: Topsides and Substructures Removal Weights 2019–2028*, Statista, 2020, https://www.statista.com/statistics/749416/forecast-ukcs-weight-of-structures-to-be-removed (accessed 13 September 2021).

6   The combined weight of the leg jackets of Beatrice A, Beatrice B, and Beatrice C is listed by Repsol Sinopec as 7517 tonnes. Repsol Sinopec, *Beatrice Decommissioning Programmes, Final Version*, 2018, https://assets.publishing.service.gov.uk/government/uploads/system/uploads/attachment_data/file/772806/Beatrice_Decommissioning_Programmes.pdf (accessed 13 September 2021).

7   In the last 13 years, the UK tax subsidies given to the UK oil industry due to decommissioning subsidies has totalled £250 billion: J. C. Boue, *The UK North Sea as a Global Experiment in Neoliberal Resource Extraction* (London: Platform London and Public and Commercial Services Union, 2020).

8   The North Sea was first "industrialized" through the development of the steam trawler in the 1880s, before being further industrialized and financialized with the discovery of oil in 1969.

In February 2018, the city demanded more than US$176,000 from a Brooklyn developer accused of committing arborcide—a term popularized by former Parks Commissioner Henry J. Stern to refer to the deliberate act of killing a tree. In the Stern case, an almost 100-year-old but still healthy 32-inch diameter pin oak perished after more than a dozen 2-inch deep holes were drilled into the tree's base. It is illegal to damage or cut down a public tree, a crime that can incur fines of up to US$15,000 and/or a year in jail, and evaluators from the Parks and Recreation Department estimate the compensation based on the size, lifespan, and health of the specimen. The developer argued against the unfair penalty on the grounds of a lack of objective evidence, but the court ruled that if the developer refused to pay the fine, they would be mandated to plant 98 new trees to replace the victimized tree. This was not the first case of arborcide in New York City (pp. 132 and 140). In 1995, a contractor hired by a billboard company to prune obstructing trees forged a city permit, and chopped down eight honey locusts and a plane tree, all on Broadway. His radical pruning resulted in a fine of US$34,500 and 500 hours of community service in city parks. Another method used when a tree is blocking a store, a sign, or some other private property is to pour salt around it, which can be quicker and less noticeable than felling the tree—it's hard to find the perpetrator too. Other times, arborcides are more bombastic. In 1996, "the Psycho of Central Park" stole a piece of construction equipment and rode it around the park, destroying two mature trees.[1] In 2018, Brooklyn celebrity chef Adam Harvey was arrested for poisoning his neighbour's 60-year-old maple tree, which prevented sunlight from reaching his kitchen's solar panels. Other high-profile cases include a 20-year-old, 30-foot-tall pear tree girdled in the West Village in 2000; 35 cedar trees cut down in Inwood Hill Park in 2008; and 67 decade-old Norwegian maple trees along the Mosholu Parkway in the Bronx that had their roots chopped by the Department of Transportation in 1989, which was ordered to replace them with 100 new trees at a cost of US$150,000.

[1]   J. Mooney, Arborcide, he wrote, *New York Times*, 4 April 2008.

LOCATION: 299 South 4th Street, Brooklyn

SPECIMEN: Pin oak (*Quercus palustris*). Slab reclaimed from fallen tree, 2018

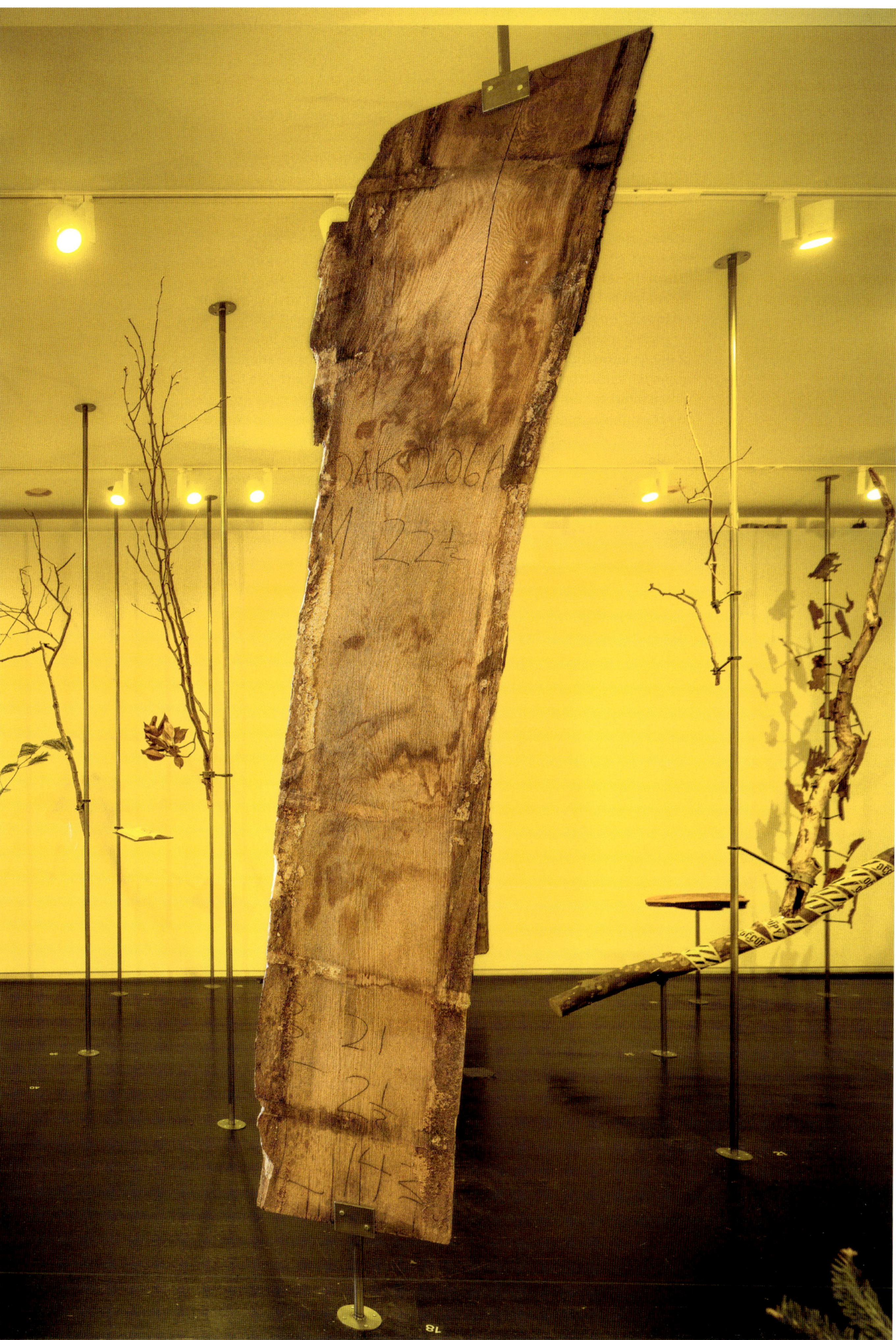
OAK 206A
M 22½
8 21
21
14

APPRAISING TREES

A callery pear tree on 11th Avenue and 25th Street was removed in 2008 to make room for three new Con Edison electrical substations supporting the 7 subway line extension. The Metropolitan Transportation Authority (MTA) eventually compensated the city US$22,500 for the loss of the tree in accordance with the NYC Parks' tree appraisal method outlined in *Tree Valuation Method*. The 2018 report calculates the replacement "value of a tree based on its size, and then takes deductions, if required, based on the tree's condition, species, and location," in an effort to mitigate canopy loss in the city.[1] Currently, the total valuation of the street tree canopy is estimated at US$5.2 billion.[2] Previously, in 2007, the MTA was allowed to remove 81 trees for the Second Avenue subway extension in exchange for paying a compensation equivalent to 430 new trees. The importance of public infrastructure for humans often outweighs considerations of green infrastructure. However, over the past few years, there has been a global effort to turn trees into assets as a way to persuade policymakers to act on the climate emergency. This move requires developing controversial metrics to perform cost–benefit analyses on trees and estimate the financial return on trees as resilient infrastructure. Other methods, like the Helliwell System, developed in 1967 in Britain and widely used worldwide, calculate the impact of felling, pruning, and planting trees, as well as their value to social and urban landscapes. This has obvious repercussions for the real estate sector's attempts to use environmental resources to increase property prices. Yet the accessibility of trees is not consistent across the city. It is often those in low-income polluted neighbourhoods—with more hard surfaces, more highways, less public transit, higher density, and less air circulation—who struggle to breathe in the scorching summer. But it is also these locally unwanted land use (LULU) areas that still have vacant post-industrial lots, the kind of lots that developers fawn over, foreseeing the potential of turning LULU brownfields into greenfields—and then gentrified neighbourhoods. The conflict between the improvement of urban transit and the preservation of tree habitats then raises questions about the potential for alternative systems that prevent trees from supplanting long-term residents.

1 NYC Parks, *NYC Tree Valuation Method*.
2 *Ibid.*

LOCATION: Lafayette Street between Prince Street and Spring Street, Manhattan

SPECIMEN: Callery pear (*Pyrus calleryana*). Branch, 2018

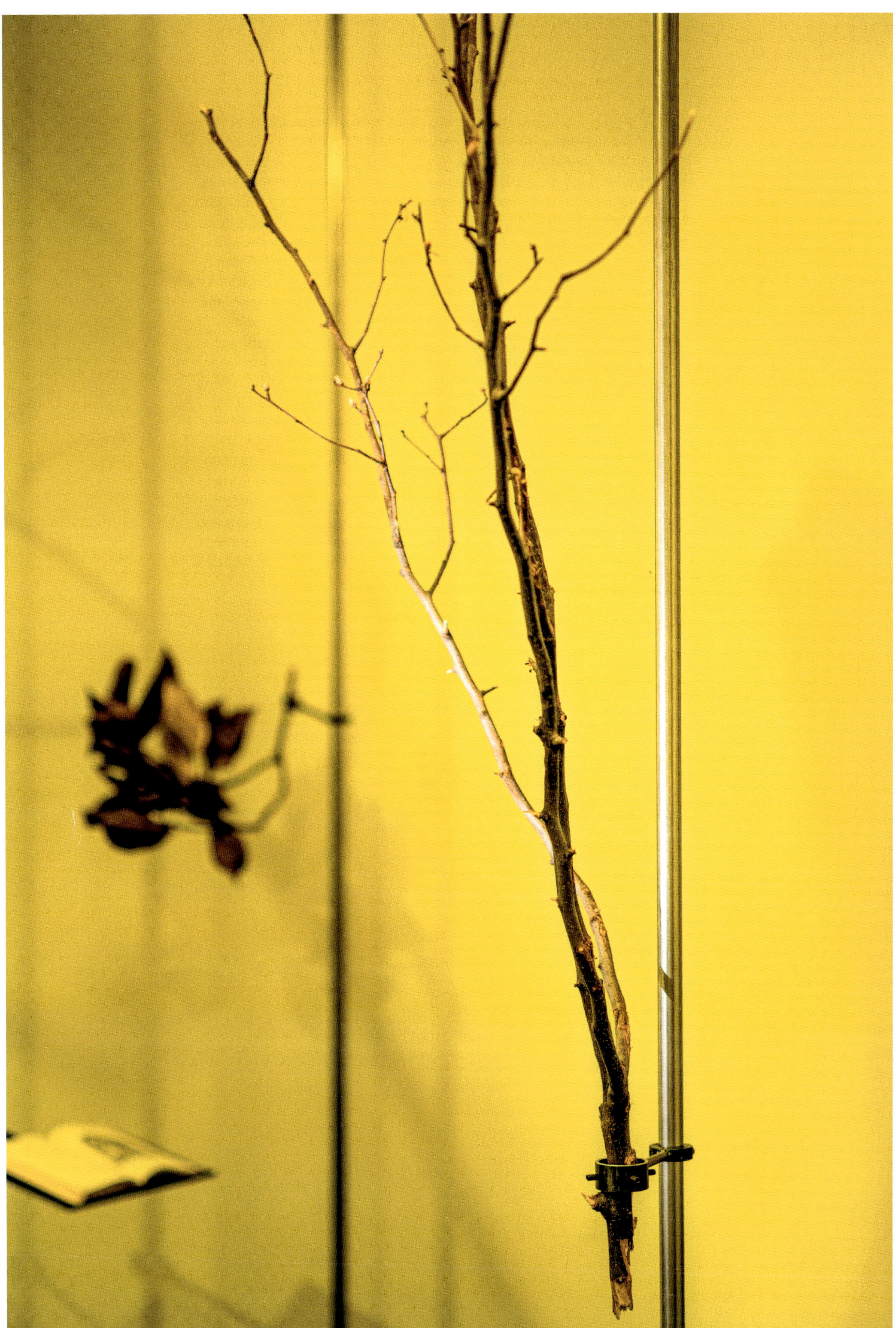

TREE BILL

In 2010, a Staten Island contractor cut down a tree that was encroaching on his driveway, unaware that it would cost him US$302,250—almost as much as the value of the house he was planning to build.[1] Since the most recent restitution law of 2010, tree replacement is a form of mandatory compensation for chopping down healthy street trees. The city calculated the replacement value of the 42-inch pin oak using its size and age, estimated at 80–100 years old. These estimates also factor in the site conditions and the location of the chopped specimen, the real-estate value and attractiveness of the neighbourhood as judged by the arboricultural appraiser, as well as the functional and aesthetic efficacy of the tree in the landscape.[2] The contractor, Molino, objected to the compensatory payment in court, arguing that the calculation was "unfair, arbitrary, and capricious."[3] He hired an external consultant to provide an alternative evaluation, which argued that the loss of the removed tree was valued at the significantly lower sum of US$14,000. Ultimately, the judge's ruling nearly halved the original penalty down to US$159,650 on the condition that Molino plant 90 3-inch trees to compensate for the public loss. However, instead of paying the Parks Department US$1,550 to plant each new tree, Molino outsourced the work to a contractor at US$250 for each tree. In such cases, it is unclear who is responsible for the trees' ongoing maintenance. Although aimed at protecting trees, the replacement value policy has inadvertently led to people avoiding planting trees in private empty lots for fear of penalties should there ever be a need to remove them.

1   A. Karni, Staten Island's $300,000 tree, *Crain's New York*, 14 July 2013.
2   NYC Parks, *NYC Tree Valuation Method*.
3   Karni, Staten Island's $300,000 tree.

LOCATION: Brooklyn

SPECIMEN: Pin oak (*Quercus palustris*). Slab reclaimed from fallen tree, 2018

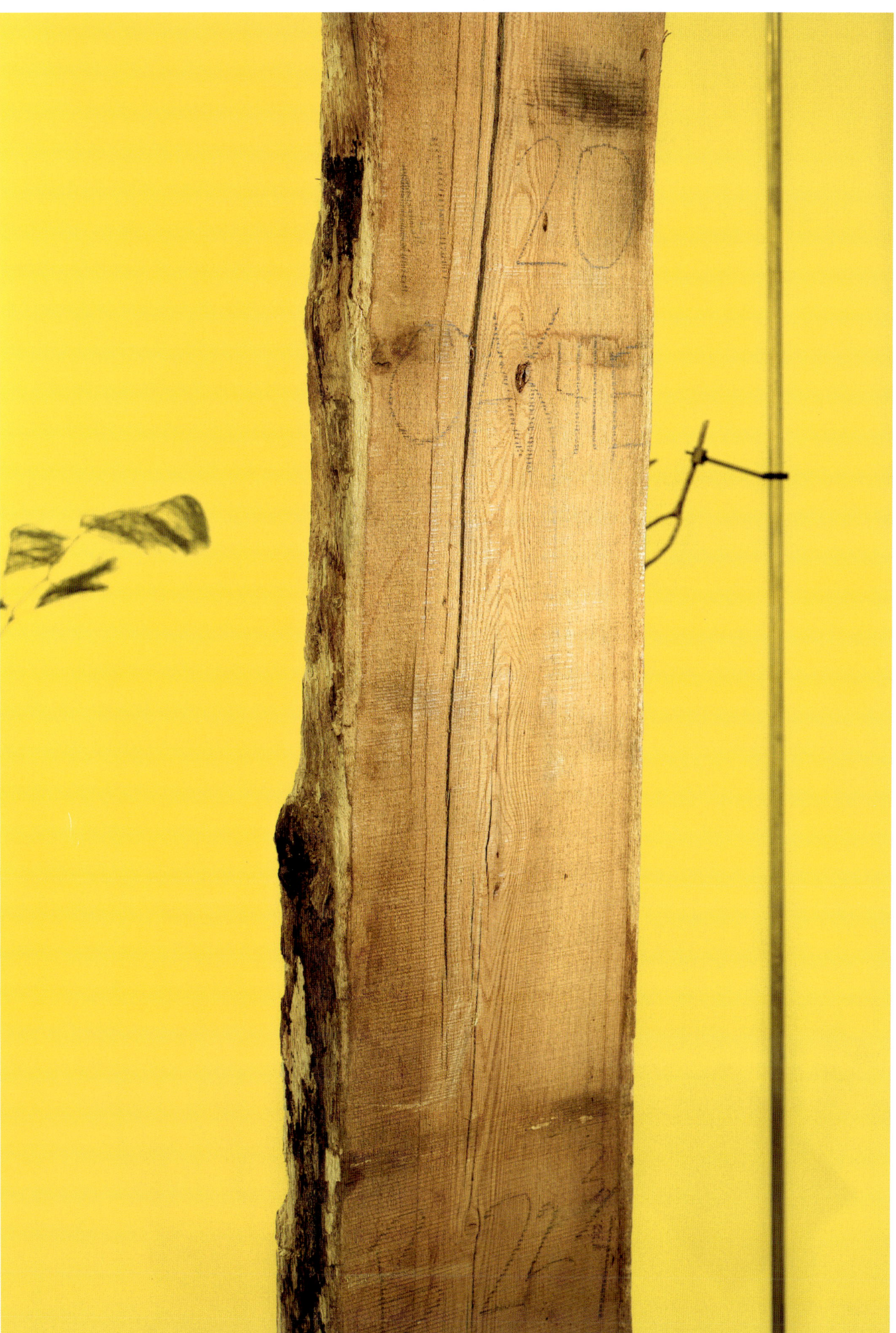

TREE TOLL

One of the largest infrastructure projects in New York City, the Robert F. Kennedy (RFK) Bridge (also known as the Triborough Bridge) has connected the Bronx, Manhattan, and Queens since 1936. In 2014, the redevelopment of one of its ramps required the removal of 16 trees, each priced at almost US$33,000. This is not an isolated case, as the city struggles to negotiate the presence of trees when trying to improve public infrastructure, revamp abandoned industrial sites, and increase accessibility to the waterfront. Similarly, in 2015, to go ahead with a ten-tower complex in Greenpoint, the developer was granted a permit to cut down five trees (two were already dead) at Newtown Barge Park for a restitution fee of US$414,000, equivalent to planting 286 new trees. As Greenpoint was already being reforested by a US$2 million project sponsored by ExxonMobil to compensate for its oil spill in Newtown Creek, the city initially thought other nearby neighbourhoods were more in need of new trees, angering local residents.[1] While these payments do help fund the management of New York street trees, the focus on the monetary value of each specimen, be it to improve bridges or waterfronts, neglects social, symbiotic, and ecosystem relationships between trees and their surroundings. In judging whether a bridge serving tens of thousands of cars per day, or a ten-tower complex housing hundreds of wealthy residents, is more or less important than a bunch of decrepit trees in highly polluted air/soil, the question presumes an economic valuation. It is the act of turning tree value into a quantifiable asset that ultimately makes trees disposable service providers for human benefit.

1   D. Furfaro, Greenpoint Landing developer pays $400k to cut down three trees, *Brooklyn Paper*, 20 July 2015.

LOCATION: RFK Bridge/Triboro Plaza, East 125th Street between First and Second Avenues, Manhattan

SPECIMEN: Sweetgum (*Liquidambar styraciflua*). Branch, 2018

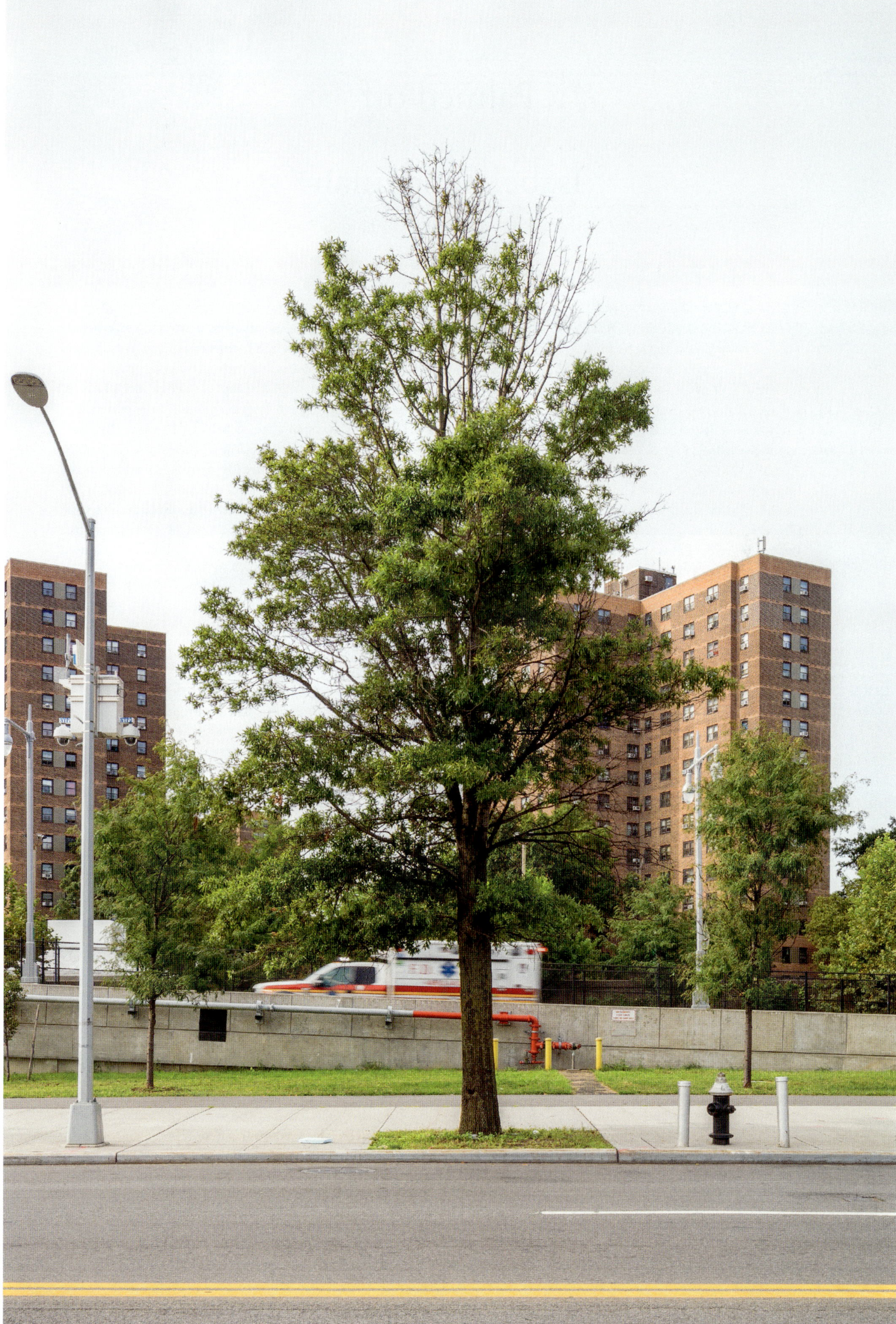

Palmed-off

Isabel Sandeman

THE ORIGINAL COMMODITY

You wash with it, you brush with it, you spread it, you eat it … It's in half of all packaged products on supermarket shelves.[1] Palm oil is used in everything from lipstick to infant formula, listed under numerous deceptive names on ingredients lists.

> Ingredients: Palm Kernel, Palmate, Palmitate, Palmolein, Glyceryl, Stearate, Stearic Acid, Palmitic Acid, Palm Stearine, Palmitoyl Oxostearamide, Palmitoyl Tetrapeptide-3, Sodium Laureth Sulfate, Sodium Lauryl Sulfate, Sodium Kernelate, Sodium Palm Kernelate, Sodium Lauryl Lactylate/Sulphate, Hydrated Palm Glycerides, Ethyl Palmitate, Octyl Palmitate, Palmityl Alcohol.[2]

This high-yield and versatile oil is produced from the orange-red fruit of the *Elaeis guineensis* species of palm tree, commonly known as the oil palm. Oil palms are native to West Africa, where they have been cultivated in colonial plantations since the 19th century. By the early 20th century, European powers had forcibly carved West Africa into land concessions, such as that granted to Lever Brothers (now Unilever) to produce palm oil for use in its soap factories.[3] Palm-oil-based soap was to become one of the first branded commodities, and was used to further the British colonial project; early advertising campaigns portrayed the simple bar of soap as a technology of social and environmental purification, transforming the imagined dirt and disorder of colonial nations into British standards of cultural "cleanliness."[4]

One such nation was British North Borneo. This was under the control of the North Borneo Chartered Company, which was set up with the explicit aim to exploit the area's natural resources for profit. The promotion of colonial plantations was the company's main economic project, while indigenous villagers, unable to pay colonial taxes, were forced to switch from subsistence to cash-crop farming. The result was an extractive, plantation-based economy oriented towards the consumption needs of the West. British North Borneo gained independence in 1963 as the Malaysian state of Sabah. However, by then, deforestation and domestication of the landscape in pursuit of productivity were already firmly embedded in the area's economic policy. Today, Sabah accounts for 27% of Malaysia's total palm oil production, with approximately 20% of its total land area used to farm oil palm.[5]

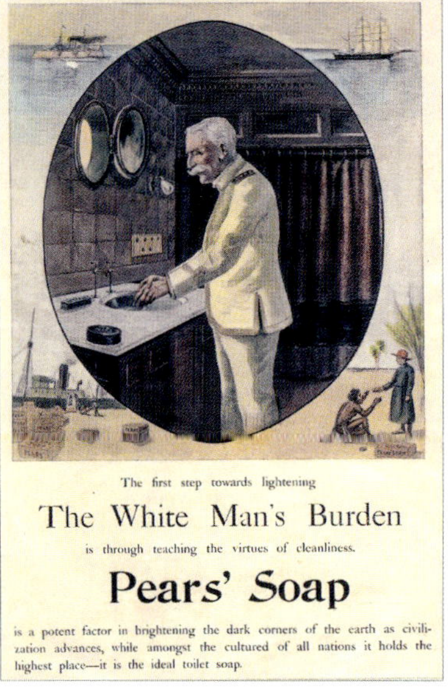

Fig. 1 Pears' Soap advertisement, "The White Man's Burden" (1899). It first appeared in *McClure's Magazine* (October 1899)

THE KINABATANGAN DICHOTOMY

The bulk of Sabah's oil palm plantations can be found on and around the lush and fertile floodplain of the Kinabatangan River. This area is one of the most naturally abundant places on the planet, but as a consequence of global demand for cheap vegetable oil, it is deteriorating into a green desert and commodity-making machine. Conflicting interests of multiple stakeholders have led to a haphazard division between depleted oil palm developments and fragmented wildlife reserves. These reserves were originally intended to form a forest corridor along the Kinabatangan. However, over time, more and more of this corridor has been levelled, terraced, and planted, destabilizing the soil and causing landslides and intensified flooding. Protected areas have become scattered islands in a sea of palms laid out in an infinite and monotonous 9-metre triangular grid.

It is this combination of fragmented forest and endless oil palm that has had the counterintuitive effect of increasing the area's ecotourism potential. As oil palm plantations expand and rainforest is lost, animals are crowded into ever-closer proximity with the river bank. With nowhere else to go, megafauna can frequently be seen in the 100 metres of rainforest immediately adjacent to the river: an area known as the riparian buffer zone. As a result, high-paying Western tourists can be guaranteed to see Sabah's Big Five—the orangutan, pigmy elephant, proboscis monkey, crocodile, and rhinoceros hornbill—all from the comfort of a river cruise. The Kinabatangan River has consequently become one of the best places in the entire world for tourists to view wildlife, while remaining blissfully unaware of the environmental destruction driven by Western demand for food oil and cosmetics.

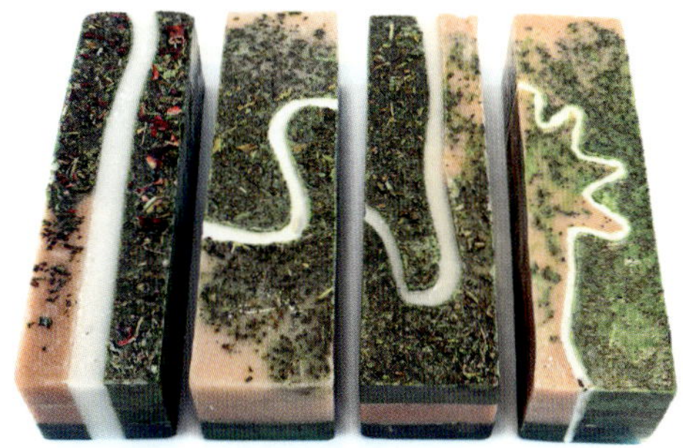

Fragmented wildlife reserves in the Kinabatangan floodplain are precariously linked by unprotected secondary forest claimed as customary land by the local Orang Sungai, a collective term coined by the colonial British, literally meaning "River People." The Sabah Land Ordinance provides a degree of protection: Indigenous people are entitled to apply for up to 8 hectares of land to be recognized under individual native title provisions. However, indigenous people are only entitled to register land that is in active use.[6] Unprotected secondary rainforest does not fit into the prevailing dichotomy of pristine wilderness and depleted development. In the eyes of the Malaysian government, it is neither efficiently productive nor worthy of protection, and is therefore considered idle and unproductive, requiring further development if it is to contribute towards the economy. Such land can be subject to state intervention and appropriated for palm oil production or infrastructure development. Fear of customary land being labelled as "idle" has prompted many natives to clear the rainforest and plant oil palm as a strategic measure to prevent land-grabbing by the state.[7]

Over 64% of idle land in the area is allocated for future oil palm, despite the fact that the majority of this land experiences severe annual flooding.[8] Flood inundation is deadly for oil palms, resulting in costly replanting and delayed harvest; factors that lead to commercially redundant plantations. Attempts at mitigating flood damage have resulted in a network of artificial channels to drain water from flood-prone plantations. Despite this extensive drainage, over 20% of plantations in the region are estimated to be underproductive.[9] Once the 25-year life cycle of these palms is complete, plantation companies are highly unlikely to replant these areas. Abandoned plantations not only fail to provide economically but are also unable to contribute the forest products, landscape connectivity, and habitat that the land provided when it was considered idle.

RECIPE FOR DECOLONIZATION

A palm-oil-free soap recipe utilizes oils and butters that come from plants and trees occurring naturally on idle land. This soap scrub contains seeds from small, seeded, pioneer species, like *Macaranga* spp., and fast-growing species of *Ficus*—the most important plant group in the rainforest ecosystem, which supplies up to 93% of many animals' diets.[10] Many of these species are epiphytes that will eventually colonize, embrace, and replace their host, acting to both sustain wildlife and destroy oil palm.

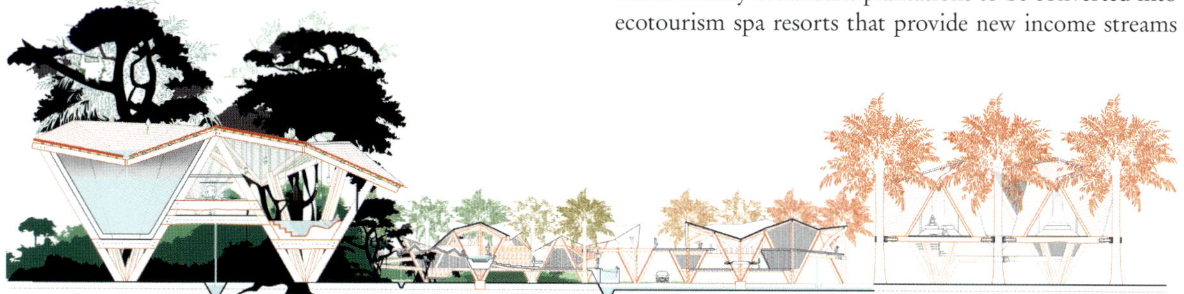

Fig. 3 *Palmed-off, Soap Sections*, Isabel Sandeman, 2017

Palmed-off proposes to use this seed soap to decolonize the landscape and restore nature's dirt and disorder. The proposal is an alternative development strategy for commercially redundant plantations to be converted into ecotourism spa resorts that provide new income streams

Fig. 4 Section of *Palmed-off*, Isabel Sandeman, 2017

for local people. The spas function as seed-distribution facilities, using cosmetic treatments to disperse seeds through the extensive channel system present in flood-inundated oil palm plantations. They are composed of a series of soaping situations: scrub therapy treatment, a seed soak, foaming footbaths, and personal pool showers. Each of these Trojan horse treatments is located directly above a drainage channel, hacking the existing oil palm infrastructure to disperse seeds and turn cosmetic consumerism into something constructive instead of destructive.

Treatment rooms are purposefully dispersed in order to exploit as many channels as possible, thereby increasing the possibility for chance to manifest itself. They are linked together in a sprawling and flexible form that takes over the plantation in the same way an epiphyte takes over its host. Through the spa's functioning—as well as active planting and maintenance of seedlings—the building itself will be slowly replaced as pioneer species establish themselves, a process that is estimated to take around

15 years. The rewilded former plantation becomes a site to forage oil crops for soap supply, and the spa resort can be relocated to a new redundant plantation. This allows for the slow transformation of the territory, through the dispersal of seeds and the manifestation of an alternative oil industry that supports idleness as productivity.

The intention is not to return the landscape to what was, but to catalyse a constructed nature from the 9-metre plantation grid. This idle land will become a habitat for endangered flora and fauna, made up of large numbers of keystone species, fruit trees, and small water bodies. Constructed nature may even become more valuable for wildlife than a natural forest of the same size, and more resilient, because this forest corridor is based on both economic and environmental conditions, rather than an arbitrary offset from the river. By rethinking human inhabitation and Western consumption habits, it may yet be possible to deliver the conservation objectives that were originally created for this area.

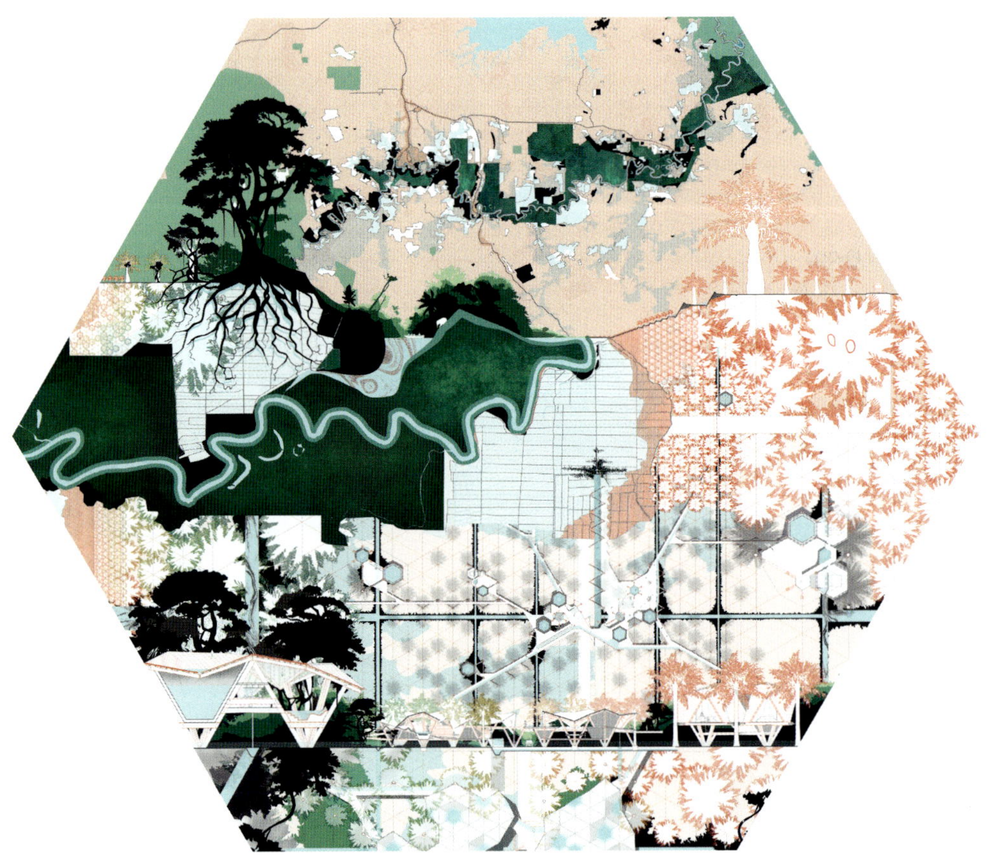

Fig. 5 *Palmed-off, the Kinabatangan Dichotomy*, Isabel Sandeman, 2017

1   WWF, *8 Things to Know About Palm Oil*, 2020, https://www.wwf. org.uk/updates/8-things-know-about-palm-oil (accessed 13 September 2021).

2   WWF, *Which Everyday Products Contain Palm Oil?*, 2016, https:// www.worldwildlife.org/pages/which-everyday-products-contain-palm-oil (accessed 13 September 2021).

3   K. Nworah, The politics of Lever's West African concessions, 1907–1913, *International Journal of African Historical Studies*, 5(2) (1972): 248–264.

4   A. McClintock, *Imperial Leather: Race, Gender, and Sexuality in the Colonial Contest* (New York: Routledge, 1995), p. 217.

5   A. Kushairi Din, Malaysian oil palm industry performance 2016 and prospects for 2017, presented at *Palm Oil Economic Review & Outlook Seminar 2017*, https://web.archive.org/ web/20180810060944/http://www.mpob.gov.my/images/ stories/pdf/2017/2017_Dr.KushairiPALMEROS2017.pdf (accessed 13 September 2021).

6   State of Sabah, Land Ordinance, 2012, https://sagclibrary.sabah. gov.my (accessed 13 September 2021).

7   F. M. Cooke, In the name of poverty alleviation: Experiments with oil palm smallholders and customary land in Sabah, Malaysia, *Asia Pacific Viewpoint*, 2012, https://doi.org/10.1111/j.1467-8373.2012.01490.x (accessed 13 September 2021).

8   N. K. Abram, P. Xofis, J. Tzanopoulos, *et al.*, Synergies for improving oil palm production and forest conservation in floodplain landscapes, *PLOS ONE* 9(6) (2014): e95388, p. 6 https://doi. org/10.1371/journal.pone.0095388 (accessed 13 September 2021).

9   Abram *et al.*, Synergies for improving oil palm production and forest conservation in floodplain landscapes, p. 8.

10   M. Shanahan, *Ladders to Heaven* (London: Unbound, 2018).

In the 1980s, Donald Trump envisioned a vast building complex crowned by a 150-storey skyscraper designed by Helmut Jahn on a former train yard south of Riverside Park—what was then the most expensive real estate development in the city's history. What came to be known as Riverside South owes its name to a group of civic organizations rallying against Donald Trump's proposal in 1989. Shortly after the Riverside South plan was approved in 1992, Trump faced bankruptcy and sold the site to a group of Hong Kong investors, with the condition that "Trump Place" would be emblazoned in gold on the main building. Initial massing schemes and a masterplan for the area were drafted by SOM. To counter resistance from civic groups, both the city and the developer committed to relocating the elevated West Side Highway that separated the community from the proposed Riverside Park South. Feeling displaced and cut off from the waterfront, local residents—grouped under the Coalition for a Livable West Side—filed a lawsuit in 1997 after the developer failed to follow through on replacing the highway with the viaduct. The construction of a new park became the token to get past the opposition.[1] As the political will to move the highway faded, the cost of its relocation became an unaffordable luxury. Although the park took more than 20 years to complete—its penultimate phase was inaugurated in October 2020—the highway between West 59th and West 72nd Streets still remains the only elevated section along the Hudson River today, splitting the park in two. Although they did not manage to create a continuous green space on the banks of the river, new trees have been planted by residents of the luxury condo towers along the park; those same residents have pushed successfully to have Trump's name removed from the façade.

1   T. S. Purdum, Trump revises project plan for West Side, *New York Times*, 6 March 1991.

LOCATION: Riverside Boulevard at West 64th Street, Manhattan

SPECIMEN: Northern red oak (*Quercus rubra*). Branch, 2018

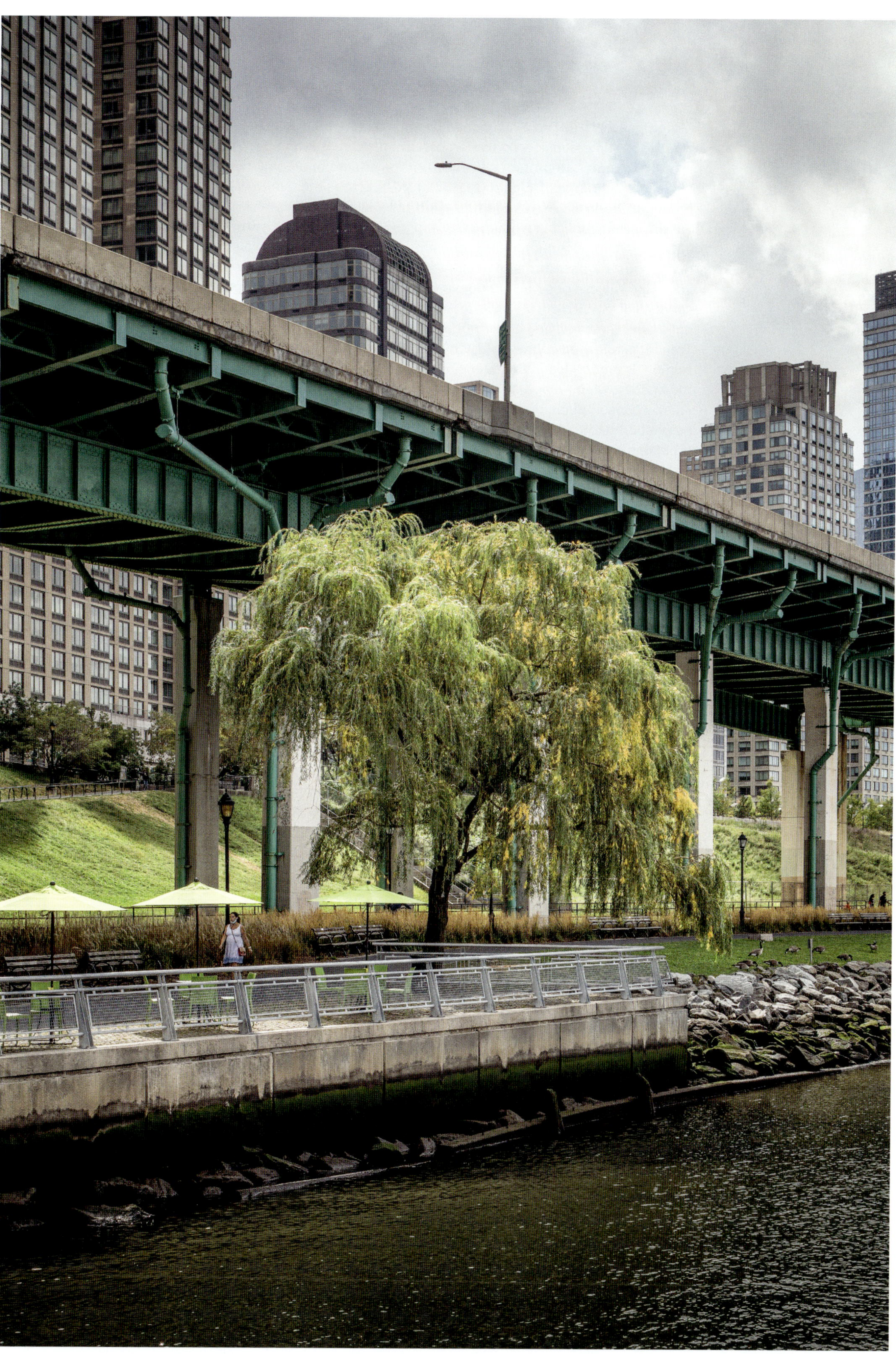

OFFSET FOREST

MillionTreesNYC (MTNYC), launched by Michael Bloomberg in 2007, was at that time considered the largest urban afforestation effort in the world. It ventured to protect citizens from the effects of air pollution and climate change by planting 1 million trees across the five New York boroughs. Such an unprecedented effort fits well into the wave of "roll-out environmentalism," whereby those in power create new institutions, initiatives, and governance arrangements to address the consequences of previous, harsher forms of neoliberalism.[1] Every street tree in New York city was assigned an economic value based on the "environmental services" it performed: stormwater intercepted, energy conserved, air pollutants removed, and carbon dioxide reduced. The New York Street Tree Map, released online in 2016 by the Department of Parks and Recreation, is embedded in the financial quantification of trees. Emphasizing the benefits of improved air quality, increased shading, and reduced energy consumption, the majority of trees were planted in low-income neighbourhoods with limited tree canopy and high levels of respiratory problems among residents. Both the first and last trees of MTNYC were planted in "Asthma Alley" in the South Bronx, and the 500,000th tree was planted in Harlem. Asthma rates in these areas are among the highest in the USA, reflecting the communities' close proximity to the waste transfer stations, incinerators, bus depots, sewage treatment infrastructure, and fossil fuel power plants that have a disproportionate impact on these particular communities of colour.[2] Long before MTNYC was even imagined, people living in these neighbourhoods were forming grassroots organizations, such as West Harlem Environmental Action Coalition (WE ACT), to fight such air-poisoning facilities, identifying them as examples of endemic environmental racism.[3] As part of a new green wave of environmental gentrification, New York's tree planting initiative was questioned for presenting itself as politically neutral, consensus-based, and ecologically and socially sensitive planning, even though in practice it subordinates equity to profit-minded development.[4] MTNYC has been a driving force of an emerging urban greening movement, both in gentrifying and long-gentrified areas. Yet, this is but one example where trees have been planted to offset pollution, offering up the city's pollutable subjects as collateral, rather than addressing the deeper root causes of pollution itself.

1 L. K. Campbell, Constructing New York City's urban forest, in *Urban Forests, Trees and Greenspace. A Policy Perspective* (L. A. Sandberg, A. Bardekjian, and S. Butt, eds) (New York: Routledge, 2014), pp. 242–260.

2 J. Sze, *Noxious New York: The Racial Politics of Urban Health and Environmental Justice* (Cambridge, MA: MIT Press, 2007), pp. 50–51.

3 See campaigns by the Organization of Waterfront Neighborhoods, South Bronx Unite, WE ACT, or Communities United for Responsible Energy, among others. As Sze remarks, these campaigns are largely undocumented in academic literature.

4 M. Checker, Wiped out by the "green wave:" Environmental gentrification and the paradoxical politics of urban sustainability, *City & Society*, 23(2) (2011): 210–229.

SPECIMEN: Carolina silverbell (*Halesia carolina*). Branch from the first tree of MTNYC, 2018
Pin oak (*Quercus palustris*). Branch from the 500,000th tree of MTNYC, 2018
Lacebark elm (*Ulmus parvifolia*). Branch from the 1 millionth tree of MTNYC, 2018

LOCATION: Teller Avenue, Morrisania, Bronx
St. Nicholas Park, Harlem, Manhattan
Joyce Kilmer Park, South Bronx

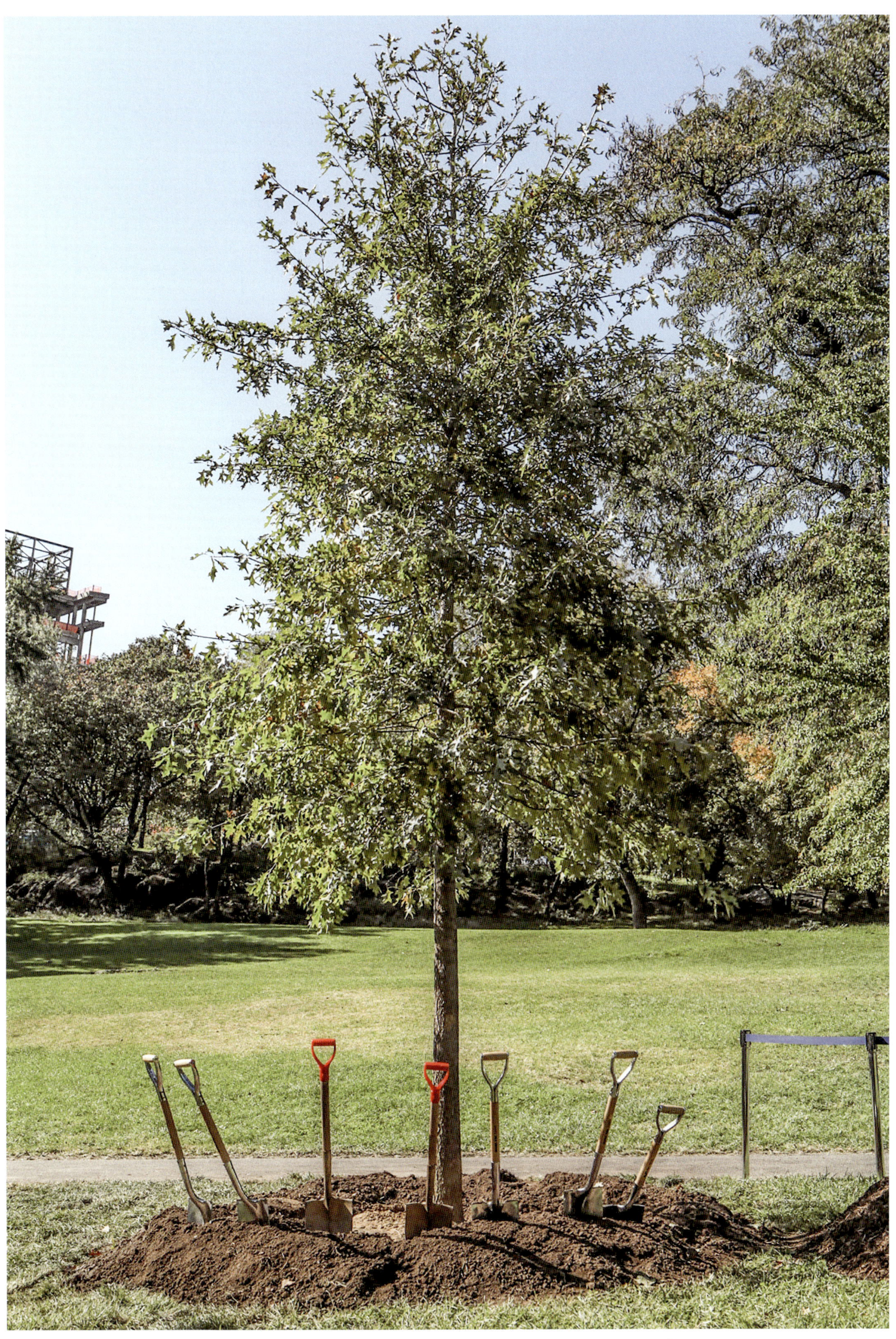

Tree rings provide invaluable climate, carbon, and ecological information. Typically accessed from felled or fallen cross-cut trunks, boring into standing trees makes these chronologies available from living specimens. This data can then be used to forecast future trends. Hundreds of core samples were extracted from living trees across Queens in 2005 as part of a survey conducted by the Columbia University Lamont–Doherty Tree Ring Laboratory to study the city's climate and weather history. The cores were later used to inform the software i-Tree, a tool developed by the USDA Forest Service to calculate the financial value of trees in proportion to their performance. Generated by GIS and algorithms, the software estimates the environmental services that could be extracted from trees. The software's Streets application aims to "improve the return on your investment dollar" by implementing "economic evaluations of tree performance" and leveraging "investment from partners for carbon credits or energy conservation."[1] The Tree Carbon Calculator—a federally approved spreadsheet developed by the Center for Urban Forest Research—tracks each tree's yearly capacity for stormwater interception, energy conservation, air pollutant removal, and carbon dioxide reduction. This circulation of value puts a price tag on urban canopies in order to protect them—a strategy that environmental scholars Bram Büscher and Robert Fletcher have critically referred to as "accumulation by preservation."[2] Corporate social responsibility schemes, together with thousands of hours of volunteer labour, have nudged many businesses to jump into the new "carbon neutrality" market and develop expertise in these carefully calculated investments. i-Tree now even quantifies the emotional impact of greenery at any point in the city, pioneering a new frontier for real estate investment and speculative valuation processes.

1   i-Tree, *i-Tree Streets Application Overview*, 29 July 2019, https://www.itreetools.org/tools/i-tree-streets/i-tree-streets-application-overview (accessed 13 September 2021).

2   B. Büscher and R. Fletcher, Accumulation by conservation, *New Political Economy*, 20(2) (2015): 273–298.

LOCATION: Various locations, Queens; Columbia University Lamont-Doherty Earth Observatory, Tree Ring Laboratory

SPECIMEN: Various species. Tree core samples, 2005

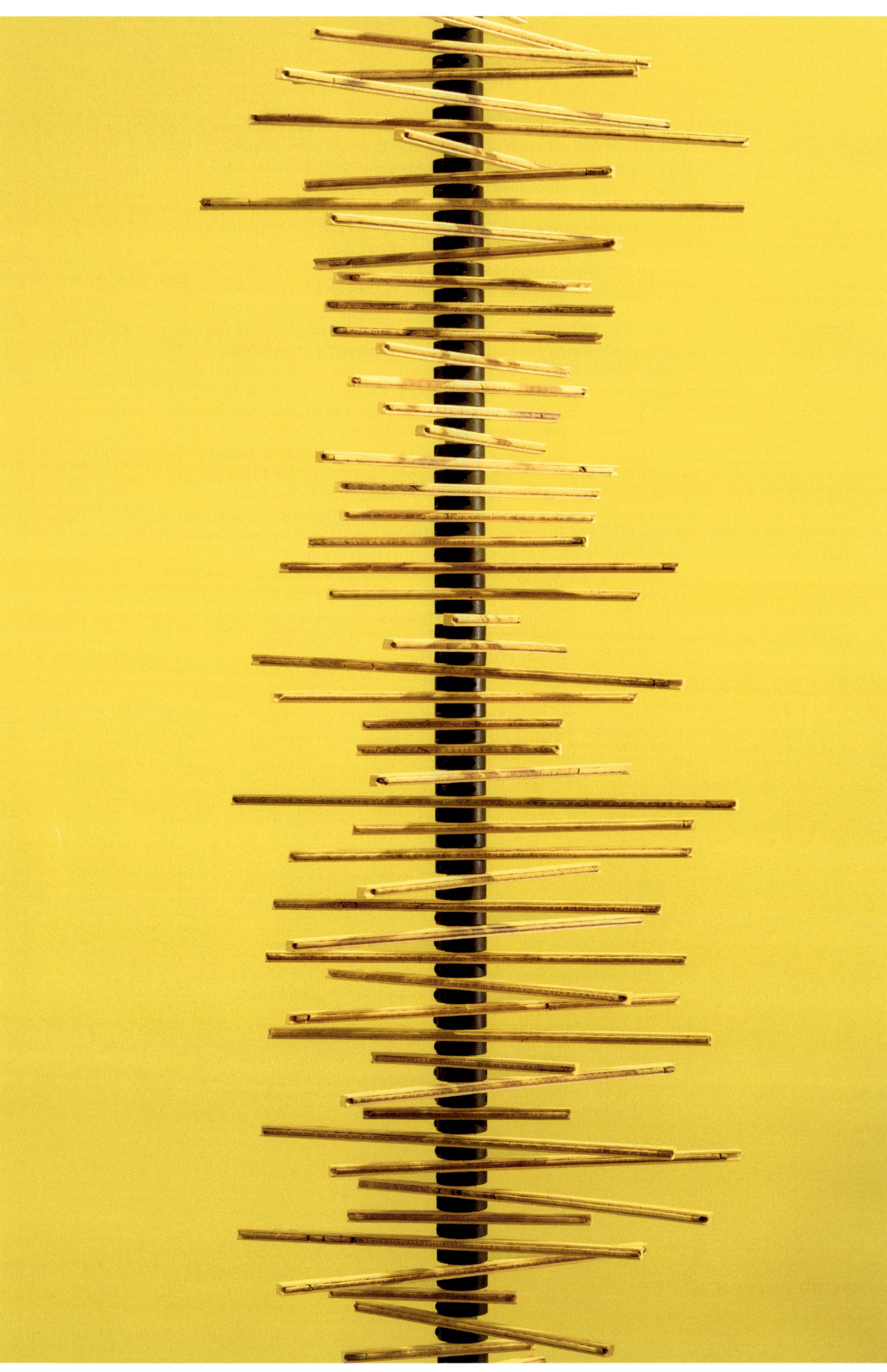

CARBON DISCREDITS

Once decision-makers were convinced of the value of planting street trees in New York, different schemes began to utilize them to trade and mitigate air pollution. Emissions trading was first instituted in the 1997 Kyoto Protocol—pushed by the US to privatize the atmosphere and effectively create "permits to pollute."[1] A few decades later, now that each street tree in New York City is valued for the amount of carbon it sequesters, a new market is emerging to sell off those environmental services. Companies such as the now-defunct Urban Offsets manage sites across the five boroughs, from Crotona Park and Soundview Park in the Bronx to Alley Pond Park in Queens, in order to "transform your offsets into assets" by planting or giving away trees to mitigate your carbon footprint and helping you become "climate resilient."[2] But when those carbon trading companies disappear, what happens to the unmaintained trees and the credits they stand for? Is the polluter alerted to the fact that they are no longer carbon neutral? This is not to say that there is something wrong with planting trees. Yet these mechanisms confuse basic understandings of "sustainability." Environmental market fraud has reached such a point that even Interpol has a publicly available guide to crime in the carbon trade. Bloomberg Green recently reported that Nature Conservancy, the world's biggest environmental group, has become a dealer of carbon offsets and sells mitigation credits to JPMorgan Chase, Disney, and BlackRock in forests that, rather than being newly planted, are in fact already well preserved.[3] Even the Vatican has been involved in carbon trade corruption, through a scam featuring offset certificates for trees that were never planted in Hungary.[4] As companies frantically chase fantasies of offsetting and carbon credits, the actual sources of fossil fuel emissions remain unaddressed.

1 Carbon Trade Watch, *The Carbon Connection*, http://www.carbontradewatch. org/index.php?option=com_content&task=view&id=32&Itemid=46 (accessed 13 September 2021).

2 Urban Offsets, https://www.urbanoffsets.co (accessed 13 September 2021).

3 B. Elgin, These trees are not what they seem, *Bloomberg Green*, 9 December 2020; see also C. Lang, The Nature Conservancy's fake forest offsets, *REDD-Monitor*, 14 December 2020.

4 D. Struck, Carbon offsets: How a Vatican forest failed to reduce global warming, *The Christian Monitor*, 20 April 2010.

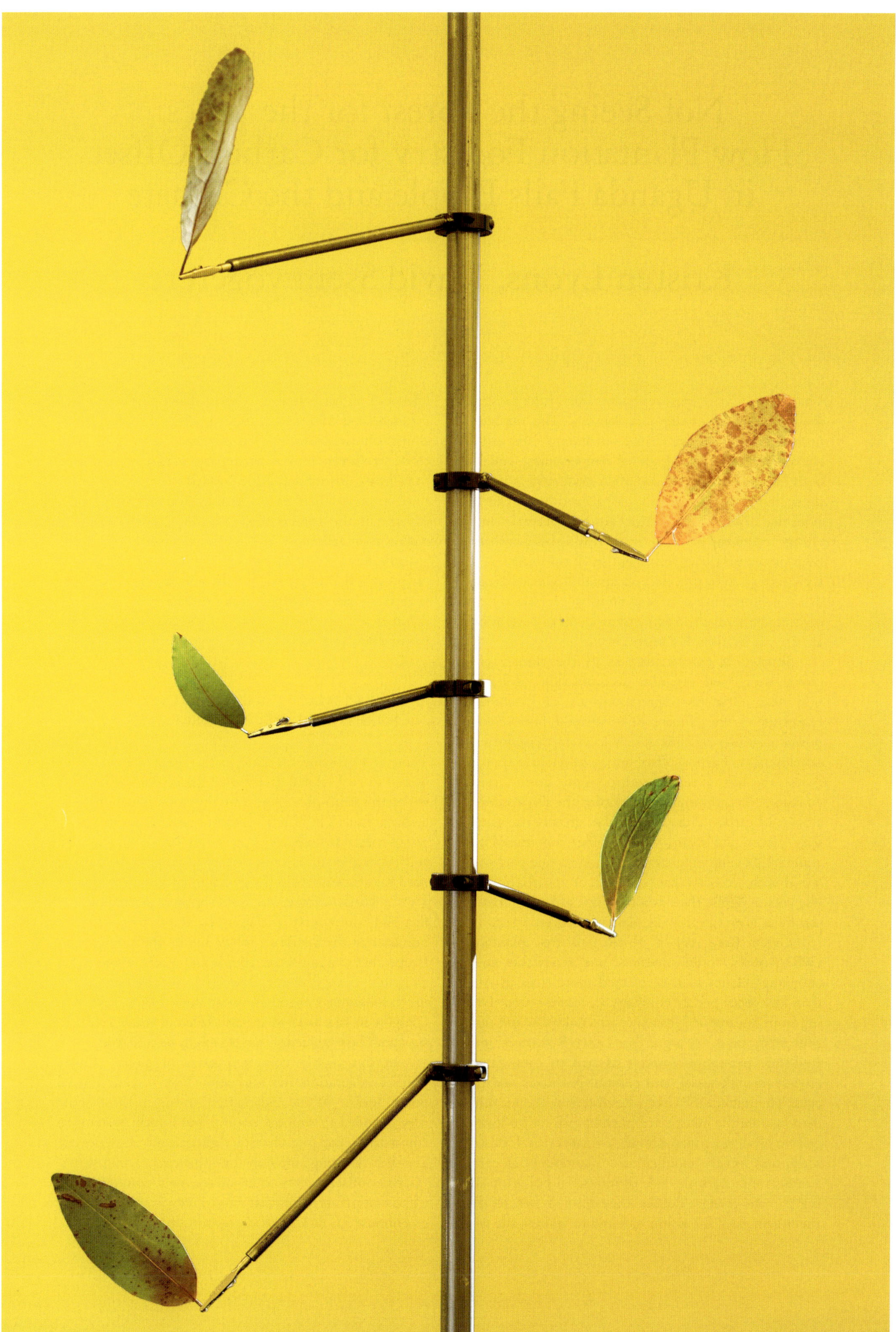

Not Seeing the Forest for the Trees: How Plantation Forestry for Carbon Offset in Uganda Fails People and the Climate

Kristen Lyons, David Ssemwogerere

The global climate crisis represents one of the most profound challenges of the 21st century. The impacts of human-induced climate change—including rising sea levels, as well as increasing global temperatures—endanger both life and livelihoods, and often most acutely threaten those least responsible for the global greenhouse gas emissions that drive climate change.[1] Anthropocentric climate change is part and parcel of the increasing burden that has been placed on the environment since colonization, and is characterized by processes of capitalist industrialization driving unsustainable carbon-intensive economies.[2] Simply put, modernist and extractivist forms of development are driving us towards climate chaos.[3]

Situated at the intersection of the climate crisis, colonization, and capitalist accumulation, global carbon offset initiatives—representing one of a number of responses to the climate crisis—extend both colonial power relations and unsustainable extractivist forms of development. Carbon offset initiatives include those activities that aim to reduce anthropogenic greenhouse gas emissions via carbon sinks—including the absorption and storage of carbon dioxide and other greenhouse gases in soils, plants, and oceans. Carbon offset is premised upon counterbalancing industrial pollution in one part of the world with activities that sequester, or absorb, pollution elsewhere.[4] While there is a diversity of such initiatives, our focus is on the growing plantation forestry sector.

Green Resources—a Norwegian tree plantation, carbon offset, forest products, and renewable energy company—claims to have planted more trees in Africa than any other private company in recent years.[5] Drawing from research in Uganda conducted by us and others over many years, we argue that Green Resources' industrial-scale plantation forestry is tied to long-standing environmental, social, and cultural problems and damages. The impacts of Green Resources at the local level demonstrate the injustice of pitching plantation forestry carbon offset as a panacea for the climate crisis. Industrial-scale, and mostly monoculture, plantations as carbon stores cannot curb the tide of industrial pollution driving climate change. Rather, they have shown to delay the urgent need for action required to address the worst effects of climate change, with evidence that some governments use offsetting to hide a failure to reduce emissions.[6] On this basis, carbon offset initiatives, including those by Green Resources, represent false solutions to the climate crisis. Such initiatives fail to see the forest for the trees, given their sustained disavowal of the profound, adverse, on-the-ground impacts for local communities, as well as their failure to curb escalating global greenhouse gas emissions. Responses to the climate crisis that centre on people, including Indigenous people and local communities—rather than markets—will be vital to unsettle colonial and corporate power. This may open up new possibilities and pathways for climate justice.

THE CLIMATE CRISIS: PLANTATION FORESTRY/CARBON OFFSET RESPONSE

There is a growing recognition that urgent action is required to curb global greenhouse gas emissions, stabilize the earth's atmosphere, and limit the worst effects of global climate chaos. The COP 21 climate negotiations in Paris in 2015—which brought together government, civil society, and private sector interests—reached a consensus on the need for action to keep the global temperature rise below 1.5°C.[7] These negotiations, however, were marred by conflict and controversy, including by the disproportionate influence of the fossil fuel lobby and by the failure to set targets that would protect people and places whose rights and interests are denied by extractivist development.[8] Similarly, subsequent negotiations—including COP 26 held in Glasgow in late 2021—have also failed to reach a consensus about how reduction targets might be realized.[9]

In this highly contested space of global climate politics, adaptation and mitigation have become central policy tools.[10] While "adaptation" refers to those activities intended to support natural and human systems to adjust to a changing climate, "mitigation" activities are aimed at reducing emissions or enhancing carbon stores. "Carbon offset" refers to an increasingly common suite of mitigation activities that aim to reduce anthropogenic greenhouse gas emissions via carbon sinks, reforestation, and afforestation. Global carbon offset is premised upon an arrangement whereby industrial pollution in one part of the world is "offset" by activities that sequester or absorb pollution elsewhere.[11] While there are many different types of offset initiatives, our focus is on plantation forestry for carbon trading.

To work, plantation forestry for carbon offset relies on the possibility of measuring the volume of carbon dioxide and other greenhouse gases sequestered (or absorbed) from the atmosphere in the wood, leaves, soil, and organic matter in plantation forestry projects. This volume is then priced and sold on to a polluting industry, company, or country. Plantation forestry initiatives claim to offset industrial pollution in one part of the world by sequestering it elsewhere, often in territories that are home to the economically poor, as in the case reported in this chapter.[12]

While plantation forestry might evoke images of clean, green, and biodiverse landscapes, particularly for largely urbanized populations in the West, the reality is far less idyllic. Plantation forestry is increasingly large scale and mostly monoculture-based, with the Food and Agriculture Organization of the United Nations estimating that industrial plantation forestry grew by 48.1 per cent between 1990 and 2010.[13] Expansion on the African continent has been especially pronounced, where large-scale investment by the private sector has enabled "corporate forestry empires" to establish themselves as key actors in the global carbon offset industry.[14] Green Resources provides an exemplar of this industrial model of plantation forestry.

MONEY DOES GROW ON TREES: PLANTATION FORESTRY AND CARBON OFFSET IN UGANDA

Uganda was at the forefront of carbon offset implementation on the African continent.[15] The first of its projects was established in 1994, via a collaboration between the FACE Foundation and the Ugandan Wildlife Authority. Despite the early euphoria that this project could deliver "win-win" benefits for local communities and the global environment, the project was quickly tarnished by accounts of violent evictions, human rights abuses, and

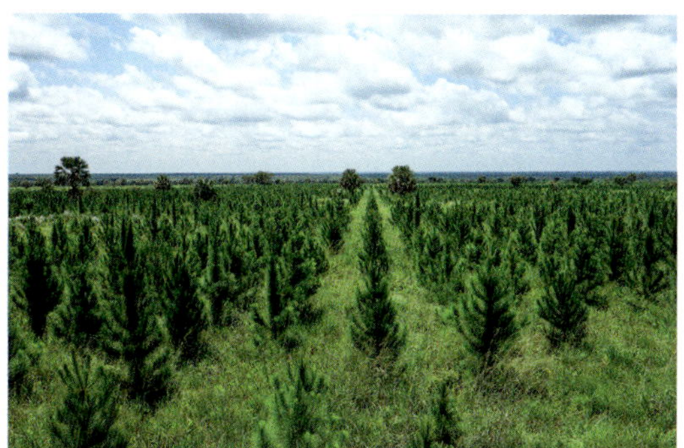

Fig. 1 The monoculture pine plantation in Green Resources' Central Forest Reserve of Kachung, Uganda. 2017

conflicts related to land ownership and access.[16] Since this first project, the number of carbon market projects—and problems—has increased.

National and international NGOs—including the World Wildlife Fund and the Jane Goodall Institute—alongside private sector interests and others, have taken leading roles in establishing afforestation, reforestation, and forest management, as well as cropland and grazing land management projects across Uganda. These initiatives are supported via international donors, including the World Bank and the Common Market for Eastern and Southern Africa (COMESA) Carbon Fund, and with national support via the Uganda Carbon Bureau and the Forest Carbon Partnership Facility's Reduced Emissions from Deforestation and Forest Degradation (REDD) Readiness Preparation process.[17] On the basis of these investments and support, Uganda is now a global market leader in carbon forestry credits.

The expansion of plantation forestry and carbon offset initiatives in Uganda has delivered sustained disruptions and problems for local communities. This is by no means unique to Uganda and, indeed, is often key to plantation forestry carbon offset projects. From the earliest initiatives, including the FACE project outlined above, projects have led to forced evictions of local communities, alongside other human rights abuses.[18] The disruption of social, cultural, and ecological connections to land and territories also drives wide-scale economic inequality, with outcomes that worsen the life chances for many affected communities.[19]

The trend of land appropriation—or "land grabbing"—to establish plantation forestry/carbon offset projects is representative of the ongoing colonial, and postcolonial, expulsion from land and appropriation of nature.[20] At the same time, this accumulation by dispossession enables industrialized countries to continue emitting high levels of greenhouse gases, thereby offering little by way of response to the urgent climate crisis.[21]

GREEN RESOURCES

Green Resources, the focus of this article, has established projects across a number of sites on the African continent. It has received significant donor support to do so (approximately US$33 million), including from public development finance institutions, such as Norfund (Norway), FMO (The Netherlands), and Finnfund (Finland).[22] In Uganda, Green Resources has obtained 50-year licences for plantation forestry at two locations, the Bukaleba Forest Reserve in the Mayuge district and the Kachung Central Forest Reserve in the Dokolo district, covering an area of around 7,300 hectares.[23] Despite aiming to implement carbon offset projects at both sites, this aim was realized—and only for a time—only at Green Resources' Kachung site.

Green Resources obtained a license to establish its industrial tree plantation in the Kachung Central Forest

Reserve from Uganda's National Forestry Authority in 1999.[24] Green Resources—operating under the names Busoga Forestry Company and Lango Forestry Company, among others—commenced its afforestation operations on an area of around 2,050 hectares in 2006. This included establishing mostly monoculture plantations, with the majority species being *Pinus caribeae*, *Pinus oocarpa* and *Eucalyptus* ssp.

This project was first certified with the Forest Stewardship Council and recognized as a Clean Development Mechanism project, as well as validated under the Climate Community and Biodiversity Standard.[25] This suite of certifications provides third-party verification that Green Resources' conduct is adequate for entry into global carbon markets. An arrangement between Green Resources and the state-owned Swedish Energy Agency (SEA) was touted as the longest carbon contract at the time of its signing—running between 2012 and 2032—and Green Resources claimed to be one of the first international companies to earn revenue via the sale of carbon credits from its forestry plantation.[26] This US$4 million deal was anticipated to sequester 365,000 tonnes of carbon.[27] However, the collaboration had barely begun before it ground to a halt when Green Resources failed to respond to the requirements of its carbon offset buyer. In 2015, the SEA—the sole purchaser of Green Resources' carbon credits—suspended payments, and subsequently terminated its contract in 2020, highlighting problems not only with Green Resources' conduct, but also with the verification systems upon which carbon offset markets depend.[28] On the basis of an audit initiated by the SEA in 2017, the buyer concluded that, as part of Green Resources' project, "villagers were deprived of vital resources and experienced threats and violence, and there [was] a lack of clarity regarding ownership in the reserve."[29]

However, the SEA itself was very late in calling out Green Resources' poor practices. Investigative journalists led by Swedish Channel 4's Camilla Ziedorn in 2015 revealed that the SEA had been aware of problems at Green Resources' Kachung site for many years.[30] Despite this knowledge, the SEA opted to both bury the facts and misrepresent local conditions. In particular, as part of its due diligence reporting in 2011, local communities were identified as being reliant on the land licensed to Green Resources. Regardless of this, the SEA claimed land licensed to Green Resources was "unused bushland."[31] When the new director of SEA—appointed in 2018—denied that SEA ever suspended payments to Green Resources, its implication in this failed project, alongside the opacity of carbon offset deals, was also exposed.[32]

While the contract between Green Resources and the SEA has now come to an end, Green Resources' activities at its Kachung site in Uganda continue. We now turn to outline some of the impacts of the presence of Green Resources in this region over many years, before reflecting on possible futures for both the company and the local communities, given the collapse of this carbon offset project.

ON-THE-GROUND IMPACTS OF GREEN RESOURCES IN UGANDA

Green Resources' Kachung project is in the Dokolo district in Northern Uganda. Here, rates of poverty are high, while life expectancy is low. Inhabitants in the region lack reasonable access to many vital services, including education, safe drinking water, sanitation, and health support services.[33] Around 80 per cent of the villagers living adjacent to the Green Resources project are subsistence farmers, and about 66 per cent live below the poverty line.[34] There are 17 villages directly adjacent to the Green Resources' licence area within Kachung Central Forest Reserve that were—and continue to be—affected by the company. So, what do these effects look like on the ground?

Dispossession from land
To begin with, the establishment of Green Resources' carbon offset project relied upon often forced and sometimes violent evictions. While forced evictions occurred prior to the arrival of Green Resources—and were likely exacerbated by the region's long-term political instability and conflict—forced relocations were part and parcel of plantation activities. Community members have described forced evictions led by government employees, as well as by the military and the police.[35] Forced removals were also documented—although quickly hidden from public view—in the SEA's own due diligence reporting, as detailed above. As further evidence, a report by the Oakland Institute published eviction notices issued to local community members by Green Resources.[36]

The changes in access and rights to land instigated by the arrival of Green Resources have effectively denied local customary land rights and traditional practices and have delivered diverse—and profound—adverse local impacts over many years. Given that most families living in proximity to Green Resources' industrial plantations rely on subsistence agriculture, the resultant land shortages have worsened the already acute challenge of meeting local food needs.

A growing food crisis
Alongside the problem of land shortages, interviews we conducted with villagers in 2017 also identified other problems that further compound the region's growing food crisis. To begin with, Green Resources' plantation forestry was described as negatively impacting agricultural production: food gardens in proximity to pine plantations have produced lower yields compared with gardens farther from the plantation.[37] These local observations are backed by a growing body of international scientific research, which attributes monoculture pine and eucalyptus plantations with declining soil and water nutrient resources.[38]

Some villagers also reported losing livestock and other food sources as a result of the chemicals utilized by Green Resources for forest management. One farmer lost most of the bees from his 20 beehives that were located near the plantation. Similarly, the company's chemical use killed off the ant population that provided an important local food source for villagers.

Despite sustained pressure from national and international civil society movements over almost 20 years, alongside criticisms from Green Resources' auditors and carbon credit buyer, Green Resources has failed to deliver even the most basic support for the local food system. For example, while Green Resources was directed to provide agricultural training and supplies in compliance with international standards, it failed to do so. Similarly, it failed to respond appropriately to firewood shortages, exacerbated by the company locking up land that villagers once relied on for firewood. As a result of this scarcity, some women we spoke with described cooking just one meal a day, foregoing a family meal to manage their constrained fuel supply.[39]

Food shortages have also been exacerbated due to the many reported cases of company staff and local police destroying villagers' food crops.[40] Notices published by the Oakland Institute in 2019 provide stark evidence of a warning by Green Resources that it would not be held responsible for any damage done to crops cultivated in the company's licence area. This report also includes details of Green Resources' request that the Ugandan government discourage local communities' "illegal cultivation" of food crops on company land, as well as its request that the government seize animals found grazing in the plantation.[41]

Damage to local ecologies and environments
Green Resources' activities have also had a negative environmental impact on the region. This stands in contrast to Green Resources' claims about itself, that it is "a sustainable forest company aiming at growing plantation forests across East Africa in a sustainable and socially just manner."[42]

Many environmental problems tied to Green Resources' activities are a result of breaches of its own Forest Management Plan, itself a requirement of its Environmental Impact Assessment. For example, the company is frequently reported for encroaching on fragile ecosystems, including spraying chemicals and planting trees within ecologically significant buffer zones adjacent to rivers and lakes. Both overuse and misuse of chemicals have also been reported, increasing runoff into rivers and lakes, and creating adverse downstream impacts, such as killing vegetation and animals.[43] Chemical pollution has also created profound problems for local communities' ability to secure safe local water supplies.[44]

Green Resources' plantation forestry system is dominated by two non-indigenous tree species (pine and eucalyptus) planted in large monoculture stands. The company has also reportedly cleared the *Combretum* wooded grasslands, comprising diverse grass, shrub, and tree species, to make way for these monoculture stands.

These inert landscapes are not conducive to the flourishing of diverse local insects, birds, and other animal life.[45]

Limited employment and poor work conditions
Green Resources claims one of its main contributions to the region is the employment opportunities it provides; it has asserted that it is the largest formal employer in the local community.[46] Yet such claims significantly overstate and misrepresent employment numbers. They also ignore the considerable decline in employment over the last decade, and the dissatisfaction and distrust among both workers and ex-workers. A number of local villagers working for Green Resources, including slashers, pruners, sprayers, and security guards, described many problems with their employment conditions. Our findings on the dissatisfaction of workers are confirmed in the Socioeconomic Impact Assessment commissioned by Green Resources in 2016.[47]

Most fieldworkers are employed by Green Resources on a casual basis, creating conditions that are both precarious and uncertain. Villagers working for Green Resources described very low rates of pay, with sprayers earning between US$2 and US$2.50 (8,000–9,000 Ugandan shillings) per day, while pruning earns just US$0.50 (or 1,800 Ugandan Shillings) per day.[48] Subcontracting also enables nepotism and patrimony to flourish, the outcome of which exacerbates local relations already tense due to the disruptions engendered by the arrival of Green Resources.

Overall, the evictions of people, destruction of food crops, and confiscation of animals, as well as flagrant breaches of environmental regulations and poor working conditions, have fuelled conflict between Green Resources and local communities. On the basis of Green Resources' poor treatment of local communities, in 2009 a group of up to 300 villagers initiated legal action against Green Resources. However, despite the SEA's demand that all legal cases against the company be resolved as quickly as possible, over 11 years later this case remains outstanding.[49]

PLANTATION FORESTRY FOR
CARBON OFFSET IN UGANDA FAILS
PEOPLE AND THE CLIMATE

Championing plantation forestry carbon offset initiatives to counter climate catastrophe relies on rendering invisible the profound injustices upon which many initiatives—including those of Green Resources—rely. It also fails to see the forests for the trees: the illusionary promises of carbon offset plantation forestry cast a shadow over the tangible reality of their negative impacts.

The collapse of Green Resources' industrial plantation forestry and carbon offset project exposes some of the failings of carbon offsetting. While local villagers have carried the social, environmental, and other costs of this project, the company profited from its destructive plantations by framing them as "carbon sinks." This extractivist form of development extends the colonial power relations that drive inequality and deploys the illusion of a so-called "clean and green" project to do so.

Green Resources' activities over many years lay bare the false solutions to climate change promoted by Western corporations and institutions in Africa. Quite simply, this is carbon colonialism at work: Uganda's natural assets and human labour are being exploited by foreign interests under the guise of curbing global greenhouse gas emissions and stabilizing the climate.[50] Further, Green Resources undermines food security and livelihoods by excluding people from their own land. A convergence of interests lined up behind Green Resources supports this model of extractivist development, including its carbon credit buyer (the SEA), international donors (Norfund, FMO, and Finnfund), carbon finance, and the auditors upon which carbon market access relies. Each is complicit in a colonial project that disavows local and indigenous peoples' rights, and drives conflict and suffering at the local level.

The termination of the contract between the SEA and Green Resources in 2020 represents a turning point for this plantation forestry project, but how significant might it be for the future of Green Resources and local communities? Green Resources has struggled with financial and legal problems for a number of years: some of its major shareholders have divested, and there is an ongoing lawsuit between its ex-CEO and the company's founder. In the face of such problems, Green Resources was salvaged by major financing from Finland and Norway and, by May 2019, Norfund controlled a 67 per cent share in the company.[51]

On the ground in the Dokolo district, however, it is unclear if local villagers are even aware of any of this. Green Resources continues its plantation forestry activities at Kachung; it is solely the carbon offset component of its activities that is curtailed. In the meantime, local communities in the Dokolo district that live alongside Green Resources industrial plantation forestry will have to continue taking the lead in ensuring their communities have secure access to food, water, and firewood, and to find autonomous zones outside Green Resources' enclosures to live and flourish. Elsewhere, as "East Africa's largest forest development and wood processing company," Green

Resources has diversified its portfolio. It also has additional plantation sites in Uganda, Tanzania, and Mozambique, where local communities suffer similar problems.

While it is difficult to imagine how the controversy at Green Resources' Kachung site could be good for its business, will it be bad? Given the ongoing significance of carbon offset initiatives in responding to climate change—especially because offsetting enable heavily polluting industries to continue to pollute, and for this reason is backed by a taskforce funded by hedge funds and comprising representatives from Big Oil, Big Finance, Big Airlines, and carbon traders—we don't see the plantation forestry industry disappearing any time soon.[52] The plantation forestry sector is enabled by carbon credit buyers, carbon finance, auditors, and international donors, all of which, in various ways, are complicit in ignoring the systemic problems in the plantation forestry carbon offset system.

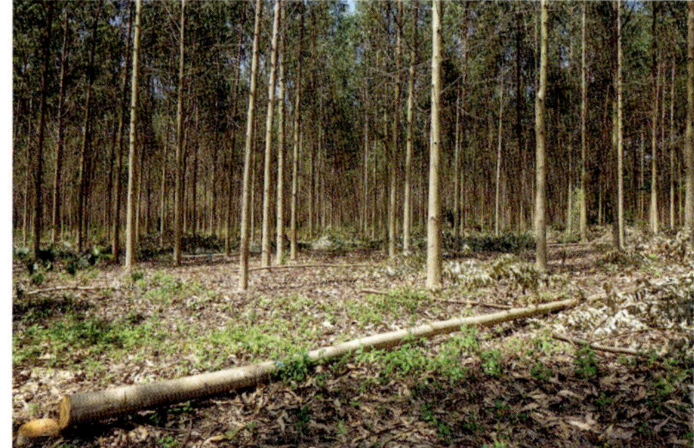

Fig. 2 Young trees in the plantation, Kachung, Uganda. 2017

ACKNOWLEDGEMENTS

The authors acknowledge financial support from the Australian Research Council and the Oakland Institute for primary data collected as part of this research. We give our deepest thanks to Anuradha Mittal (founder and executive director) and Frederic Mousseau (policy director) at the Oakland Institute for their sustained support of critical research and advocacy on global carbon markets. Their critical insights, research, and editorial support have contributed to our ongoing thinking and understandings in this space.

1   I. Baños Ruiz, Talanoa dialogue: Giving everyone a voice in the climate conversation, *DW*, 9 February 2018, https://p.dw.com/p/2sEud (accessed 13 September 2021); Presidents of COP 23 and COP 24, *Talanoa Call for Action*, 2018, https://unfccc.int/sites/default/files/resource/Talanoa%20Call%20for%20Action.pdf (accessed 13 September 2021).

2   K. Whyte, Way beyond the lifeboat: Allegory of climate justice, in *Climate Futures: Reimagining Global Climate Justice* (D. Munshi, K. Bhavnani, J. Foran, and P. Kurian, eds) (Berkeley, CA: University of California Press, 2020).

3   K. Lyons, A. Esposito, and M. Johnson, The pangolin and the coal mine: Challenging the forces of extractivism, human rights abuse and planetary calamity, *Antipode Online*, 1 February 2020, https://antipodeonline.org/2021/02/01/the-pangolin-and-the-coal-mine (accessed 13 September 2021).

4   A. Nel and D. Hill, Constructing walls of carbon: the complexity of community, carbon sequestration and protected areas in Uganda, *Journal of Contemporary African Studies*, 31(3), (2013): 421–440.

5   See K. Lyons, C. Richards, and P. Westoby, *The Darker Side of Green: Plantation Forestry and Carbon Violence in Uganda—The Case*

of Green Resources' Forestry Based Carbon Markets (Oakland, CA: The Oakland Institute, 2014), https://www.oaklandinstitute.org/darker-side-green (accessed 13 September 2021).

6   C. Lang, Open letter to Mark Carney's Taskforce on Scaling Voluntary Carbon Markets: Carbon offsets are "riddled with fraud and human rights abuses, *REDD Monitor*, 27 January 2021, https://redd-monitor.org/2021/01/27/open-letter-to-mark-carneys-taskforce-on-scaling-voluntary-carbon-markets-carbon-offsets-are-riddled-with-fraud-and-human-rights-abuses (accessed 13 September 2021).

7   O. Hoegh-Guldberg, D. Jacob, M. Taylor, *et al.*, The human imperative of stabilising global climate change at 1.5 °C, *Science*, 365(6459) (2019).

8   See P. Bond, Climate change casino: Carbon trading reborn in new generation mega-polluters, *Counter Punch*, 4 December 2015, https://www.counterpunch.org/2015/12/04/climate-change-casino-carbon-trading-reborn-in-new-generation-mega-polluters (accessed 13 September 2021); H. R. Hughes and M. Paterson, Narrowing the climate field: The symbolic power of authors in the IPCC's assessment of mitigation, *Review of Policy Research*, 34(6) (2017): 744–766.

9   M. McGrath, Climate change: COP 24 fails to adopt key scientific report, *BBC News*, 8 December 2018, https://www.bbc.com/news/science-environment-46496967 (accessed 13 September 2021).

10   A. Hanafi, COP 24: Transparency, ambition and carbon markets on the Paris Rulebook Agenda in Katowice, Environmental Defence Fund (blog), 3 December 2018, http://blogs.edf.org/climate411/2018/12/03/cop-24-transparency-ambition-and-carbon-markets-on-the-paris-rulebook-agenda-in-katowice (accessed 13 September 2021).

11   See Bond, Climate change casino; L. Lohmann, The endless algebra of climate markets, *Capitalism Nature Socialism*, 22(4) (2011): 93–116.

12   A. Bumpus, The matter of carbon: Understanding the materiality of tCO2e in carbon offsets, *Antipode*, 43(2) (2011): 612–638.

13   M. Kroger, Globalization as the "pulping" of landscapes: Forestry capitalism's north–south territorial accumulation, *Globalizations*, 10(6) (2013): 837–853; M. Kroger, The political ecology of global tree plantation expansion: A review, *Journal of Peasant Studies*, 41(2) (2014): 235–261.

14   Kroger, Globalization as the "pulping'" of landscapes, 2013; L. German, A. Mandondo, F. Paumgarten, and J. Mwitwa, Shifting rights, property and authority in the forest frontier: "Stakes" for local land users and citizens, *Journal of Peasant Studies*, 41(1) (2014): 51–78.

15   C. Cavanagh and T. Benjaminsen, Violent accumulation: Unpacking the "spectacular" failure of carbon offsetting at a Ugandan national park, *Geoforum*, 56 (2014): 55–65; A. Nel, "Zones of awkward engagement" in Ugandan carbon forestry, in *Carbon Conflicts and Forest Landscapes in Africa* (M. Leach and I. Scoones, eds) (London: Earthscan, 2015); K. Lyons and P. Westoby, Carbon colonialism and the new land grab: Plantation forestry in Uganda and its livelihood impacts, *Journal of Rural Studies*, 36 (2014): 13–21.

16   Nel, "Zones of awkward engagement."

17   A. Bomuhangi, C. Doss, and R. Meinzen-Dick, *Who Owns the Land? Perspectives from Rural Ugandans and Implications for Land Acquisitions* (unpublished, April 2012).

18   For another high-profile plantation forestry case in Uganda, see M. Grainger and K. Geary, *The New Forests Company and Its Ugandan Plantations* (Oxfam International, 2011), https://oxfamilibrary.openrepository.com/bitstream/handle/10546/142858/cs-new-forest-company-uganda-plantations-220911-en.pdf?sequence=6&isAllowed=y (accessed 13 September 2021).

19   See Lyons and Westoby, *Carbon colonialism and the new land grab*.

20   See J. Borras, M. Margulis, and N. McKeon, Land grabbing and global governance, *Globalizations*, 10(1) (2013): 1–23.

21   D. Harvey, The "new" imperialism: Accumulation by dispossession, *Socialist Register* 40 (2004): 63–87; P. Bottazzi, D. Crespo, H. Soria, *et al.* Carbon sequestration in community forests: trade-offs, multiple outcomes and institutional diversity in the Bolivian Amazon, *Development and Change*, 45(1)(2013): 105–131.

22   Green Resources: http://greenresources.no (accessed 13 September 2021).

23   A. Garberg, Tree planting project threatens food security, *Framtiden*, 3 May 2012, https://www.framtiden.no/english/other/tree-planting-project-threatens-foodsecurity.html (accessed 13 September 2021).

24   See Lyons *et al.*, *The Darker Side of Green*.

25   M. Hardy and K. Whittington-Jones, *Kachung Community Development Plan Performance Audit: Busoga Forestry Company Limited* (BFC), *Kachung Forestry Plantation: Lira Region, Uganda: Final Report*, prepared by EOH Coastal and Environmental Services, March 2017.

26   See Lyons and Westoby, *Carbon colonialism and the new land grab*.

27   Sweden freezes carbon payments to Green Resources due to land conflicts, *Development Today*, 1 December 2015, https://www.development-today.com/archive/2015/dt-15/sweden_freezes_carbon_payments_to_green_resources_due_to_land_conflicts (accessed 13 September 2021).

28   Sweden drops Uganda forest carbon deal with Green Resources due to unresolved land disputes, *Development Today*, 10 March 2020, https://development-today.com/archive/dt-2020/dt-2--2020/sweden-drops-uganda-forest-carbon-deal-with-green-resources-due-to-unresolved-land-disputes (accessed 13 September 2021).

29   Cited in C. Lang, The Swedish Energy Agency has stopped buying carbon credits from Green Resources' destructive plantations in Uganda, *REDD Monitor*, 11 March 2020, https://redd-monitor.org/2020/03/11/the-swedish-energy-agency-has-stopped-buying-carbon-credits-from-green-resources-destructive-plantations-in-uganda (accessed 13 September 2021).

30   K. Fakta, *The Forbidden Forest*, TV4 Sweden, 11 November 2015, https://www.youtube.com/watch?v=COoPVXlNbqQ (accessed 13 September 2021).

31   F. Mousseau, *Evicted for Carbon Credits. Norway, Sweden and Finland Displace Ugandan Farmers for Carbon Trading* (Oakland, CA: The Oakland Institute, 2019), https://www.oaklandinstitute.org/evicted-carbon-credits-green-resources (accessed 13 September 2021).

32   Mousseau, *Evicted for Carbon Credits*.

33   D. Kyalimpa and S. William, *Socioeconomic Impact Assessment of Busoga Forestry Company Operations Dokolo District*, prepared for Busoga Forestry Company Limited, 2016.

34   Climate Focus, *Kachung Forest Project: Afforestation on Degraded Land*, August 2011, https://www.scribd.com/doc/303944478/Due-Diligence-Kachung (accessed 13 September 2021).

35   Lyons *et al.*, *The Darker Side of Green*.

36   Mousseau, *Evicted for Carbon Credits*.

37   K. Lyons and D. Ssemwogerere, *Carbon Colonialism*.

38   F. Bernhard-Reversat, *Effect of Toxic Tree Plantations on Plant Diversity and Biological Soil Fertility in the Congo Savanna. With Special Reference to Eucalypts*, Centre for International Forestry Research, 2001, http://www.fao.org/forestry/42677-0641c6b278b5916899e198a24444dc455.pdf (accessed 13 September 2021).

39   Lyons and Ssemwogerere, *Carbon Colonialism*.

40   Lyons *et al.*, *The Darker Side of Green*.

41   Mousseau, *Evicted for Carbon Credits*.

42   Green Resources website, 2020, https://web.archive.org/web/20200618231428/http://greenresources.no/ (accessed 16 November 2021).

43   Lyons *et al.*, *The Darker Side of Green*.

44   Lyons and Ssemwogerere, *Carbon Colonialism*.

45   Lyons *et al.*, *The Darker Side of Green*.

46   Hardy and Whittington-Jones, *Kachung Community Development Plan*.

47   Kyalimpa and William, *Socioeconomic Impact Assessment of Busoga Forestry Company Operations Dokolo District*.

48   Lyons and Ssemwogerere, *Carbon Colonialism*.

49   *Ibid.*

50   See Lyons *et al.*, *The Darker Side of Green*.

51   Mousseau, *Evicted for Carbon Credits*.

52   Lang, *Open letter to Mark Carney's Taskforce on Scaling voluntary carbon markets*.

THE TREE THAT ALMOST FELLED A MILLION TREES

In August 2013 the limb of an under-maintained oak tree in Kissena
Park in Queens fell, killing a pregnant woman sitting on a bench nearby.
Residents in the neighbourhood had been complaining about the poor
state of the park's trees, a problem endemic across the city. In 2009, a
man who was severely injured by a falling branch in Central Park was
compensated more than US$11 million. The following year, there were
another two fatal tree-related accidents in Central Park—a man and
a baby who were also killed by falling branches. These tragic events
raised questions about the city's budget for tree upkeep. State Senator
Tony Avella and NYC Park Advocates called on Mayor Michael Bloomberg
to shift all funds from MillionTreesNYC to better maintenance of existing trees. With mounting pressure after the Kissena incident, the city
announced that it would cut down and remove 2,000 trees damaged
by Hurricane Sandy to prevent future accidents. As carbon credits are
awarded for new planting rather than maintaining existing stock, corporate investment is heavily skewed toward the former, despite old trees
absorbing more carbon than new saplings. The 2021 city budget cut
funding for street tree maintenance by US$7.2 million, hardly future-
proofing pedestrian safety.[1]

1   C. Kessler, Tree pruning budget cuts raise fears of falling branches, *The City*,
13 July 2020.

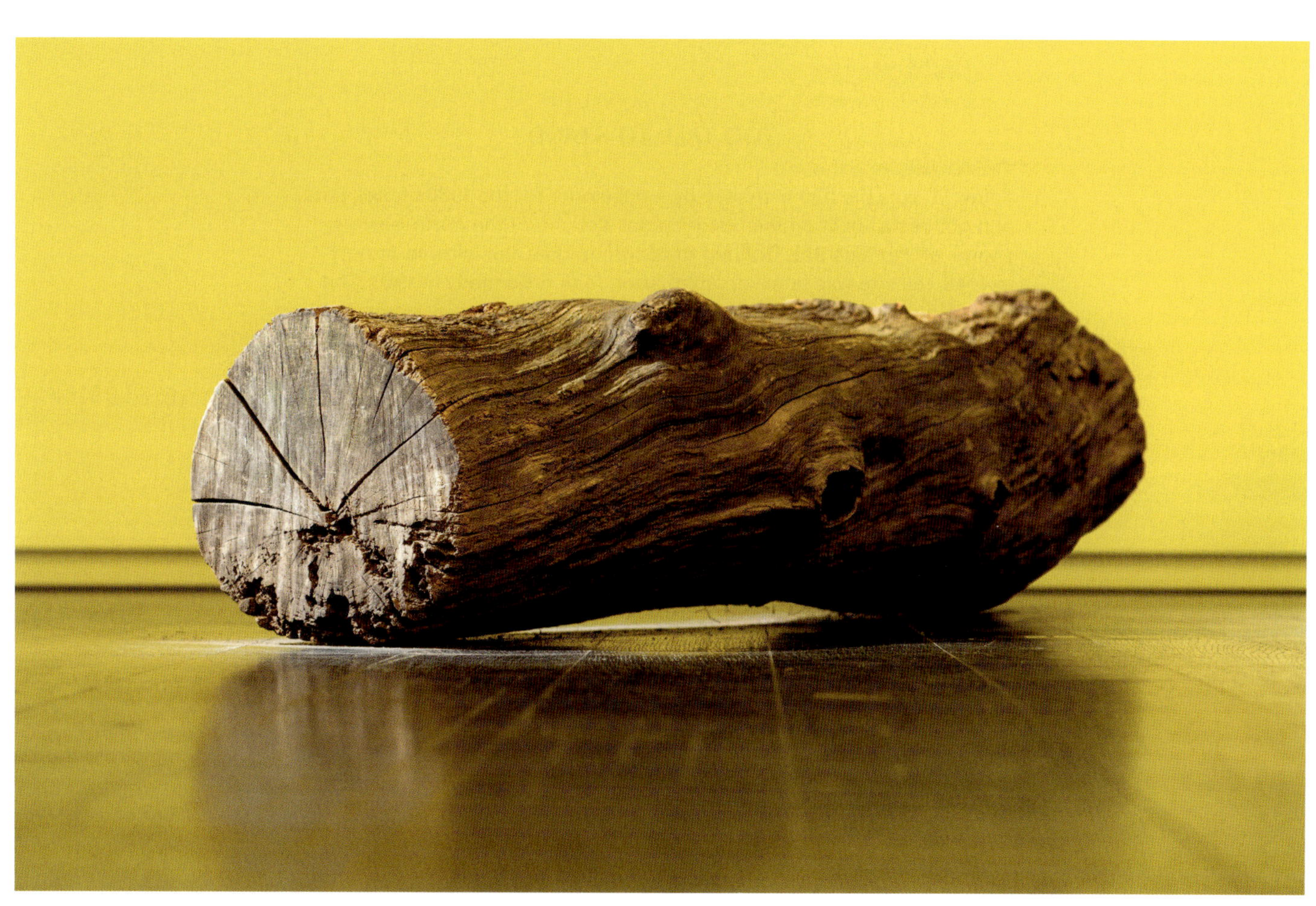

TOO TALL TO STAND

"Idlewild" was the name chosen by a developer for the 1930s hotel, park, and golf resort built on the historic tidal wetland of the north-eastern shores of Jamaica Bay. Drained to accommodate the Idlewild Airport in 1948, the site was later renamed after John F. Kennedy in 1963. The remaining swamps are today called Idlewild Park Preserve, a protected area included in the New York City Department of Parks and Recreation's Forever Wild Program, which seeks to preserve the 51 most ecologically valuable, undisturbed lands in the city. Adjacent to the runway, Idlewild is a protected forest plagued by the hazards of low-flying planes. In 2013, local residents protested against the Port Authority of New York and New Jersey's plans to remove 800 "invasive" trees in order to extend the runway. Civic pressure succeeded in modifying the plans, and the Port Authority agreed to consider installing lights to alert pilots to the presence of trees as an alternative to their removal.[1] Nonetheless, Forever Wild had to compromise when it came to trees growing too close to the runway. These had their tops trimmed to stunt their growth and to prevent them from interfering with air traffic, thereby exposing frictions between the preservation of urban environments and the future health of the trees. Even where obstruction was not apparent, a Federal Aviation Administration formula insisted the trees were simply in the way.[2]

1 JFK runway plans modified to save 800 trees in Southeast Queens, *Inhabitat*, 30 October 2013.

2 J. Yapalater, Idlewild Park's too-tall trees coming down, *QNS*, 6 April 2018.

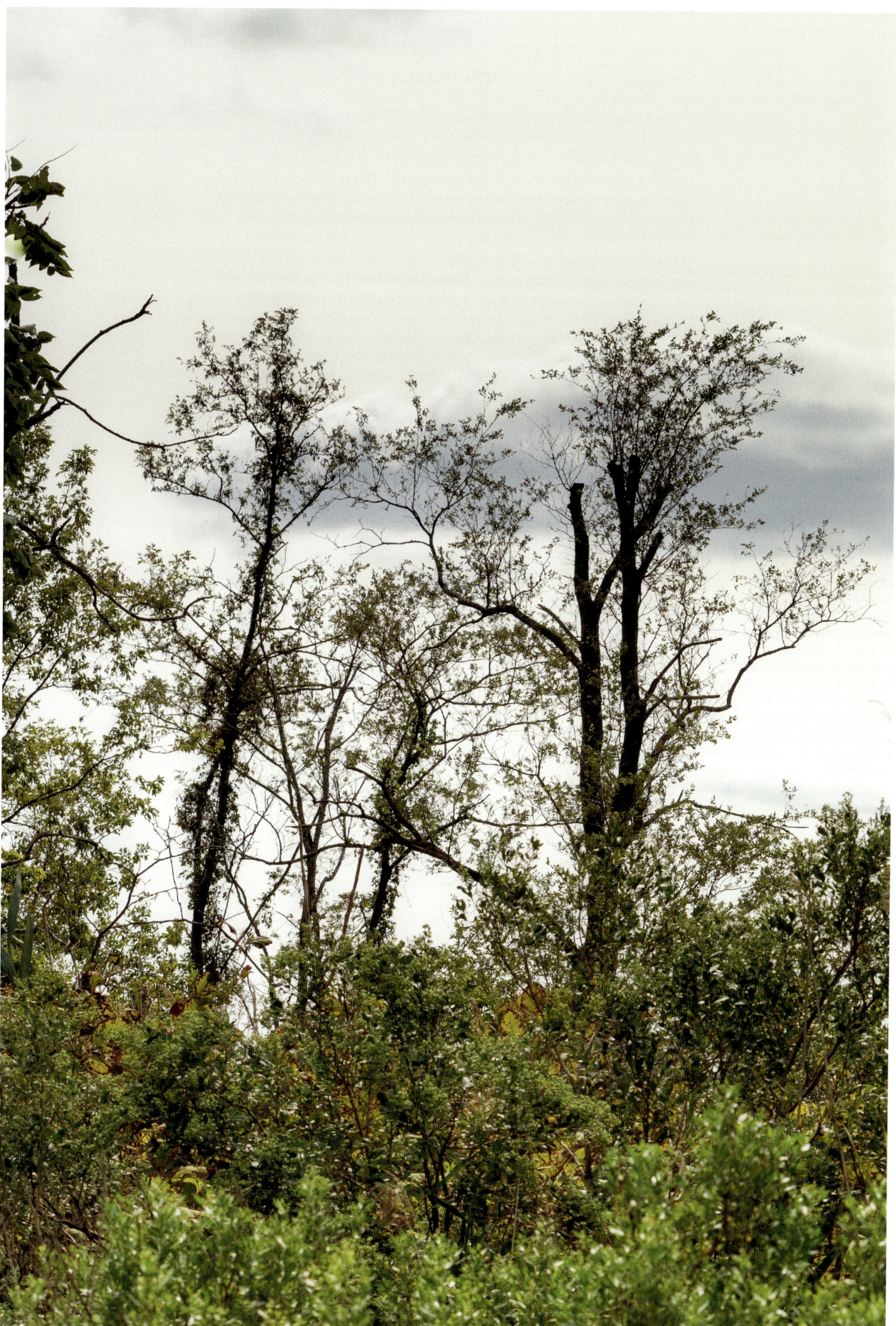

POST RETREAT

In 2017, new financial opportunities galvanized the southern shore of Staten Island into becoming the site of the first mitigation banking scheme in New York. Located along Saw Mill Creek, the wetland was restored in order to sell credits to private developers or government agencies and compensate for the loss of natural saltmarsh, mitigating the unavoidable impact of waterfront development. Run by the New York City Economic Development Corporation, the Saw Mill Creek Wetland Mitigation Bank has seen the restoration of over 50 acres of land and has removed dozens of thousands of tons of debris and contaminated sediment. The bank is open to requests for proposals to offset wetland destruction elsewhere. Competitive offers must be greater than the reserve price, currently at US$1.5 million for one credit.[1] After Hurricane Sandy, coastal dwellers began to demand that the city purchase their damaged waterfront properties and restore the public wetlands that would protect against future storms. Staten Island homeowners organized their own buyout groups—a collective action to retreat from the coast and receive pre-storm values for their property—as the best flood defence, and lobbied for their neighbourhoods to be literally unbuilt.[2] They perceived their environments to be no longer habitable, and thus preferred to vacate the land and return it to nature in perpetuity. The New York City metropolitan area has lost about 85 per cent of its coastal wetlands over the last century. While the rise of "managed retreat" initiatives to higher ground has helped to restore some of those lost ecologies, they also run the risk of accelerating a new mitigation market that appropriates good intentions to mask the destruction of coastlines elsewhere.

1   NYC Economic Development Corporation, 29 March 2020.
2   L. Koslov, The case for retreat, *Public Culture* 28 (2016): 374.

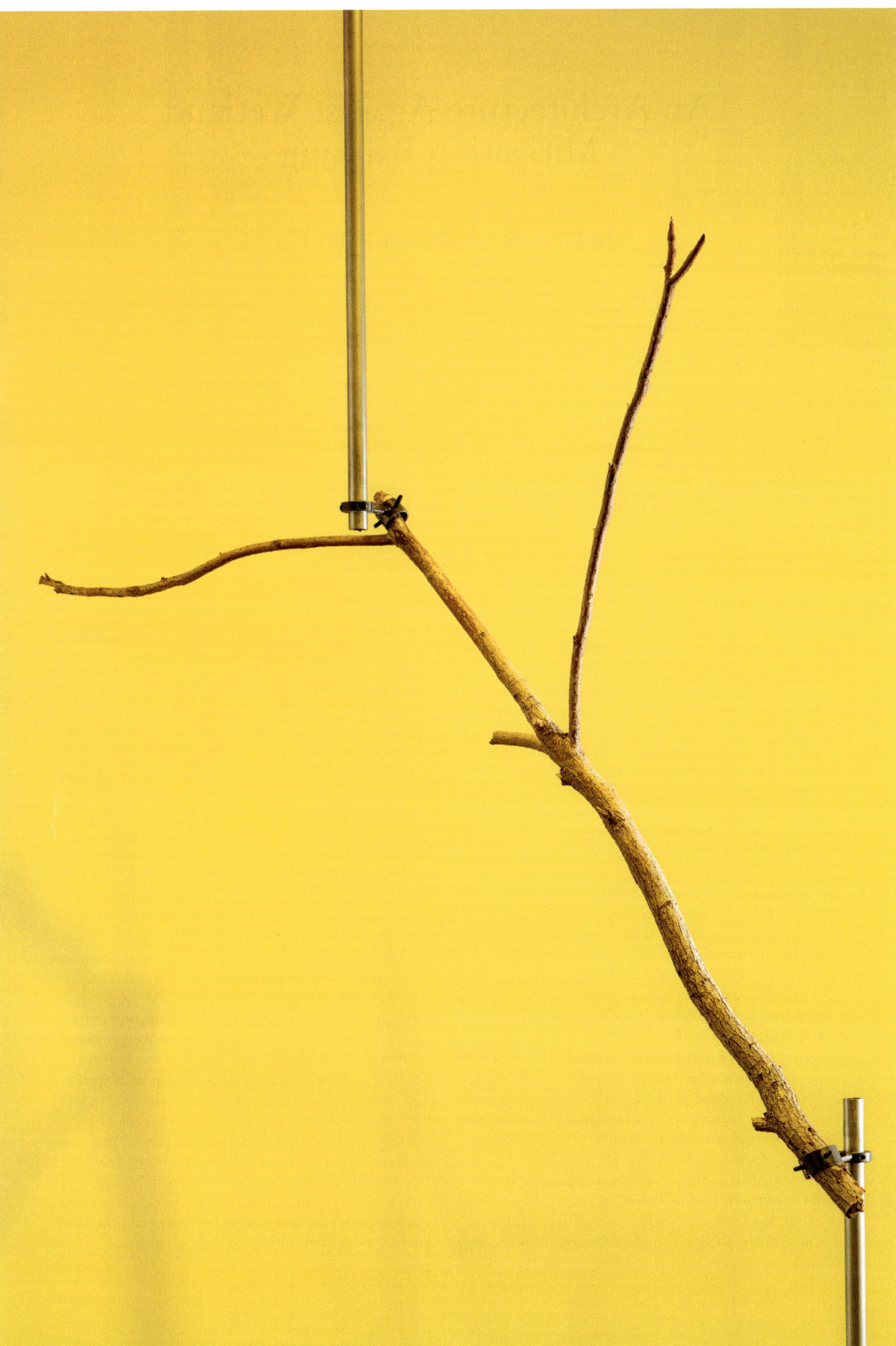

An Architecture Against Wetland Mitigation Banking

Matthew Darmour-Paul

As a space of refuge or domination, of stolen land or the centre of the settler universe, "home" has long been the site of the struggle between humans and nature, markets, and one another. Only recently have natural zones across the USA been more broadly recognized as sites of struggle for the homes of *non*-human lives, and for claims for and against their accelerating eviction and relocation.

Following centuries of public vilification, drainage, and infilling of marshes and swamps in the USA, private mortgage lenders have now turned to the inherent biodiversity and regenerative propensity of wetlands as spaces for capital accumulation.[1] Backed by environmental legislation enacted in the H. W. Bush era, charitable "land development" organizations can create, restore, or preserve wetlands in disused agricultural lands in anticipation of ecologically adverse property developments in city centres. Property developers pay the owners of these "wetland mitigation banks" for restoration credits that regulatory bodies deem equivalent to the environmental destruction of new housing developments. With little competition between property developers and land developers—at times they collaborate to inflate value—bioregions around the country are witnessing the systematic relocation of valuable ecosystems from highly populated city centres (where property values are high) to privatized rural areas (where property values are low).[2]

When a non-human species is nominated under the 1973 Endangered Species Act, state and federal actors like the United States Fish and Wildlife Service must consider whether there are specific habitats believed to be essential to the species' conservation.[3] Those areas may then be designated as a "critical habitat," which, when measured and valued (an absurdity in practice), functions as a kind of ecological surplus that can be traded for destruction through a scheme separate from (but related to) mitigation banking, known as "conservation biodiversity banking."

How did these perverse credit mechanisms come to entangle housing and environmental conservation efforts? In *Life as Surplus*, Melinda Cooper documents the rise of the commercialized life sciences in the USA, writing that "Post Fordism does not dispense with industrial production (and pollution), it simply displaces it— moving it offshore or legally by fighting regulation."[4] At the newly purchased wetland mitigation bank, soils depleted by decades of industrial activity no longer require reparations to people or the land. Rather, neoliberal economic policies focus on the vitalism of endangered wetland species and their wetland habitats elsewhere for renewed sources of wealth, equating "the evolution of life with that of capital."[5] As Cooper argues, biology and finance become fused around the concept of self-(re)generation. The autopoietic capacity of, for example, a critically endangered seasonal shrimp to defy "limits to growth"—autopoiesis being a highly resilient and regenerative life force—is conflated with speculative capital and its promise of endless surplus value.

This ecological surplus mobilized to offset destruction happens in space (in the newly constructed wetland bank), but also in time. The destruction of a wetland habitat today is imagined to be sufficiently paid for by the promise of a new wetland constructed tomorrow. Loaded with offsets, financialized ecology is future-oriented, sidestepping the present as an inconvenient structure of experience.[6] This is in keeping with the nationwide focus on bioremediation technology rather than cleaning up toxic waste sites: the promise of a technically efficient clean-up is more valuable than the actual cleaning up. It's in these poorly surveilled moral territories that new types of "bio-entrepreneurialism," like wetland mitigation banking, thrive.

In simpler terms, ecological surplus means those organisms and environments that are seen as more than what is required (which begs the question, required for what?). Ecological surplus is nature after undergoing a simple but radical devaluation, what Jason Moore and Raj Patel describe as "cheap nature." "Cheap natures" are produced through surveying, exploiting, and calculating environments for the express purpose of capital accumulation— environments necessarily without humans, so that they can then be used to negate all-too-human developments. They rely on other cheap categories (labour, energy, food, lives, etc.) in a cheap ecosystem to keep them useful for capitalists.[7] In the case of wetland mitigation banks, wetlands can no longer house and support endangered species "for free." The inherent contradiction of species biodiversity conservation banking is thus: to be a non-human species community at the cusp of extinction is to be valuable, and to be a flourishing species is to be cheap.

Sovereignty in these spaces, as exercised by the state, means selecting who matters and who is disposable. Elizabeth Povinelli has argued that this power tends to rely on an overlooked distinction between "the lively and the inert," or what she describes as a kind of "geontopower" that subtends biopower. In the murky spaces of the wetland, where many species exist inchoate, or in suspended animation (as in the case of the hibernating frog), a gradient of liveliness might prove the most useful for considering the precious-nearly-extinct and the too-many-to-be-valuable non-human species of Northern California.[8]

The endemic and constructed vernal pools associated with wetland mitigation banking in Northern California continue a longer narrative around financially driven displacement. Cities such as Oakland and San Francisco routinely evict poor residents on the basis of "environmental improvements."[9] This greenwashing and environmental gentrification abuses the moral ambiguity associated with tree planting and nature preservation as too necessary to question. This is especially true in the case of wetland mitigation banks and their residents.

Endemic vernal pools are miraculous four-dimensional ecological events. They are defined in biological terms as mostly dry, ephemeral pools that obligate species (those restricted to a particular habitat or environmental conditions) take advantage of. For three-quarters of the year, amphibians such as the spadefoot and California red-legged frog bury themselves alive in the dried, cracked pool bed, anticipating spring rains to come to resurrect them. Similarly, crustaceans known as fairy shrimp, believed by scientists to be hundreds of millions of years old, lay thousands of extremely resilient eggs in the pool bed that are brought to life by the rains of spring. The obligate species that cohabit in vernal pools are protected there from larger streams or waterways and from the hungry fish and human-induced pollution that tend to accompany them. When the anticipated rains arrive, the pools erupt in concentric floral ring patterns, brought on by plants that flower in radically different ways based on millimetre differences in water levels [Fig. 1]. The coming to life of thousands of amphibians and crustaceans extends the otherwise dormant food web into uplands, forests, and bird migration routes, providing productive breeding, feeding, and sheltering grounds for animals on the move.[10] Constructed wetland mitigation banks, on the other hand, are designed on a reduced model: wet circles are drawn, built, and injected with crustaceans—it is the image of a whole but only admits those singular participants worthy of being banked.

An Architecture Against Wetland Mitigation Banking seeks to formalize the struggles of ecological sovereignty and the "gradient of liveliness" that challenges the hard-lined distinctions between the living and the inert. By reconfiguring the ruins of industrial agriculture and suburban sprawl—linear irrigation machines, agricultural mesh, terracotta roof tiles, weatherboard, and reclaimed lengths of timber—I offer a new means to house humans at the edges of these generous, expanding wetland pools, both endemic and constructed [Fig. 2]. For three-quarters of the year, human residents are allowed to live among the pools, on the condition that they leave for the rainy months of non-human breeding. Sharing knowledge of the vernal pool ecology with the residents establishes a community based on care, not competition, while an experimental conservation basic income moves beyond market-based instruments and the extractive relationship typical of productivist agriculture.[11]

This speculative project questions how we might reposition architecture as a worthy spatial practice in the pursuit of multi-species flourishing. Might we see the abundant form of vernal pools beyond the emotional distance of entrepreneurial biologists—a bankrupt relationship at best—but as obligate species, reliant on a specific temporariness, fully engaged in an unfolding and unfinished gradient of liveliness?

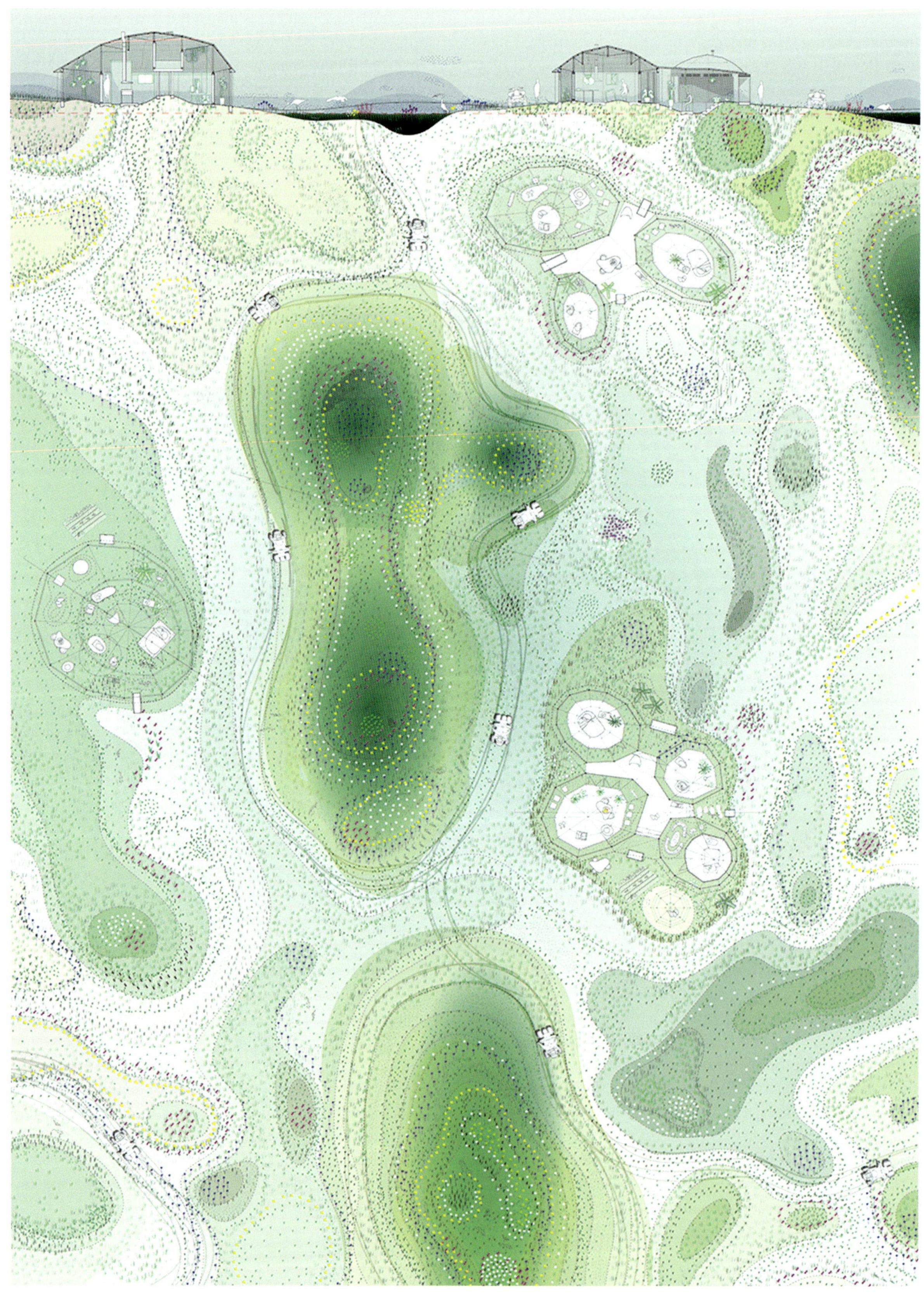

Fig. 2 Plan and section of a rewilded mitigation bank, Matthew Darmour-Paul, 2018.

1   This turn is epitomized by former Goldman Sachs managing di-
     rector and partner Mark Tercek who, after 24 years with the firm
     and profits from the 2007/8 financial crash in his pocket, left the
     mortgage market to become CEO of The Nature Conservancy, a
     land development company responsible for "conserv[ing] the lands
     and waters on which all life depends." For more on this savvy finan-
     cial refocusing, see *Banking Nature*, directed by Sandrine Feydel and
     Denis Delestrac (Java Films, 2015).

2   J. B. Ruhl and James E. Salzman, *The Effects of Wetland Mitigation
     Banking on People*, 1 January 2006, Florida State University College
     of Law, Public Law Research Paper No. 179.

3   Listing a particular species says more about human attitudes to-
     wards displaceable species communities than stewardship, as both
     frogs and flowers are entangled in what Jacques Rancière would call
     "the politics of who counts:" the political decision happens in the
     designation of becoming a non-human tradeable population, not in
     the translation of any political process toward an outcome.

4   M. Cooper, *Life as Surplus: Biotechnology and Capitalism in the
     Neoliberal Era* (Seattle, WA: University of Washington Press, 2008),
     p. 23.

5   Cooper, *Life as Surplus*, p. 42.

6   The regulatory bodies of wetland banking delay their checks and
     assessments of financialized wetlands until the data on these key
     habitats will be more favourable—a time which often never comes.

7   R. Patel and J. Moore, *A History of the World in Seven Cheap Things;
     A Guide to Capitalism, Nature, and the Future of the Planet* (Berkeley,
     CA: University of California Press, 2017).

8   M. Chen, *Animacies: Biopolitics, Racial Mattering, and Queer Affect*
     (Durham, NC: Duke University Press, 2012), p. 6.

9   For a humorous introduction to the issue of environmental gentrifica-
     tion in Oakland, see *The North Pole*. http://www.thenorthpoleshow
     .com (accessed 13 September 2021).

10   Traditional ecosystems theory assumes that energy, in the form
     of nutrients, travels either up from decomposers or down from
     consumers to reach a kind of ecological "climax." But this is mis-
     leading, at least in the case of the vernal pool. Species don't reach
     some fantasized optimization level, they come and go as they please,
     taking advantage of conditions they find favourable. It is better to
     approach this ecology of beings as an open gathering: a necessarily
     contingent and unfinished assemblage that has diverse participants
     but no wholes.

11   B. Büscher and R. Fletcher, *The Conservation Revolution. Radical
     ideas for Saving Nature beyond the Anthropocene* (London: Verso,
     2020)

TREE THAT CARES FOR ITSELF

In 2012, artist and engineer Natalie Jeremijenko installed her project *TREExOFFICE* at the Socrates Sculpture Park in Long Island City. The project consisted of a co-working space, in the form of a tree-fort-like open-plan office sited around a poplar tree on the grounds of the park, facing the East River with views of Manhattan. Complete with Wi-Fi, and locally produced power, *TREExOFFICE* provided a place to rethink the relationships between working habits and ecological habitats. The project imagined the park as a productive workspace rather than a passive resource, where humans could rent a spot in the tree canopy. Earnings went towards augmenting soil quality with carbon-rich biochar, introducing companion plantings around the tree to protect it from potential pests, and hiring a professional gardener, providing a framework under which the tree benefits directly from its use. Formerly a landfill, a grassroots coalition of artists and community members led by sculptor Mark di Suvero transformed the site in 1986 into a sculpture park. The less toxic environment that we see today (at least at ground level) has hosted hundreds of public art installations over the decades since. Above the sculptures, however, heavy air pollution is still persistent. The nearby Ravenswood Generating Station, identified as the largest carbon polluter state-wide in 2014, together with the Astoria Generating Station also located nearby, provide nearly half of the city's electricity by burning number 6 fuel oil, one of the most polluting energy sources in the world.[1] The area has been rebranded as "Asthma Alley." Socrates Park is free to visit and is open 365 days a year, but its well-intentioned agenda may not have helped to slow the alarming gentrification rates in Astoria, despite the polluted air. Trees can certainly enjoy being serviced, but it will take another wave of green gentrification to shut down the remaining fossil-fuel-burning facilities, and let the tree just be a tree.

1   S. Chalise, Astoria is tired of nickname: "Asthma Alley" and is calling for clean electricity, *2019 Op-Eds*, 9 (Schenectady, NY: Environmental and Natural Resource Economics, Union College Digital Works, 2019).

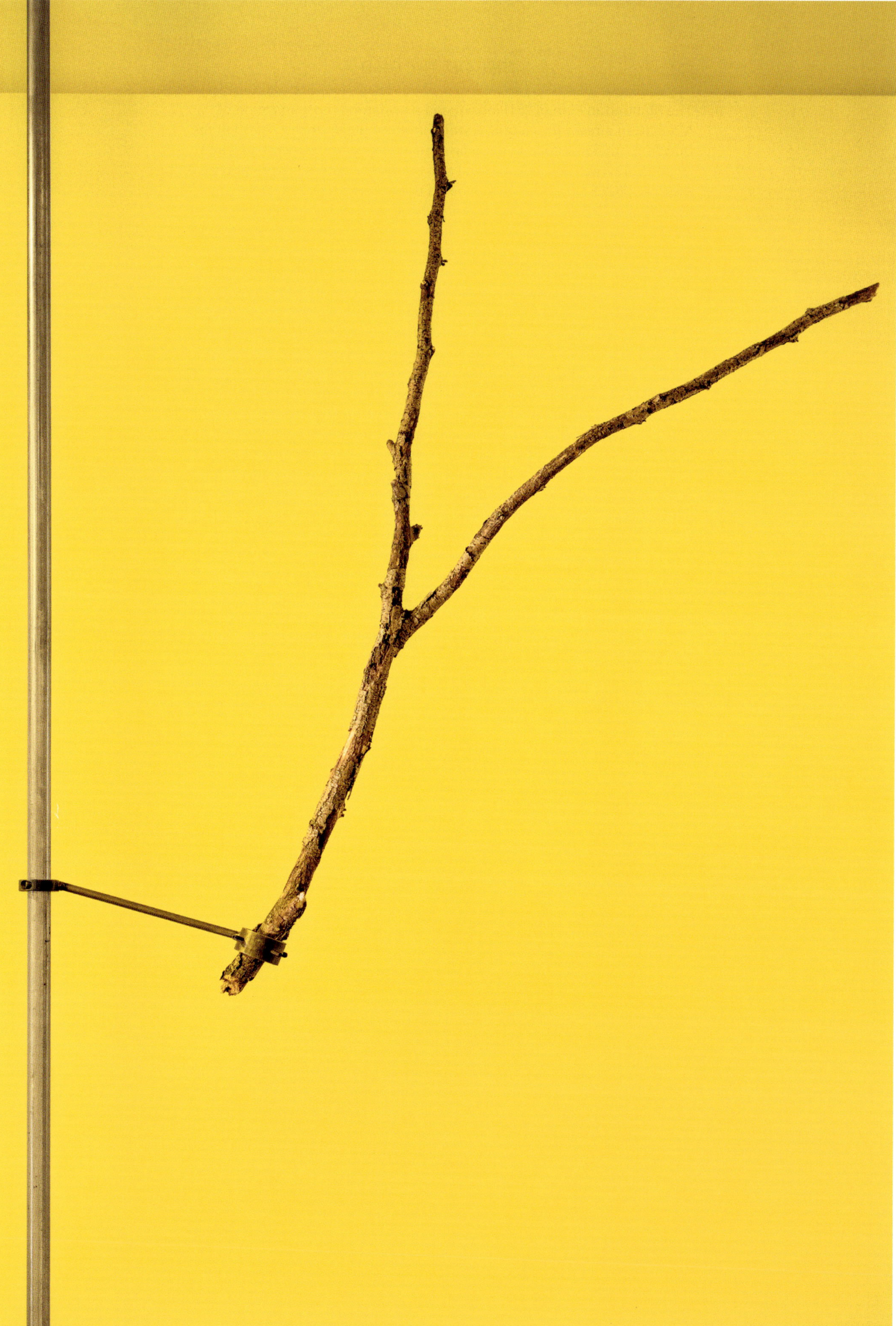

TREE OFF THE GRID

The Manhattan Plan of 1811 introduced a sweeping reorganization of Manhattan streets into a grid system of rectangular blocks. Through the power of eminent domain, the plan erased farms and homesteads, and levelled and reordered the natural and built environment. As it happened, the so-called Stuyvesant Pear Tree on the estate that had historically belonged to Dutch director-general of New York City Peter Stuyvesant—carefully maintained by 40–50 enslaved people—stood right on one corner of the forthcoming grid, sparing it from urban development.[1] The tree, allegedly brought by Stuyvesant from The Netherlands when he assumed control of the colony in 1647, managed to survive the implementation of the urban grid, but not the new traffic system that came with it. Despite the iron guard protection that enclosed it, the pear tree was felled after a wagon crashed into it in February 1867. It was eventually chopped into pieces and crafted into mementos, ranging from collectable slices to a wooden cane. In 2003, a new tree was planted in the same location as the original. Unlike the pear tree, Stuyvesant's former bouwerie farm site was rapidly absorbed into the grid. Once the largest and best of the farms set aside by the Dutch West India Company for its head officer, it became the site for gas storage tanks in 1842, giving the area the name of Gas House District. Its 18 city blocks, a mix of industrial and residential use, were razed in the 1940s to make space for Stuyvesant Town and its 8,757 new apartments. The slum clearance project removed around 11,000 people from 600 buildings. In 1945, the *New York Times* called the Stuy Town displacement the greatest and most significant mass movement of families in New York's history. Trapped in a misfitting geometry a few blocks from where the tree once stood, Stuyvesant Street remains a discrete trace of the farmstead structure as it collided with the 1811 grid.

1 U. P. Hedrick, *The Pears of New York* (Albany, NY: J. B. Lyon, 1921).

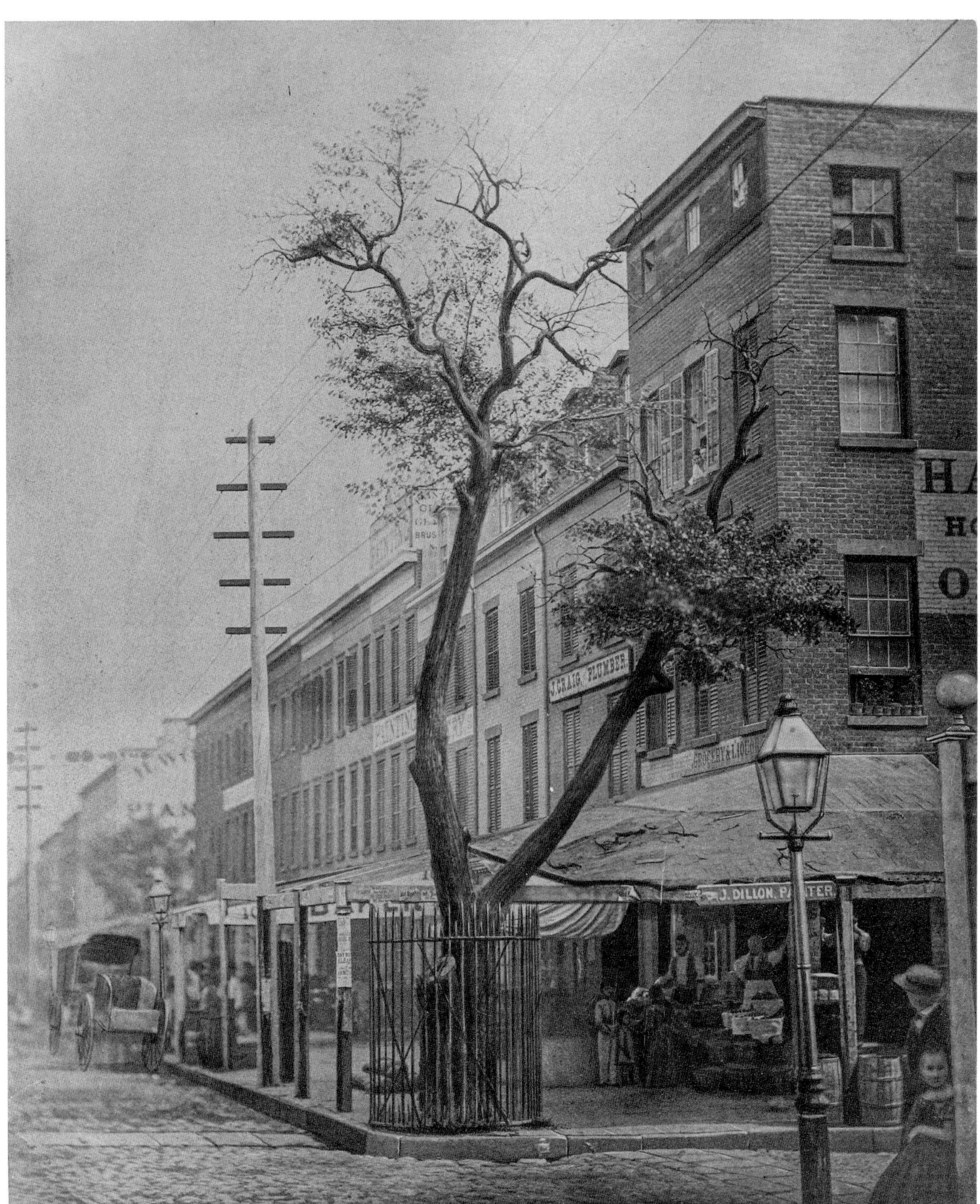

J. CRAIG PLUMBER
GROCERY & LIQUOR
J. DILLON, PAINTER

Known as "the Dinosaur," the English elm at the corner of St Nicholas Avenue and 163rd Street in Washington Heights has long been praised for its strength and resilience. Planted near the Morris–Jumel Mansion estate, the oldest remaining colonial house in Manhattan, the tree has witnessed the many stages of building the city. St Nicholas Avenue's serpentine layout itself still follows an Algonquian trail known as Weekquaeskeek—after the common "birch bark kettle," the "birch bark country" that lined it, or "the end of the marsh"—which the Manhattan grid did not manage to fully assimilate, only surround. In 2008, the New York City Parks Department chose the tree as one of 25 New York trees with valuable genetic material: it predates the Manhattan grid, and has survived polluted air and toxic industrialization for more than 230 years. In their long journey from the Mediterranean to North America, English elms arrived in England with the Romans to support vine-training. Recent DNA studies have proved that the elms actually derive from a single clone that was taken from Italy to Britannia around 2,000 years ago.[1] Once the technology became available, geneticists began to clone buds of still-standing mature American elm trees to prepare for future epidemics, like the Dutch elm disease that ran rampant in the 1970s. As only one in 100,000 elms is "field resistant," the survivors might be key to bringing back the long-lost elm population. As part of the MillionTreesNYC project, cuttings from the trees were also "cloned" to reproduce their success elsewhere in the city (no genetic manipulation involved).[2] Ten samples of each tree were sent to a nursery in Oregon and sent back to New York once they reached 2–3 inches in height. The trees are valued for their biological resilience and their perceived ability to provide long-term environmental services to the city—i.e. through their genes.

1   L. Gil, A. Soto, M. T. Cervera, and P. Fuentes-Utrilla, Phylogeography: English Elm is a 2,000-year-old Roman clone, *Nature*, 431 (2004): 1053.
2   B. Swett, *New York City of Trees* (New York: Countryman Press, 2013), p. 78.

LOCATION: St Nicholas Avenue at 163rd Street, Washington Heights, Manhattan

SPECIMEN: English elm (*Ulmus procera*). Branch, 2018

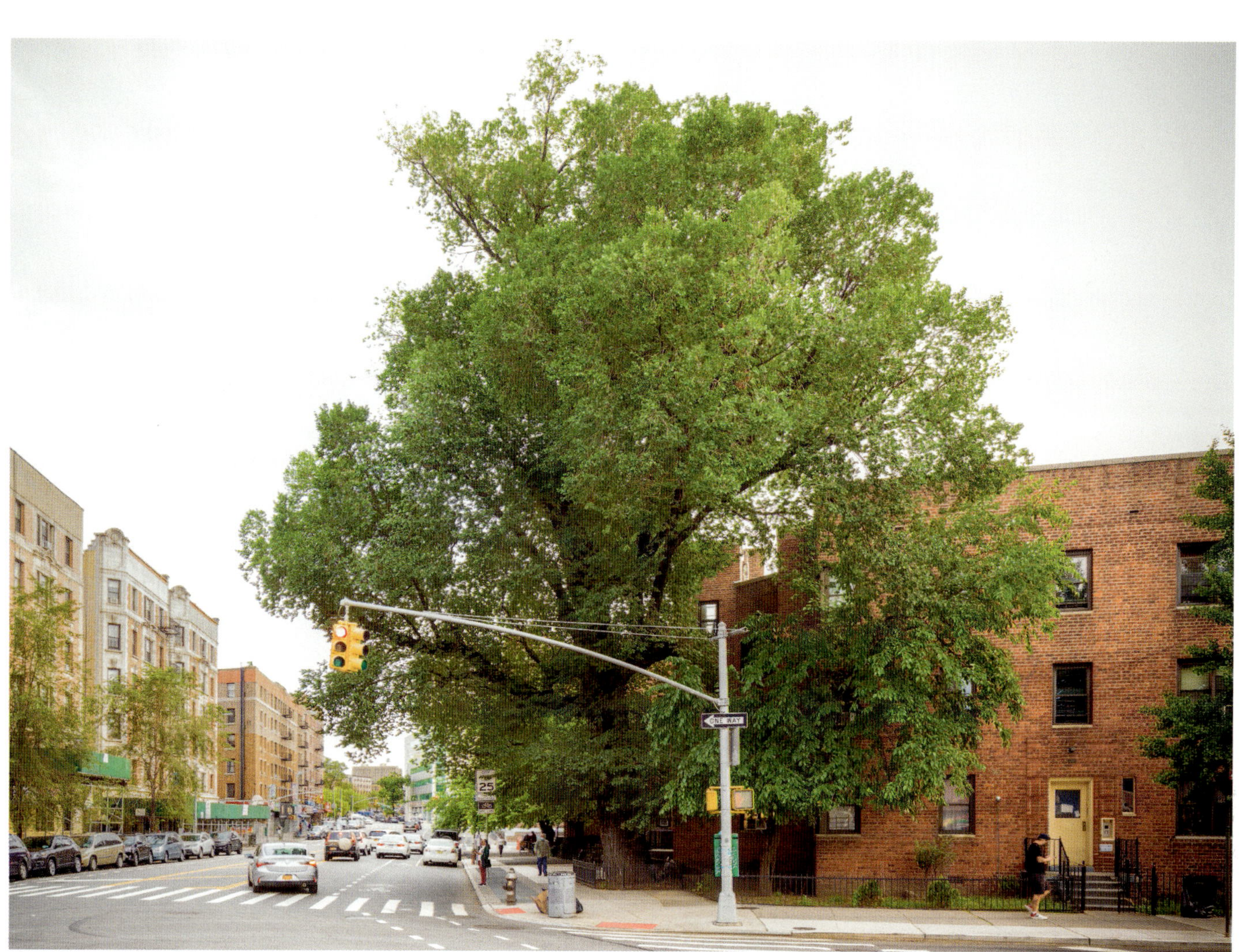

REQUIEM FOR A TREE

Four London plane trees, each over 20 years old, died in the "Temple Square Massacre" in Flatbush in April 1988 when a group of local shop owners cut them down to make their storefronts more visible. This case of flagrant arborcide prompted the then Parks Commissioner Henry J. Stern to hold a funeral in memoriam, a practice he enjoyed performing for other vanished trees (pp. 90 and 140). During the event, Stern wore a black armband and paid his respects as Giuseppe Verdi's *Requiem* wafted through the air. Afterwards, a seven-year-old linden tree was planted in the centre of Temple Square to compensate for the loss of the four mature specimens. At the time, Stern estimated the replacement value of each tree, measuring 16–18 inches in diameter, at US$10,000 apiece. One of the most common tree species in New York City, London planes are a hybrid of American sycamore and Oriental plane, which were cross-bred to be highly resistant to urban pollution. The bark of this resilient tree absorbs airborne PM_{10} toxins—particles less than or equal to 10 micrometres in diameter that can infiltrate the lungs. This biological retention process causes the tree to continuously shed its bark, or exfoliate itself, throughout the year. The weakness of this tree is saltwater, as was seen when hundreds resisted the winds from Hurricane Sandy in the Rockaways only to succumb to the seawater that followed. Most threats to these trees are human. In 1988, Stern also witnessed the largest settlement for an arborcide case when a contractor ripped up 26 trees (including oak, poplar, sassafras, and sycamore maple) in Bayside, Queens, after clearing a view of Little Neck Bay for two homes built on 218th Street. The contractor agreed to furnish 180 trees with an average diameter of 4 inches, with an estimated value of US$100,000. "The Bayside 26," Stern reported to the media, "shall not have died in vain."

LOCATION: Temple Square, at the corner of Schermerhorn Street and Flatbush Avenue, Brooklyn

SPECIMEN: London plane (*Platanus x hispanica*). Bark, 2018–19

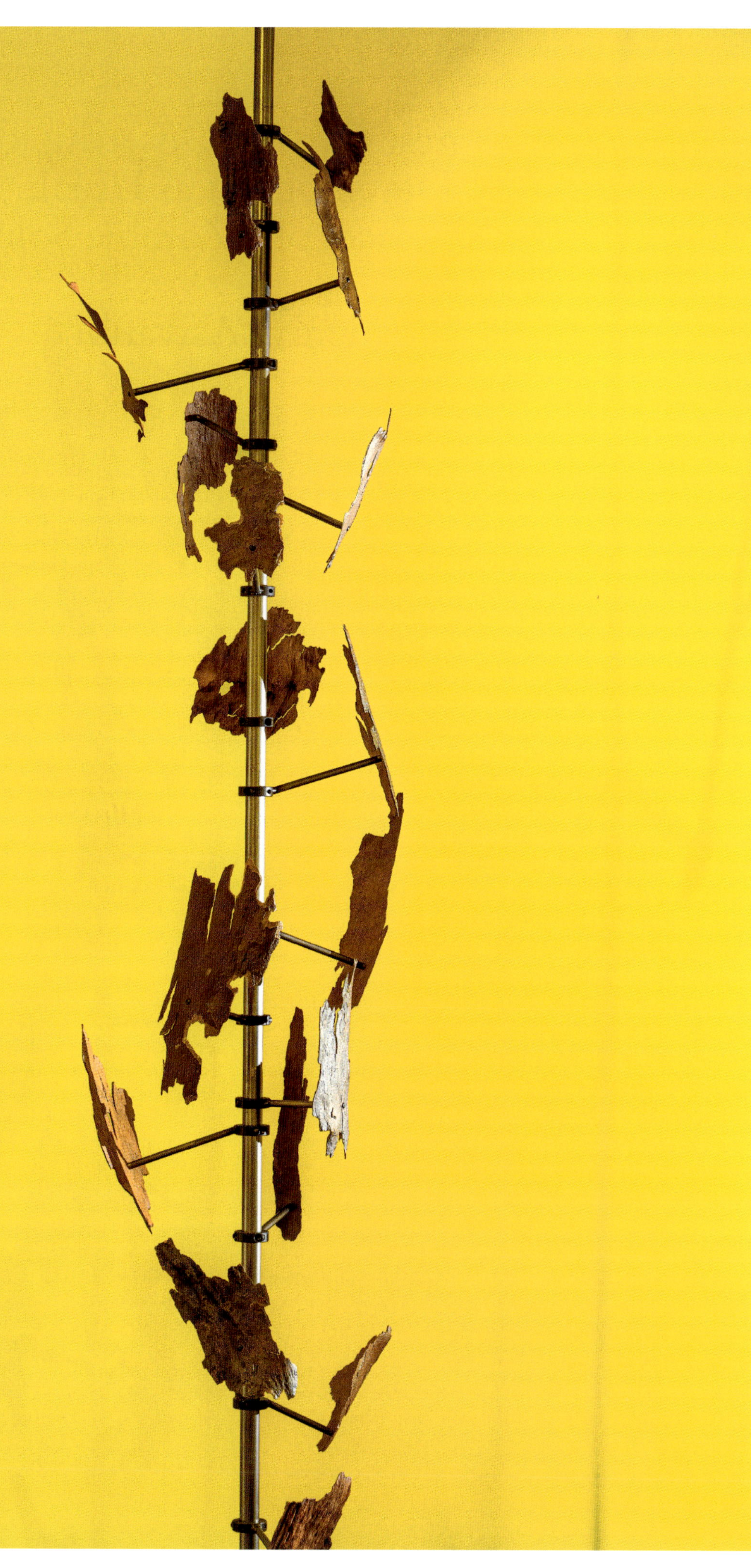

Forest Carbon Offsetting or Development as Usual: Three Spaces of a Zombie Solution

Adeniyi Asiyanbi

The last few decades have seen the rise of offsetting as a way to address growing environmental crises, from climate change and biodiversity degradation to wetland degradation and air pollution.[1] Carbon offsetting as a form of climate change mitigation now constitutes perhaps the largest kind of environmental offsetting globally. Yet, not only has carbon offsetting been unable to put a dent in the steady upward trajectory of global carbon emissions, the conceptual and material bases of carbon offsetting remain deeply contested. Indeed, carbon offsetting, particularly in its dominant forest-based form, appears to legitimize and enable development as usual. This warrants a scrutiny of forest carbon offsetting as a zombie solution—dead with respect to its core aim of reducing emissions, but reanimated through a variety of optimistic initiatives that ultimately legitimize the status quo of fossil fuel production, rapacious resource extraction and consumption, and capitalist growth.

The flagship tropical forest-based carbon offsetting programme REDD+—REDD+ is an abbreviation for "Reducing Emissions from Deforestation and Forest Degradation," plus conservation, sustainable management of forests, and enhancement of forest carbon stocks—was first introduced as "compensated emissions reduction" in 2005.[2] When the Coalition for Rainforest Nations proposed the initiative within the United Nations Framework Convention for Climate Change (UNFCCC), it was tapping into an idea with a long history. The Clean Development Mechanism (CDM), a precursor to REDD+, had allowed for the generation and sale of carbon offsets from afforestation and other non-forest-based projects. The CDM in turn emerged within a contested international climate change arena that reflects the dominance of a market oriented with an emphasis on carbon sinks.[3]

If the foundational theoretical work of the British economist Ronald Coase prepared the ground for refiguring environmental pollution as something that could be "solved" through economic exchange rather than simply stopped, British physicist Freeman Dyson's theoretical computations made it thinkable that the world's carbon emission problem could be effectively addressed by planting enough trees.[4] These theoretical postulations were, at best, reductionist apprehensions of complex socio-ecological processes, allowing climate change to be reduced to a purely physical problem in the latter and a purely economic problem in the former. Yet, seized upon by proponents of market environmentalism, these two ideas became the building blocks for carbon offsetting, not merely as a solution to a supposedly existential climate change crisis but, paradoxically, as another frontier for capital accumulation and economic growth.[5] This approach proceeds with a disavowal of the ways in which the uneven geographies and temporalities of global carbon offsetting, along with its inherent moral hazards, significantly amplify climate injustice.[6]

Such is the provenance of REDD+, which over the last one-and-half decades has mobilized over US$10 billion in public funds alone. The programme seeks to address climate change by mobilizing public and market finance to countries of the global South in order to encourage forest-based emission reduction by increasing forest carbon stock against set baselines. Yet, as the World Bank puts it, the promise of REDD+ is even more expansive: to "transform rural landscapes, conserve forests, make a difference in climate change trajectories and, most importantly, to bring prosperity to the rural poor."[7] REDD+ boasts an expansive network of actors, including over 60 participating countries from the global South, multilateral organizations, international NGOs, indigenous groups, market actors, certification organizations, and independent researchers and consultants. Proponents espouse a win-win discourse of economic growth and ecological sustainability, disseminating a string of claims that the initiative is "cheap," "natural," "quick," and offers "co-benefits." Some even hold up REDD+ as a model for post-Paris Agreement global climate governance architecture.[8] Extending the promise of REDD+ and forest-based climate change mitigation, more than 100 countries now list forest-based actions in their commitment to the Paris Agreement.

Yet, more than a decade of REDD+ has left a trail of unmet expectations. Proponents and critics alike agree that REDD+ has failed to deliver tangible results.[9] Global deforestation continues to escalate, with an estimated

24.2 million hectares (an area approximately the size of the UK) of tree cover lost in 2019 according to Global Forest Watch. Reviews of several REDD+ studies point to widespread tension and conflict.[10] Others report frequent instances of rights abuses and violence in attempts to secure forests for REDD+.[11] REDD+ has, in some cases, problematically reinforced state control over forests, land, and resources.[12] In others, it has given power to international consultants, NGOs, and for-profit organizations, often outside the frame of democratic mandates and accountability.[13] In some cases, REDD+ and associated activities have also further marginalized forest communities and other local actors, particularly those with weak or unrecognized claims to forests and resources.[14] Meanwhile, REDD+ "safeguards," which were conceived precisely in anticipation of these problems, are not always effective.[15]

On the more technical side of things, REDD+ continues to be plagued by the long-standing difficulties of avoiding or even quantifying "leakage" (i.e. the displacement of economic activities to forests outside the intervention zone), and ensuring "additionality" and "permanence." For instance, "additionality" requirements entail proving that a REDD+ project prevents deforestation that would otherwise have happened—something that is virtually impossible to know. This is because the complex interactions of socio-economic and environmental factors operating across scales to shape tropical forests make it difficult to ascertain for sure what *would have* happened to the forest aside from what has *historically* or is *actually* happening to it. At best, such counterfactuals are political decisions. Beyond the unpredictable global economic dynamics shaping forest-intensive commodity chains that drive significant global deforestation, uncertainties regarding how climate change impacts forests through fires, drought, pests, and other "disturbances" raise important questions about the reliability of carbon offsets from forests generally.[16] Faced with these complexities and the messy reality of REDD+ across many countries, even the Centre for International Forestry Research (CIFOR), which had a sympathetic view of REDD+, has stopped just short of declaring REDD+ "dead."[17]

A closer review of REDD+ in Nigeria, while not in any way representative of the diversity of experiences across over 60 REDD+ countries, provides a glimpse into how messy, even counterproductive, some REDD+ projects can (and have) become. By 2008, Cross River State had begun groundwork for REDD+. The state, with a population of about 3.7 million people, living in an area of about 20,156 km² (an area approximately the size of Wales), hosts what is now widely regarded as Nigeria's "last rainforest." With REDD+ readiness funds and technical support from the World Bank's Forest Carbon Partnership Facility (FCPF), the United Nations Programme on Reducing Emissions from Deforestation (UN-REDD), and the California-based Governors' Climate and Forests Taskforce, local actors, and international consultants worked to develop REDD+ proposals. With no more

than a couple of visits to a handful of communities, and with NGOs often taken as representative of communities, proposals went ahead to map out three REDD+ clusters—groupings of contiguous forests belonging to more than 100 communities.[18] This clustering of community forests soon exacerbated existing boundary tensions between communities, while at the same time creating new tensions over representation and potential benefit sharing.[19]

Meanwhile, the state government declared a statewide ban on timber logging in preparation for REDD+ in 2008, a decision that was praised by international REDD+ partners. The state expected the programme to attract significant international finance. The ban, to continue indefinitely, was enforced by a militarized Anti-deforestation Task Force (ATF) that zealously extended enforcement to non-timber forest products. Consequently, a wide range of local forest uses was criminalized and "forest offenders" piled up so quickly that a mobile forestry court had to be created. Thus, multitudes of people and communities in Cross River who depended on the forest and the forest value chains lost forest-based income. Communities also lost their official timber royalties, which for most were never replaced by the much-touted carbon benefits from REDD+. Instead, the ATF created an atmosphere of violence and abuse, which led to protests, litigation, and confrontations with local communities.[20]

Meanwhile, the ban on forest use exempted industrial agricultural plantations. By 2014, at the peak of the ban, deforestation also reached a 14-year peak in Cross River, due partly to forest clearing for industrial agriculture, which was untouched by REDD+ restrictions.[21] Moreover, illegal timber extraction also continued under the ATF's watch. Its inability to prevent actual logging across the vast landscape meant that the ATF resorted to the confiscation and auction of timber deemed illegally sourced. By 2015, when REDD+ champion Governor Imoke was handing his office over to his successor, a national newspaper reported his lament "that REDD+ did not yield a return on investment" for the state.[22]

In contrast to the messiness of REDD+ across many tropical countries and pockets of "model" cases, a resurgent optimism propels REDD+ afresh at the global level, with international institutions like the World Bank and donor countries like Norway celebrating "results" and "progress."[23] International REDD+ proponents now rally around the new notion of natural climate solutions (NCS), claiming that "nature" is the forgotten bulwark in the fight against climate change and can be mobilized to "provide a third of the solutions to climate change."[24] While REDD+ seeks to mobilize tropical forests in the global South specifically, NCS refers to all carbon-sequestering landscapes and ecosystems (including grasslands and oceans), of which forests are only the most important. A growing array of powerful corporations—from the oil industry to the aviation industry—now champion NCS. NCS is at the heart of plans by Mark Carney (the former Bank of England governor and UN special envoy on

Climate Change and Finance) and his team to catalyse the ailing global carbon offset market into a US$100 billion per year market. In short, a raft of initiatives seeks to, in Chris Lang's words, "bring REDD+ back from the dead."[25]

THREE SPACES OF A ZOMBIE SOLUTION

So how should we understand the persistence of REDD+ and forest-based climate action despite the historically poor performance? It appears useful to think of "the zombie," a metaphor that has been used to make sense of carbon off-setting, particularly under the CDM.[26] Writing about a decade ago, Oscar Reyes (2011) analysed the abysmal record of CDM projects, the carbon markets they underlie, and the paradoxical enthusiasm of proponents seeking "to 'move beyond' the CDM and 'scale up' mitigation actions in the global South." Reyes describes these optimistic efforts as the stumbling forward of the "zombies of new carbon market mechanisms." Today, Reyes' critique aptly explains REDD+ and the voluntary carbon market it underpins. If REDD+ is dead, at least with respect to its core aims, then various attempts to revitalize it are perhaps the forward floundering of a zombie solution.

But a key feature of a zombie is that it is "taken over," as it were, and repurposed towards other ends. So how is the zombie of REDD+ (and forest-based carbon offsetting more generally) being "possessed" by a range of interests and projects? What functions does the zombie of REDD+ ultimately serve? Lane and Stephan ask that we go beyond the simple admission of the "unkillable" yet vacuous carbon markets as zombies to decipher what carbon market zombies actually *do*.[27] They invite us to grapple with the "politics inherently involved in the development, ongoing maintenance and contestation of the carbon markets" as zombies.[28] In what follows, I briefly outline only three spaces of development as usual that illustrate the diverse spatial co-constitution of the REDD+ carbon-offset zombie.

1) Extractive, forest-decimating development in the global South

Not only has REDD+ largely failed to stop tropical deforestation, it has co-existed with or fostered extractive and forest-decimating agro-industrial development in many REDD+ countries. This is the case in Colombia,[29] Nigeria,[30] and the Amazon region.[31] REDD+, in theory at least, claims to incentivize a voluntary shift from extractive, forest-intensive land uses to forest conservation. Yet, to accept this claim at face value is to ignore both the reality of the convenient co-existence of REDD+ and extractivist development and the logic that clearly indicates that this co-existence is not (at least not completely) incidental.

REDD+ is not merely a tool for environmental amelioration. It is also envisioned and pursued as a tool to expand private capital, and in this sense it is not unlike extractivist development.[32] This is why even the largely public international REDD+ funds have been clear that a fundamental aim is to ensure that in-country REDD+ programmes leverage private investment not only in carbon forestry but also in a wide range of other activities about which carbon-sequestration *claims* can be made, from industrial plantations to "climate smart agriculture" to "sustainable mining." For instance, Biocarbon Fund, a US$350 million fund financed by the governments of Germany, Norway, and the UK, stipulates that all projects create an "enabling environment" for large-scale commercial investments. Selected countries supported by the fund are said to host large investments in industrial agriculture involving international corporations in "sustainable cotton production" in Zambia, and "sustainable coffee production" in Ethiopia and Kenya.[33] And when oil corporations such as Equinor and Petrobras invest in or fund REDD+ activities in Brazil (as I explain further below), they do so not with the aim of displacing or limiting their own oil production but precisely to legitimize production and the expansion of production capacity.

A similar logic is evident in the finance sector, where fund managers investing impact funds in REDD+ are perfecting the strategy of diversifying their asset portfolios beyond carbon offsets. This is done to not only hedge risk but also to maximize investment returns, particularly in the face of uncompetitive carbon prices.[34] For example, AlphaSource Climate Fund, a US$250 million fund with a portfolio and pipeline of REDD+ projects across Africa, Southeast Asia, and Latin America, targets landscapes where REDD+ investments can cover a range of projects, including "responsible mining," "sustainable timber," and "climate-smart commodities," among others.[35] In the Kasigau Corridor REDD+ project, which has received investments of €101 million from the Althelia Climate Fund and the International Finance Corporation's US$152 million Forest Bond, revenue sources included not only carbon credit sale but also the production and sale of charcoal, ecotourism, and the marketing of locally produced arts and crafts.[36] In short, not only have various forms of extractivist development continued on the REDD+ landscape in the global South, but the logic underpinning this phenomenon is very much internal to carbon offsetting as a tool for expanding resource extraction, markets, and the circuit of capital.

2) Development of fossil-fuel economies in the global North

Fossil fuel emissions from energy generation still account for about three-quarters of total global greenhouse gas emissions. This is only one of many reasons why the oil industry wields enormous political and economic power to influence governments and intergovernmental institutions, shape public perception, and sway science-policy debates on climate change. When such an industry throws its weight behind carbon offsetting, then one needs to pay keen attention. As analysts continue to show, the new language of "net zero emission" or "negative emissions" through offsetting partly serves to skew climate change debates in ways favourable to the fossil fuel industry. By championing carbon offsetting, the fossil fuel industry seeks primarily to defer the imminent shift away from fossil production and use. It seeks to defer the imminent devaluation of fossil assets while harnessing moral capital to neutralize public concern about climate change.[37] In short, REDD+ and carbon offsetting allow the oil industry to continue to produce fossil fuels while claiming (to work towards) future emission neutrality targets.

For instance, Equinor, the Norwegian-state owned multinational oil company, announced investments in the Brazilian REDD+ programme just as the company was expanding its oil production capacity in Brazil. Equinor's promise only adds to the broader Norwegian government's leading support for REDD+, which analysts have interpreted as a clear strategy for the protection of the country's interest in the fossil fuel industry.[38] Other oil majors have also thrown their support behind REDD+. Shell announced a plan to invest US$200 million in nature-based solutions between 2020 and 2021 alone—part of its commitment to net zero emissions by 2050—and has since invested in REDD+ offsets in Indonesia and Peru.[39] Eni has REDD+ offset agreements with Zambia, Mozambique, Vietnam, Mexico, Ghana, the Republic of the Congo, the Democratic Republic of the Congo, and Angola. BP has made contributions to the World Bank-managed REDD+ platform, Forest Carbon Partnership Facility. Chevron, which has invested US$1.1 billion in carbon capture, utilization, and storage (CCUS) technologies, has also invested in REDD+ type projects in Brazil. In short, the zombie of REDD+ carbon offsetting *does* enable continued production and use of fossil fuel, the largest footprints of which come from the global North and few large economies in the global South.

3) Urban development proceeds with empty claims of carbon neutrality

Cities and urban centres are important sites of carbon emissions. Although relatively small in terms of their spatial coverage (about 3 per cent of the global surface area), urban centres are associated with significant levels of emissions. In fact, some accounts suggest that about 70 per cent of global carbon emissions associated with final energy use are based in cities.[40] Moreover, cities—in all their density of people, things, and ideas within very fluid boundaries—are also important sites of climate leadership, innovation, and activism.[41] For instance, carbon-neutral design and construction are becoming popular in most global cities. Utility companies, particularly energy supply companies, are increasingly marketing net-carbon-neutral energy to users. Apart from these material ways in which cities figure as important loci of carbon emissions and mitigation, urban centres are also an important site for symbolic performances and enunciations of carbon neutrality agendas and for contesting those agendas.

While significant structural innovations to reduce emissions are emerging in cities, offsets continue to be used to address so-called "residual emissions." As "residual emissions" is typically a loose category, urban net carbon neutrality claims rely on offsetting to such an extent that some analysts call for a restriction on how much offsetting can be used to account for net carbon neutrality in urban initiatives.[42] For instance, since 2010, the government of British Columbia has consistently maintained net carbon neutrality across all public sector organizations, mainly (up to 80 per cent) through offsets generated partly from forest protection and management in British Columbia and elsewhere.[43] Besides governments, global corporations with a significant urban presence, such as Facebook and Amazon, have recently announced net-zero emission plans, with some already channelling funds towards natural climate solutions.[44] For instance, Amazon's Jeff Bezos has directed the first instalment (US$791 million) of his pledged US$10 billion climate intervention fund towards natural climate solutions. One implication of all this is that claims *in* and *by* cities of carbon neutrality need to be taken seriously, not only for what they mean for the future of cities as sites of decarbonization, but also for how they authorize and legitimize development underpinned by questionable claims of carbon neutrality. And, as urban development is tightly bound up with the growth of capitalism, the role of offsetting should be understood as fostering the "production of space(s), place(s) and nature(s) in line with contemporary patterns of capitalist urban growth."[45]

STUMBLING FORWARD

The zombie of forest-based carbon offsetting stumbles forward. Evidence that these supposedly "natural," "cheap," and "quick" climate "solutions" fail to achieve the desirable impacts stands in sharp contrast to the enthusiasm that is swelling around them at the international level. The metaphor of the zombie allows us to grapple with this tension, while a focus on what the carbon-offset zombie *does* opens up space to appreciate the many stakes here, of which only a few have been highlighted in this chapter. What is clear is that these zombie solutions, in their failure to meaningfully depress carbon emission trajectories, merely provide ways to double-down on development as usual and capitalist growth, while distracting from more ambitious actions that hold the possibility of averting the worst of the climate crisis. Justice for those who already suffer the most from climate change is what makes the critique of carbon offsetting even more urgent.

1 "Carbon offset" is used to refer to a range of instruments, which have different technical names depending on the programme under which they are generated and traded.

2 M. Santilli, P. Moutinho, D. Nepstad, *et al.*, Tropical deforestation and the Kyoto Protocol, *Climatic Change*, 71(3) (2005): 267–276.

3 W. Carton, A. Asiyanbi, S. Beck, H. J. Buck and J. F. Lund, Negative emissions and the long history of carbon removal, *WIREs Climate Change*, 11(6) (2020): e671.

4 R. H. Coase, The problem of social cost, in *Classic Papers in Natural Resource Economics* (Berlin: Springer, 1960), pp. 87–137; F. J. Dyson, Can we control the carbon dioxide in the atmosphere?, *Energy*, 2(3) (1977): 287–291.

5 P. Newell and M. Paterson, *Climate Capitalism: Global Warming and the Transformation of the Global Economy* (Cambridge: Cambridge University Press, 2010); A. G. Bumpus and D. M. Liverman, Accumulation by decarbonization and the governance of carbon offsets, *Economic Geography*, 84(2) (2008): 127–155; K. McAfee, Green economy and carbon markets for conservation and development: A critical view, *International Environmental Agreements: Politics, Law and Economics*, 16(3) (2016): 333–353.

6 C. Okereke and K. Dooley, Principles of justice in proposals and policy approaches to avoided deforestation: towards a post-Kyoto climate agreement, *Global Environmental Change*, 20(1) (2010): 82–95; W. Carton, J. F. Lund, and K. Dooley, Undoing equivalence: Rethinking carbon accounting for just carbon removal, *Frontiers in Climate*, 3 (2021).

7 Forest Carbon Partnership Facility (FCPF), *Foreword, Forest Carbon Partnership Facility 2015 Annual Report*, 2015, p. 7.

8 A. Savaresi, A glimpse into the future of the climate regime: Lessons from the REDD+ architecture, *Review of European, Comparative and International Environmental Law*, 25(2) (2016): 186–196.

9 A. Angelsen, M. Brockhaus, A. E. Duchelle, *et al.*, Learning from REDD+: A response to Fletcher *et al.*, *Conservation Biology*, 31(3) (2017): 718–720; R. Fletcher, W. Dressler, B. Büscher, and Z. R. Anderson, Questioning REDD+ and the future of market-based conservation, *Conservation Biology*, 30(3) (2016): 673–675; A. Asiyanbi and J. Friis Lund, Policy persistence: REDD+ between stabilization and contestation, *Journal of Political Ecology*, 27(1) (2020).

10 S. Milne, S. Mahanty, P. To, *et al.*, Learning from "actually existing" REDD+: A synthesis of ethnographic findings, *Conservation & Society*, 17(1) (2019): 84–95; M. Leach and I. Scoones, *Political Ecologies of Carbon in Africa* (M. Leach and I. Scoones, eds) (Abingdon: Routledge, 2015); Asiyanbi and Lund, Policy persistence.

11 A. P. Asiyanbi, A political ecology of REDD+: Property rights, militarised protectionism, and carbonised exclusion in Cross River, *Geoforum*, 77 (2016): 146–156; C. J. Cavanagh, P. O. Vedeld, and L. T. Traedal, Securitizing REDD plus? Problematizing the emerging illegal timber trade and forest carbon interface in East Africa, *Geoforum*, 60 (2015): 72–82.

12 T. Krause, Reducing deforestation in Colombia while building peace and pursuing business as usual extractivism?, *Journal of Political Ecology*, 27(1) (2020): 401–418; A. B. Setyowati, Governing the ungovernable: Contesting and reworking REDD+ in Indonesia, *Journal of Political Ecology*, 27(1) (2020): 456–475.

13 D. McNeill, M. Furuly, and A. Vatn, REDD+, NGOs and local government in Tanzania, *International Forestry Review*, 20(3) (2018): 375–389; E. O. Nuesiri, Feigning democracy: Performing representation in the UN-REDD funded Nigeria-REDD programme, *Conservation and Society*, 15(4) (2017): 384–399.

14 Asiyanbi, A Political Ecology of REDD+; M. M. Kansanga and I. Luginaah, Agrarian livelihoods under siege: Carbon forestry, tenure constraints and the rise of capitalist forest enclosures in Ghana, *World Development*, 113 (2019): 131–142; C. Luttrell, E. Sills, R. Aryani, A. D. Ekaputri, and M. F. Evinke, Beyond opportunity costs: Who bears the implementation costs of reducing emissions from deforestation and degradation?, *Mitigation and Adaptation Strategies for Global Change*, 23(2) (2018): 291–310; S. Chomba, J. Kariukib, J. F. Lund, and F. Sinclair, Roots of inequity: How the implementation of REDD+ reinforces past injustices, *Land Use Policy*, 50 (2016): 202–213.

15 M. Poudyal, B. S. Ramamonjisoa, N. Hockley, *et al.*, Can REDD+ social safeguards reach the "right" people? Lessons from Madagascar, *Global Environmental Change*, 37 (2016): 31–42.

16 Asiyanbi and Lund, Policy persistence. Even more complex are the problems associated with assumed equivalence in carbon emissions across fossil fuel carbon, which formed in complex and slow Earth-shaping conditions over thousands of years, and relatively quick-forming biomass carbon in trees, which has a much shorter recycling period. Moreover, different carbon emissions have very different social origins, with significant ethical implications—for instance, carbon emissions from a luxury flight compared to carbon emissions from a household using firewood to make its only main meal for the day.

17 Angelsen *et al.*, Learning from REDD+; Mexico and Nicaragua (two of the flagship REDD+ countries in the Americas) had their agreements with the World Bank's FCPF Carbon Fund cancelled in March 2021.

18 Nuesiri, Feigning democracy.

19 U. Isyaku, A. A. Arhin, and A. P. Asiyanbi, Framing justice in REDD+ governance: Centring transparency, equity and legitimacy in readiness implementation in West Africa, *Environmental Conservation*, 44(3) (2017): 212–220.

20 Asiyanbi, A political ecology of REDD+; I. Ekott, Investigation: How a $4 million UN climate programme impoverished Nigerian communities, *Premium Time Newspaper*, 21 April 2016.

21 G. C. Schoneveld, The politics of the forest frontier: Negotiating between conservation, development, and indigenous rights in Cross River state, Nigeria, *Land Use Policy*, 38 (2014): 147–162.

22   Ekott, Investigation: How a $4 Million UN Climate Programme Impoverished Nigerian Communities, p. 2.

23   A. Asiyanbi and K. Massarella, Transformation is what you expect, models are what you get: REDD+ and models in conservation and development, *Journal of Political Ecology*, 27(1) (2020): 476–495.

24   B. W. Griscom, J. Adams, P. W. Ellis, *et al.*, Natural climate solutions, *Proceedings of the National Academy of Sciences of the United States of America*, 114(44) (2017): 11645–11650.

25   C. Lang, The green gigaton challenge: Bringing REDD back from the dead, using Norway's oil money to "grease the wheels," REDD, 3 December 2020, https://redd-monitor.org/2020/12/03/the-green-gigaton-challenge-bringing-redd-back-from-the-dead-using-norways-oil-money-to-grease-the-wheels (accessed 13 September 2021).

26   R. Lane and B. Stephan, Zombie markets or zombie analyses?, *Revivifying the Politics of Carbon Markets* (B. Stephan and R. Lane, eds) (Routledge: Philadelphia, PA, 2015), pp. 1–23; O. Reyes, Zombie carbon and sectoral market mechanisms, *Capitalism Nature Socialism*, 22(4) (2011): 117–135.

27   Lane and Stephan, Zombie markets or zombie analyses?

28   Lane and Stephan, Zombie markets or zombie analyses?, p. 3.

29   Krause, Reducing deforestation in Colombia while building peace and pursuing business as usual extractivism?

30   Schoneveld, The politics of the forest frontier.

31   G. M. Thaler, The land sparing complex: Environmental governance, agricultural intensification, and state building in the Brazilian Amazon, *Annals of the American Association of Geographers*, 107(6) (2017): 1424–1443.

32   J. Fairhead, M. Leach, and I. Scoones, Green grabbing: A new appropriation of nature?, *Journal of Peasant Studies*, 39(2) (2012): 237–261.

33   BioCarbon Fund, Private sector engagement, https://www.biocarbonfund-isfl.org/theme?title=Private%20Sector%20Engagement (accessed 17 November 2021).

34   The average carbon price in the voluntary carbon market has continued to decline since 2006, reaching a historic low of US$3.01 in 2018 (Ecosystem Marketplace, 2019). Prices have rebounded more recently.

35   S. Zwick, *Seven Lessons from a Decade of Impact Investing*, Ecosystem Marketplace, 2017, https://www.ecosystemmarketplace.com/articles/seven-lessons-from-a-decade-of-impact-investing (accessed 13 September 2021).

36   J. Kill, *The Kasigau Corridor REDD+ Project in Kenya: A Crash Dive for Althelia Climate Fund* (Re:Common, Counter Balance, and Jamaa Resource Initiative, 2016), p. 15, https://redd-monitor.org/wp-content/uploads/2020/11/2017-The-Kasigau-Corridor-REDD-Kenya.pdf (accessed 13 September 2021).

37   W. Carton, "Fixing" climate change by mortgaging the future: Negative emissions, spatiotemporal fixes, and the political economy of delay, *Antipode*, 51(3) (2019): 750–769.

38   H. Svarstad and T. A. Benjaminsen, Nothing succeeds like success narratives: A case of conservation and development in the time of REDD, *Journal of Eastern African Studies* 11(3) (2017): 482–505.

39   Investigative journalists have reported evidence of leakage in both REDD+ projects underlying Shell's offsets in Peru and Indonesia. Shell, *Nature-Based Solutions*, https://www.shell.com/energy-and-innovation/new-energies/nature-based-solutions.html#iframe=L3dlYmFwcHMvMjAxOV9uYXR1cmVfYmFzZWRfc29sdXRpb25zL3VwZGF0ZS8 (accessed 13 September 2021).

40   M. Balouktsi, Carbon metrics for cities: Production and consumption implications for policies, *Buildings and Cities*, 1(1) (2020).

41   Carbon Neutral Cities Alliance (CNCA), *Our Reports—*, https://carbonneutralcities.org/what-we-do/resources-and-reports (accessed 13 September 2021); H. Bulkeley, L. B. Andonova, M. M. Betsill, *et al.*, *Transnational Climate Change Governance* (Cambridge: Cambridge University Press, 2014); A. Walnycki, *Climate Activism and Cities: A Shared Agenda*, International Institute for Environment and Development, 2020, https://www.iied.org/climate-activism-cities-shared-agenda (accessed 13 September 2021).

42   Balouktsi, Carbon metrics for cities.

43   British Colombia, Public sector Climate Change Accountability Reports, https://www2.gov.bc.ca/gov/content/environment/climate-change/public-sector/cnar (accessed 13 September 2021).

44   S. Zwick, Natural climate solutions win big in first Bezos grants, *Ecosystem Marketplace*, 16 November 2020, https://www.ecosystemmarketplace.com/articles/natural-climate-solutions-win-big-in-bezos-grants (accessed 13 September 2021).

45   E. Apostolopoulou and W. M. Adams, Cutting nature to fit: Urbanization, neoliberalism and biodiversity offsetting in England, *Geoforum*, 98 (2019): 215.

In December 1998, the mother of all weeping beech trees in North America—all future weeping beeches were grown from cuttings of this first tree imported from Belgium to Flushing in 1847—was declared dead. Numerous attempts to save her, using support cables and fertilizer injections, failed. Designated as one of two living landmarks in New York in 1966, the city publicly mourned the loss of the 151-year-old tree at the full funeral held for her by Parks Commissioner Henry J. Stern, as he had done for other specimens (pp. 90 and 132). "This is the vegetable equivalent of an Egyptian pharaoh going into his sarcophagus surrounded by his adoring little offshoots," eulogized Stern.[1] The tree's remains were repurposed as heritage trail benches and memorial logs—a proposal also called for dicing the tree into millions of souvenir toothpicks, or even pencils. The sales revenue from the remnants was to be "inherited" by the progeny of the weeping beech: eight branches around the mother tree that over the years had touched the ground and re-rooted around its large canopy were to be invested in paying for special gardener's care. Since the tree's passing, the area surrounding Weeping Beech Park is also experiencing something of an afterlife. An influx of transnational capital and the rise of luxury condos led by Chinese American developers and wealthy Chinese immigrants has displaced previous generations of immigrant residents and small business owners.[2] The 69 per cent Asian population now struggles to preserve this historically working-class neighbourhood and its culinary charm. The weeping beech's death almost coincided with the city's new vision for Flushing's waterfront in the early 2000s, which had previously been neglected (p. 56). Organizations like the Flushing Anti-Displacement Alliance and other coalitions will keep fighting to stand in place. Margaret I. Carman Green in Weeping Beech Park honours her efforts in setting up the Flushing Freedom Trail, which connects spaces in the area that sheltered formerly enslaved people in their emancipation struggle.

1 A. C. Meier, On the trail of New York's greatest trees, *Citylab*, 17 April 2017.
2 S. Ngu, "Not What It Used to Be:" in New York, Flushing's Asian residents brace against gentrification, *The Guardian*, 13 August 2020.

LOCATION: Northern Boulevard Park, now at 143-35 37th Avenue, Flushing, Queens

SPECIMEN: Weeping beech (*Fagus sylvatica*). Fragment of weeping beech tree, 1998

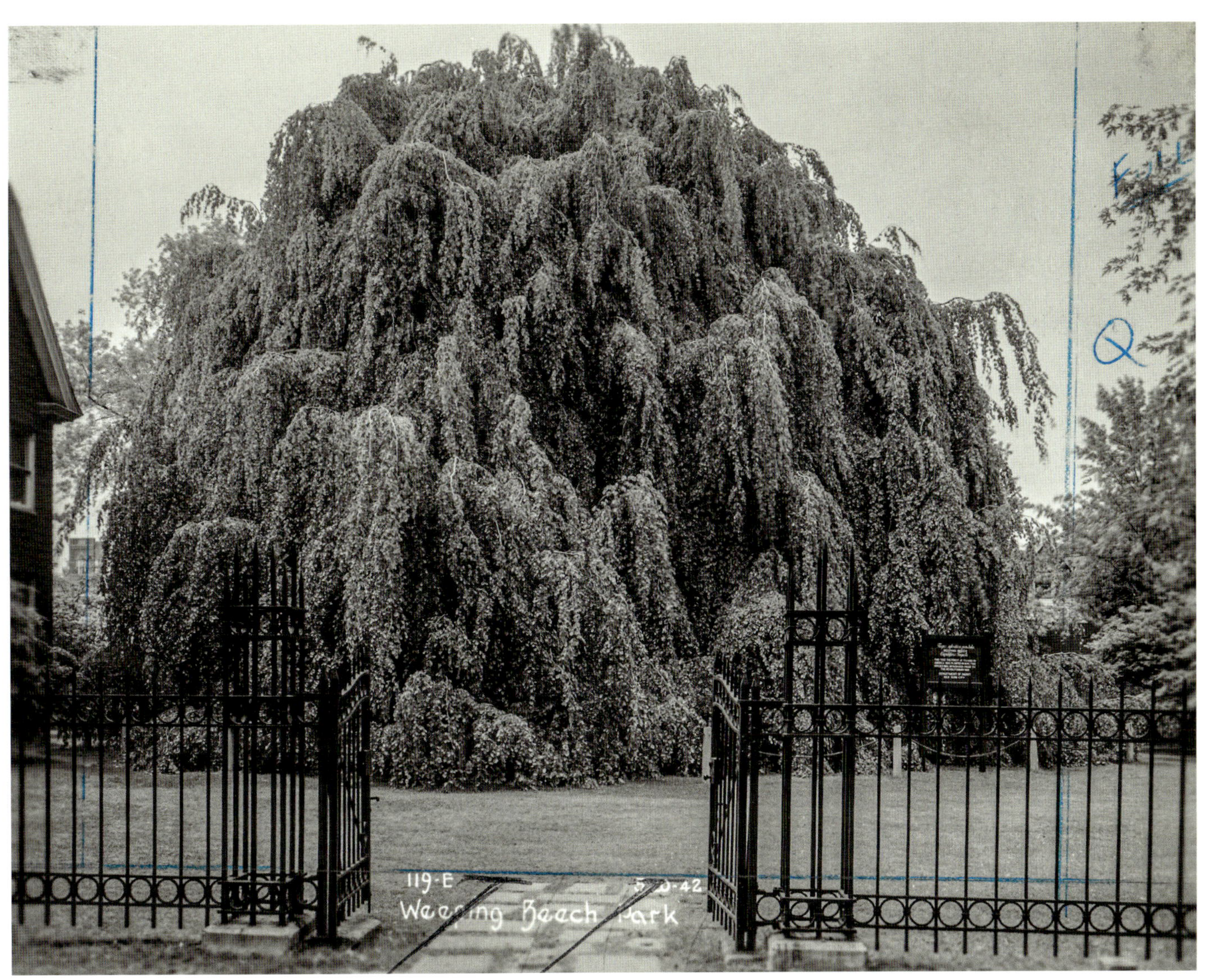
119-E
Weeping Beach Park

OCCUPY TREE

In 2011, participants of Occupy Wall Street designated a London plane tree standing at the eastern edge of Zuccotti Park the "Tree of Life." They gathered around it daily to publicly express nationwide anger at the seemingly insurmountable inequality between the wealthiest 1 per cent of the population and the remaining 99 per cent, as well as to protest corporate influence on democracy. The tree was the locus for public speeches during the peaceful occupation of the park, itself a privately owned public space built in the 1960s in a trade of air rights for more office space (p. 76). Carved out of speculative zoning tactics, this privately owned public space incongruously allowed sometimes up to 200 protesters to remain in the park 24 hours a day and set up camp. After 9/11, the park had been refurbished with 54 honey locust trees and the larger London plane, which was surrounded by semi-circular granite benches, on one of which was perched a bronze statue of a businessman inspecting his open briefcase. Turned into a makeshift altar composed of candles, seashells, incense, and other offerings, the Tree of Life briefly galvanized the possibility of a new American dream. In the camp, other DIY sanitation, learning, reading, and dining services were set up, promoting alternative economic models alongside poetry sessions, musical performances, and protest chants. After protesters were evicted on 15 November 2011, the Tree of Life was chopped down. Its symbolic load was unbearable for the surrounding environment. In September 2018, ten years after the collapse of Lehman Brothers and seven years after Occupy, a 26-feet tall, half-ton, rose-shaped sculpture by the German artist Isa Genzken was unveiled in the same spot that the Tree of Life once occupied.[1]

---

1   C. Swanson, On Occupy's anniversary, a rose blooms in Zuccotti Park, *Vulture*, 17 September 2018.

SPECIMEN: Tree of Life—London plane (*Platanus* × *hispanica*). Branch and Occupy Wall Street Tape, 2011/2019

LOCATION: Zuccotti Park, Manhattan Branch, 2018; Tompkins Square Park, Manhattan

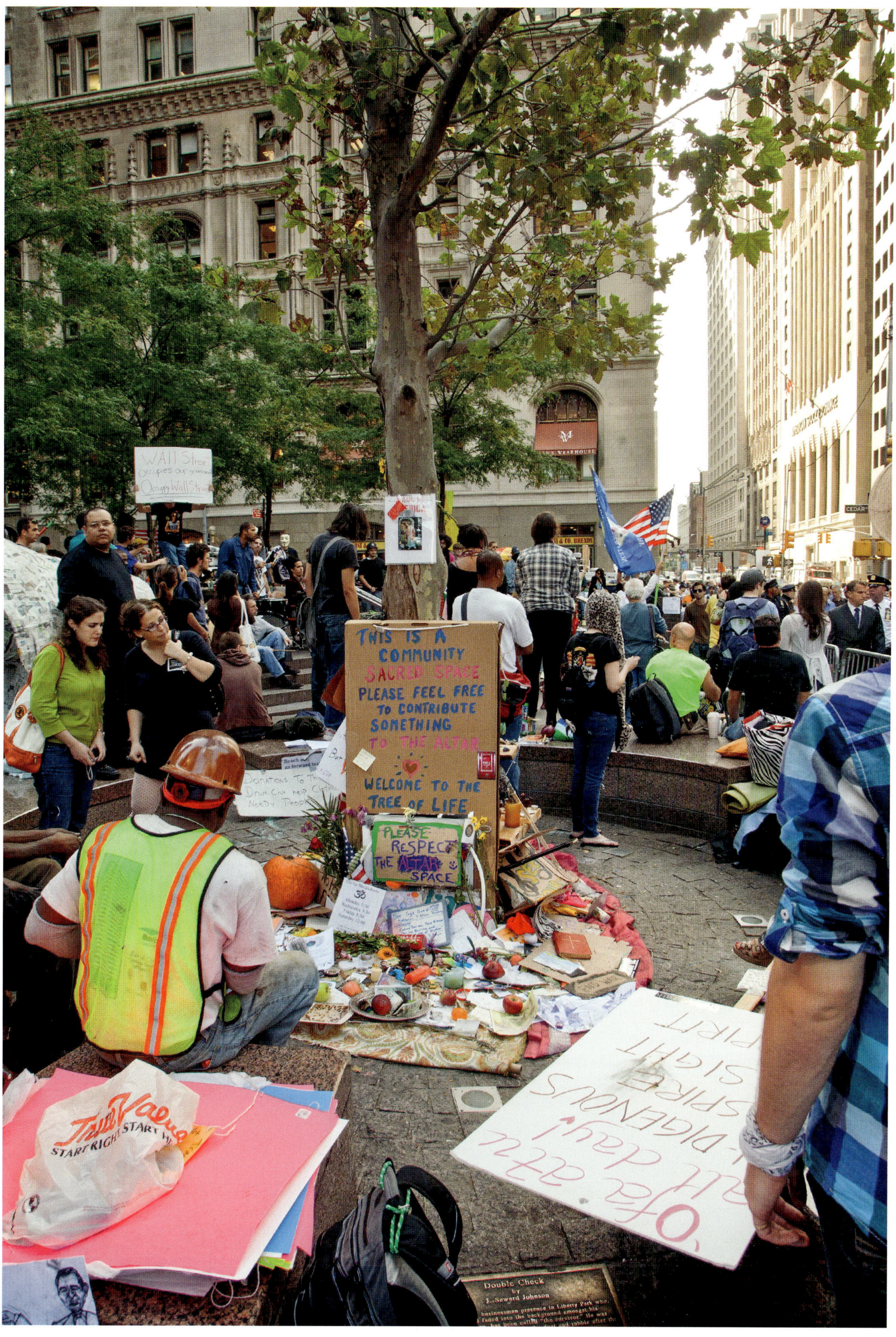

THIS IS A
COMMUNITY
SACRED SPACE
PLEASE FEEL FREE
TO CONTRIBUTE
SOMETHING
TO THE ALTAR
WELCOME TO THE
TREE OF LIFE
PLEASE RESPECT
THE ALTAR &
SPACE
True Value
START RIGHT START HERE
Double Check
by
J. Seward Johnson

TREE BUILD-AROUND

In 1983, Bronx resident Bruce Snowden noticed that the roots of a nearly 200-year-old American sycamore tree were being suffocated by the surrounding sidewalk.[1] American sycamores are commonly confused with London plane trees because of their similarly exfoliating bark, but the former keep a band of dark bark at their base and are found near water bodies or where the water table is close to the surface, while the latter exfoliate all the way down to the roots. Advocating for the city to save the unique sycamore, Snowden launched a fundraising and media campaign, which included a symphony composed and performed by local residents.[2] Eventually, the concrete around the tree was removed.[3] In the late 1990s, when the adjacent vacant lot was bought, residents pressured the developer into altering the design of a new building to prevent root damage by making enough space for the tree's canopy. Before going ahead with plans, the developer decided to resell the lot, and the next owner inherited the challenge. At 87 feet high and 49 inches in diameter, this tree may be one of only a handful that have successfully forced a developer to redesign a building according to its needs. Modelled around it, the U-shaped structure required a recessed middle void to ensure the sycamore received adequate sunshine. Even pedestrians have to detour around the generous tree pit to continue straight on the sidewalk. The Sycamore Court condos on 3050 Corlear Avenue, Bronx, still carry the history of the tree around which they were built in their name. American sycamores, also known as buttonwood trees, are also the namesake of the foundation of today's New York Stock Exchange (NYSE). Beneath an American sycamore on Wall Street, where merchants gathered to close deals, the Buttonwood Agreement established organized securities trading in the city in 1792. Soon there were too many brokers to meet under the tree and a new building was needed. Unlike the Bronx condos, the NYSE did not bend to the needs of a single tree.

1 R. McElroy, Neighborhood Report: New York Trees: In Kingsbridge, a sycamore faces unwelcome neighbor, *New York Times*, 1 October 2000.

2 B. Snowden, The "symphony" that saved the tree, *Riverdale Press*, 10 July 2008.

3 B. Swett, *New York City of Trees* (New York: Countryman Press, 2013), p. 70.

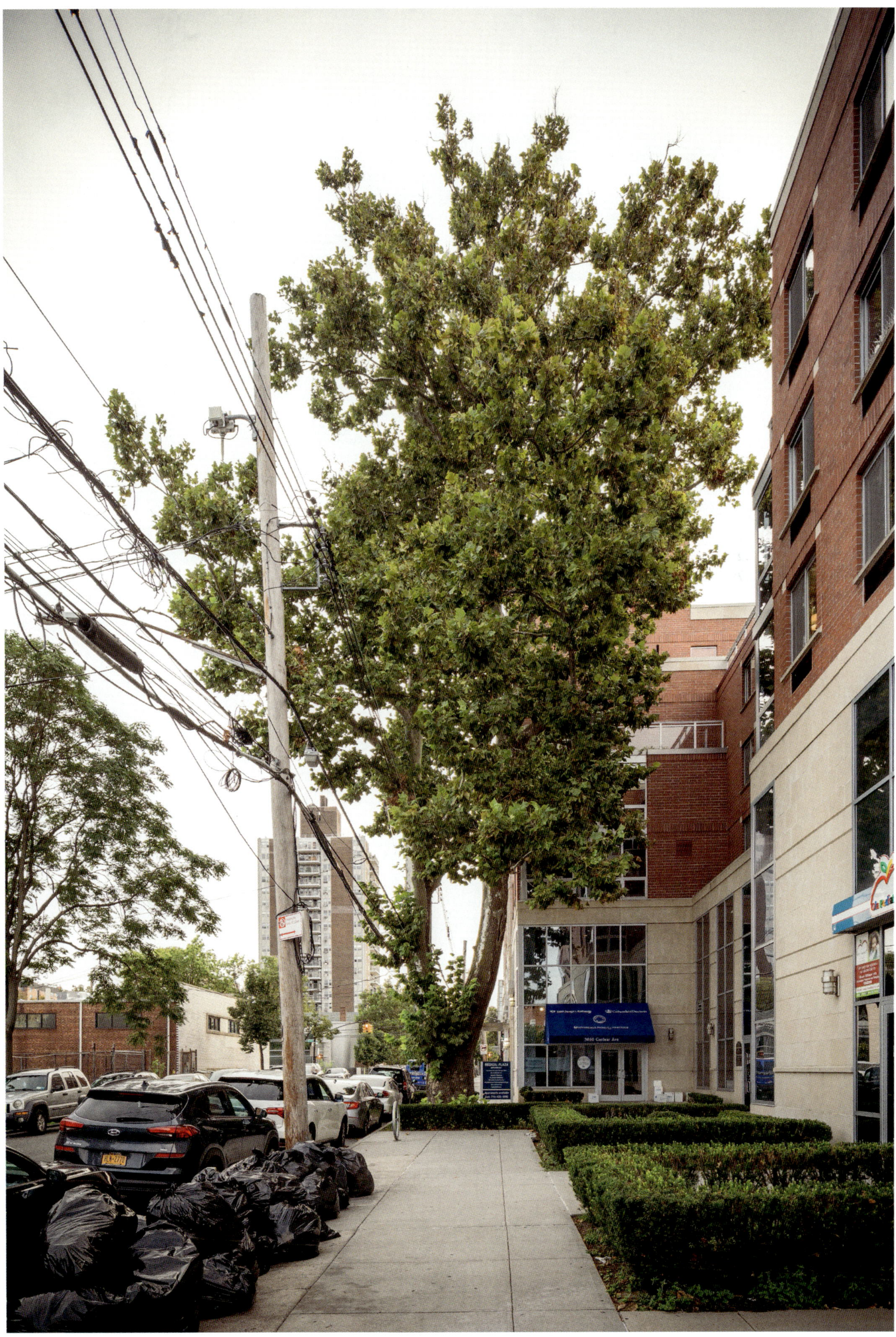

"We've already lost too many trees, houses, and people," said African American activist Hattie Carthan after she witnessed the decrease in trees in Bedford–Stuyvesant in the early 1960s. She sent postcards to everyone on her block, and formed the T&T Vernon Avenue Block Association in 1964 to raise funds to buy and plant new trees and to revitalize a street that had once been completely tree lined, but had slowly yielded to concrete and asphalt. Her tree-planting initiative was supported by both her neighbours and the city, allowing her to form the Neighborhood Tree Corps and the Green Guerrillas to care for the trees and even distribute "seed bombs" to surrounding abandoned plots. Under the umbrella of the Bedford–Stuyvesant Beautification Committee, Carthan eventually presided over 100 block associations, planted more than 1,500 gingko, sycamore, and honey locust trees throughout Bedford–Stuyvesant, and advised the New York City Parks Department on city-wide tree planting programmes.[1] In 1968, when Carthan and her neighbours discovered that their prized, local magnolia tree was threatened by a future development project, they made a collective effort to protect it. The magnolia was shipped from North Carolina in 1885. A rare specimen in the north-east of the USA, it had managed to resist New York frosts and grow to 40 feet in height. Local activist efforts eventually blocked the apartment complex and garage, saving both the magnolia tree and the three brownstones sheltering it. Carthan's perseverance also secured the adjacent houses as the Magnolia Tree Earth Center, the headquarters of a community horticulture non-profit fighting for food justice in the area. Carthan, "The Tree Lady of Brooklyn," managed to have the magnolia tree designated as a living landmark, the only one still standing in the city. In the official declaration, she was acknowledged as "the person who, almost single-handedly, ha[d] been responsible for arousing local appreciation of the tree and in directing this appreciation towards practical steps for its preservation."[2]

1 F. Ferretti, Urban Conservation: A one-woman effort, *New York Times*, 8 July 1982.

2 New York Preservation Archive Project (NYPAP), *Hattie Carthan*, https://www.nypap.org/preservation-history/hattie-carthan (accessed 13 September 2021).

SPECIMEN: Bedford–Stuyvesant magnolia tree (*Magnolia grandiflora*, renamed *Magnolia × brooklynensis* "Hattie Carthan"). Branch, 2018

LOCATION: 677 Lafayette Avenue, Bedford–Stuyvesant, Brooklyn

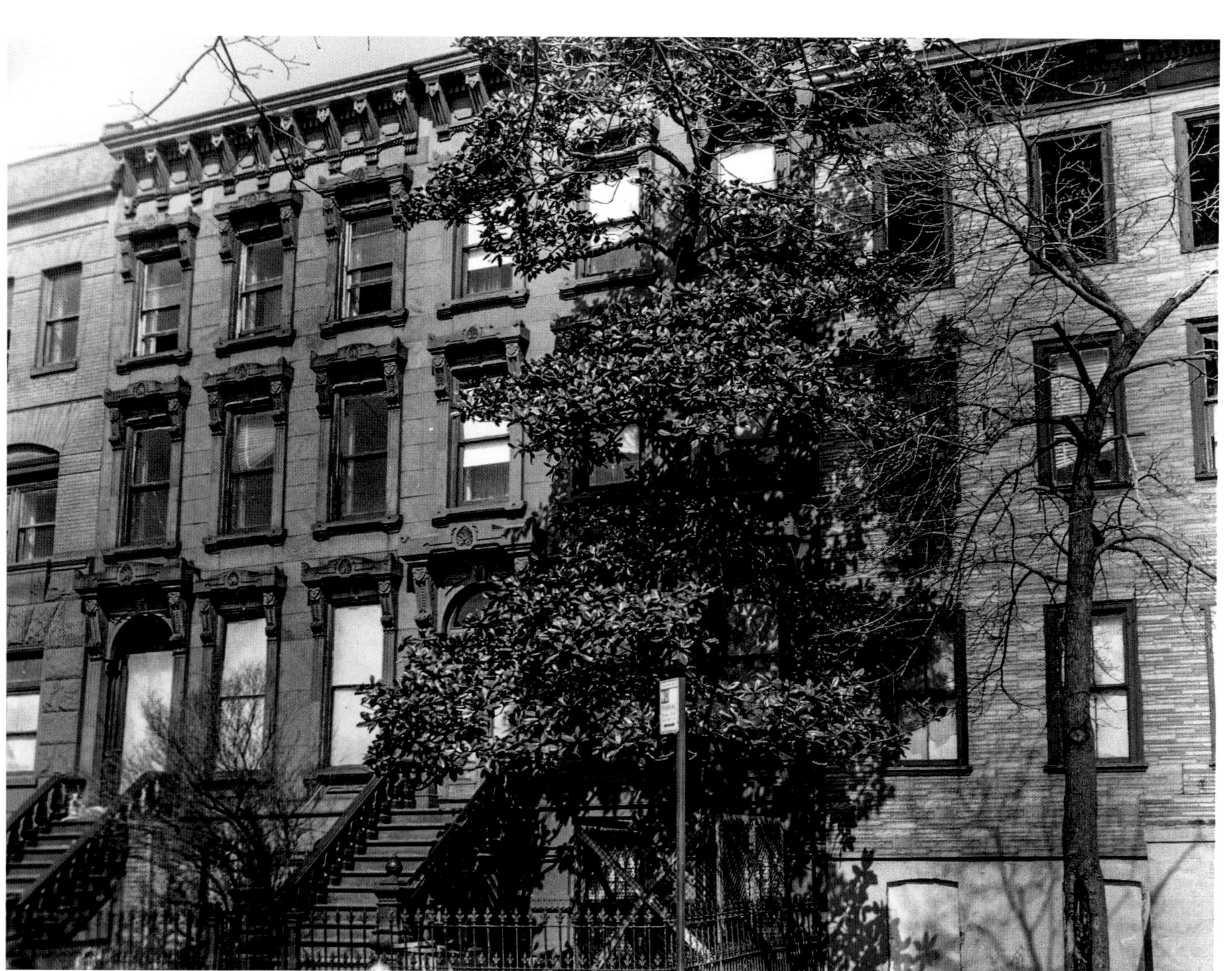

WHITEWASHING GREEN

In *What Are We Going to Do, Michael?* (1973), author Nellie Burchardt portrays the struggle of a young boy, Michael, to save a magnolia tree with the help of his neighbour, Mrs Jacobson. The book is based on the story of activist Hattie Carthan, who campaigned to save a Bedford–Stuyvesant magnolia tree threatened by development in the 1960s (p. 146). Although the neighbourhood was then primarily African American (as was Carthan herself), Burchardt nonetheless depicts the protagonists of her book as white.[1] In doing so, the book failed to recognize the grassroots environmentalism of African American communities, led by figures such as Elsie Richardson and Shirley Chisholm, among others.[2] Perhaps the book was already anticipating the current wave of displacement. Bedford–Stuyvesant, today one of Brooklyn's hottest housing markets, saw a 633 per cent increase in its white population between 2000 and 2010, the biggest population increase of any racial or ethnic group in any New York City neighbourhood.[3] After years of struggle, long-standing community efforts to improve the neighbourhood's streetscape have attracted high-income outsiders, causing property values to skyrocket. Community horticulture initiatives have become victims of their own success, serving as a mechanism for environmental gentrification. But it is rather housing shortages, insecurity, and market deregulation that are uprooting original dwellers from the places where their long-fought for plants and trees stand.

1   S. Dümpelmann, *Seeing Trees: A History of Street Trees in New York City and Berlin* (New Haven, CT: Yale University Press, 2019), pp. 97–98.

2   M. Woodsworth, *Battle for Bed-Stuy: The Long War on Poverty in New York City* (Cambridge, MA: Harvard University Press, 2016), p. 98.

3   K. S. Hymowitz, The Blossoming of Bed-Stuy: Is gentrification racist?, *The Bridge*, 28 June 2017.

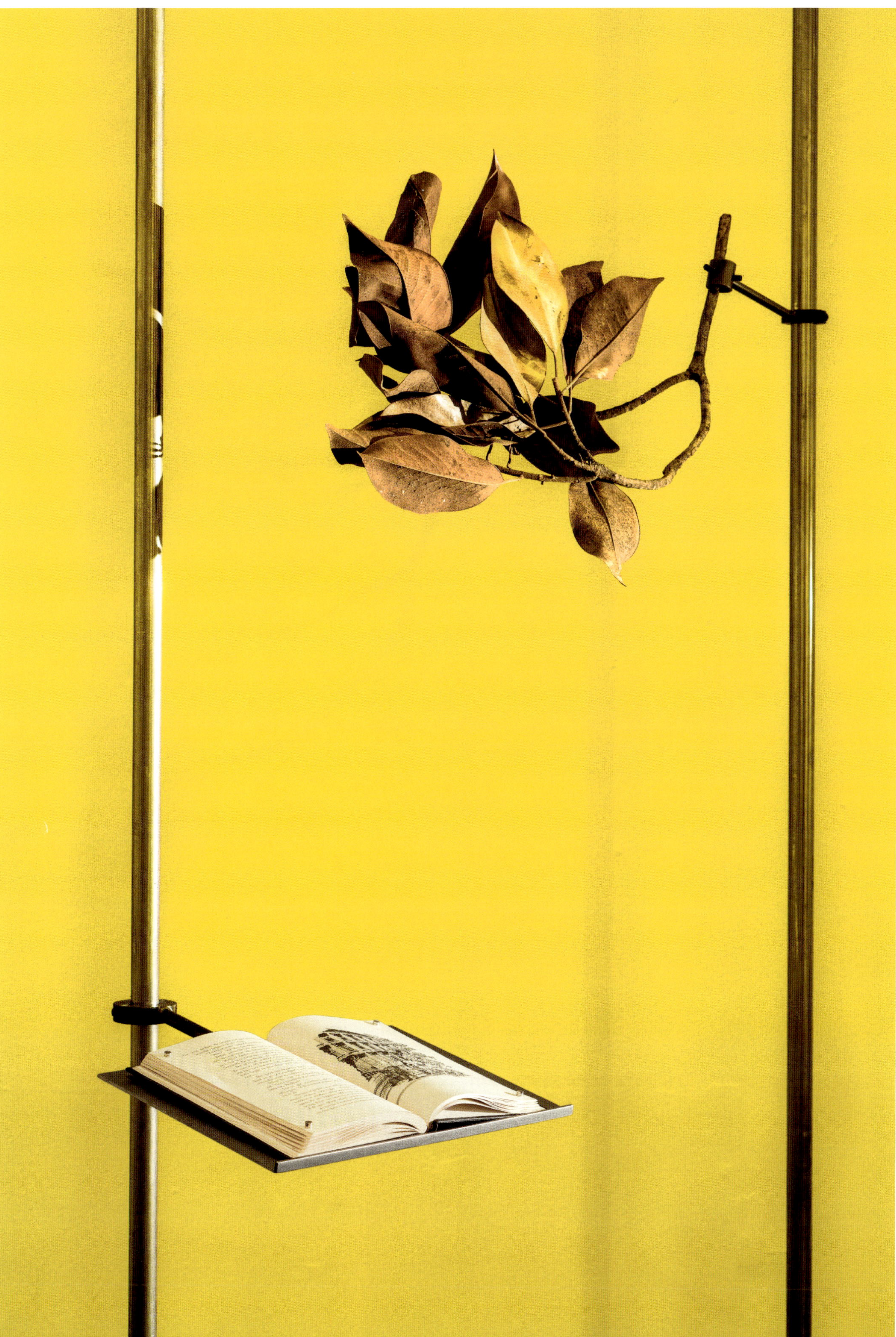

WOMEN'S LEAGUE FOR TREES

In March 1924, seven years before the Rockefeller Center Christmas Tree lighting tradition began, the Women's League for the Protection of Riverside Park (WLPRP) planted a conifer tree to light up on that Christmas Eve. The WLPRP was formed in 1916 in opposition to the West Side Improvement Project, which proposed a new expressway and elevated railroad track (the tracks that are today the site of the High Line). The organization, which at its peak counted 500 members, aimed to add a feminist perspective to the ornamental or economic visions laid out by male planners.[1] The League planted 72 trees in Riverside Park, as well as a memorial tree dedicated to an unknown soldier from each state in the Union, the District of Columbia, Alaska, and Puerto Rico. The arguments put forward by the WLPRP to protect Riverside Park emphasized the benefits for both children's health and real estate property value.[2] The League also created the Bird Sanctuary to record migratory species, and organized school children of public schools Nos 54 and 179 to regularly plant trees in the park. After years of intense negotiations with the city, the WLPRP managed to protect the park, restore the southerly end, provide boating and recreational facilities along the river, remove old shacks along the river front and coal pockets from 96th Street, pave the promenade north of 96th Street, and, more importantly, require the New York Central Railroad Company to cove the train tracks between 72nd and 82nd Streets. In 1938, the WLPRP's main mission was accomplished, and it ceased its activities.

1   New York Historical Society, *Guide to the Women's League for the Protection of Riverside Park Records*, 1916–1938 (Bulk 1916–1931), http://dlib.nyu.edu/findingaids/html/nyhs/womansleague (accessed 13 September 2021).

2   A. L. Buttenwieser, *Manhattan Water-bound: Planning and Developing Manhattan's Waterfront from the Seventeenth Century to the Present* (New York: New York University Press, 1987), p. 131.

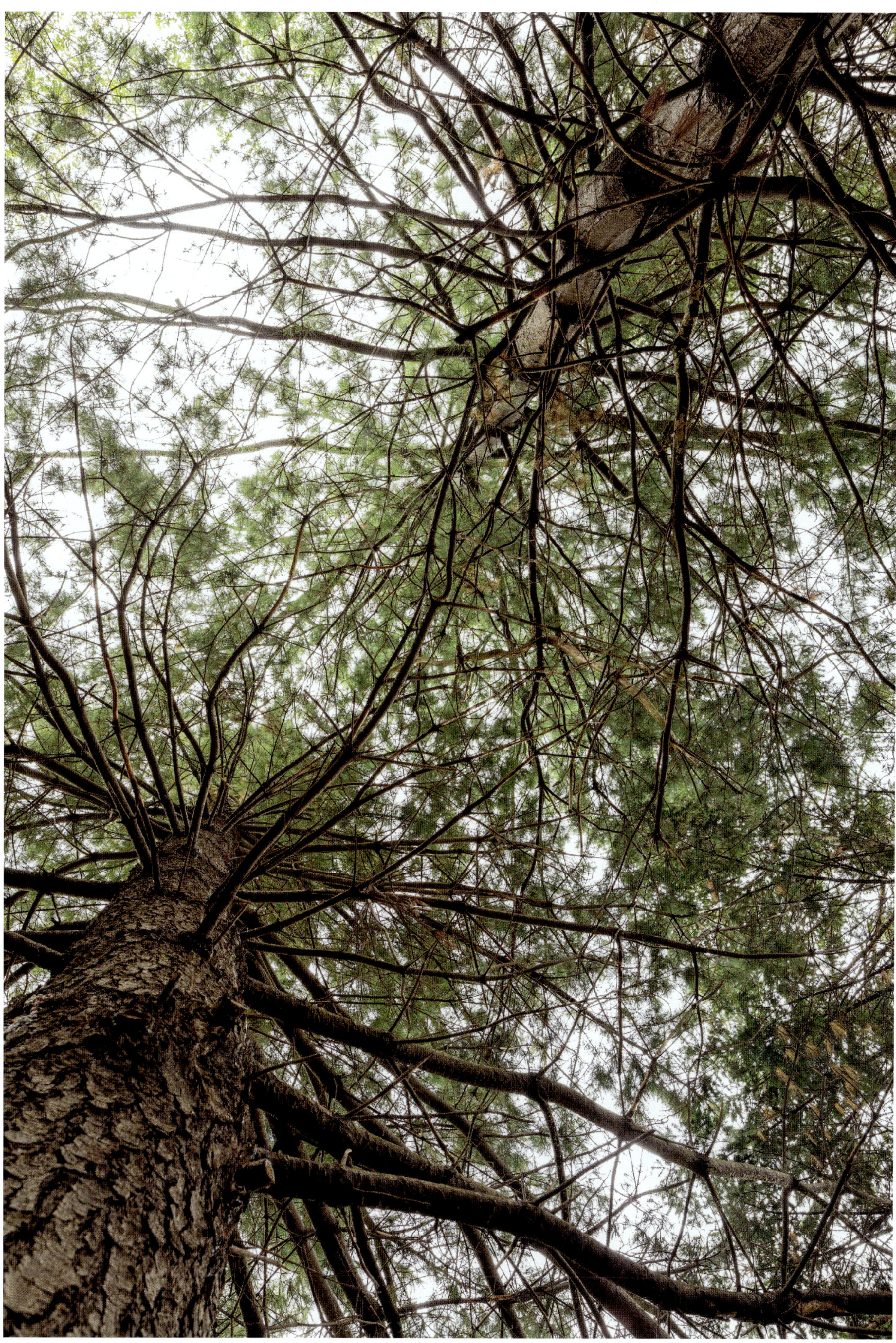

Buen Vivir
in Times of Chaos

Pablo Solón

We cannot speak about Vivir Bien, or Buen Vivir, without looking at context. Buen Vivir is not a list of good practices for all circumstances.[1] As with all systemic alternatives, Buen Vivir has to be rethought in light of new realities. The world has left the period of neoliberal globalization that began in the 1970s and entered a new phase. This phase of systemic crises in a capitalism of chaos probably started with the financial crisis of 2008, and has now manifested itself in all its morbid splendour.[2] Capitalism has never before been through a moment like this. This is neither a temporary disruption of the old normality nor the emergence of a new one. This is the end of all kinds of normality and the beginning of chaos. This is a phase of increasing unpredictability: the convergence of different systemic crises at environmental, economic, social, health, political, institutional, and geopolitical levels. Crisis, polarization, and conflict are already escalating, and will continue to escalate at different levels. Any movement towards new eco-societies will be filled with contradictions.

Time will move fast, faster than ever. Change will be neither gradual nor smooth. In times of chaos, people move from one extreme to the other, and embrace contradictory opinions at the same time. Many old concepts and institutions will disappear, and new categories, relations, and entities will emerge.

In times of chaos, we have to rethink systems, not only as an end goal but also as a pathway toward new societies. In times of chaos, Buen Vivir can help with some pieces of the puzzle—but it itself has to be flexible.

WHAT IS BUEN VIVIR?

In the Andes of South America, this question has many different answers. The most sceptical and critical will tell you that it's just a discourse of neo-populist governments and some left-wing political parties. Others will focus more on the concrete cultural practices of certain indigenous communities. Some will say that Buen Vivir is a set of rules of behaviour, others will describe its cosmovision. The concept of Buen Vivir began to emerge towards the late 20th and early 21st century from ideas centred in the systems of knowledge, practice, and organization of indigenous peoples of the Andes of South America.[3] For our purposes here, perhaps the most vital elements of Buen Vivir are its vision of the whole or the *Pacha*, co-existence in multipolarity, the pursuit of equilibrium, the complementarity of diverse subjects, and decolonization.[4]

The overarching cosmovision of Buen Vivir is most different from other paradigms in its understanding of the whole, or the *Pacha*. The *Pacha* is a holistic world view that encompasses the sky and all of its life-giving elements, such as the sun and the guiding lights of the moon and the stars. The world above is referred to as *Hanaq Pacha*. *Ukhu Pacha* refers to the world below, which is the place where the dead and the spirits live. Then, of course, the rest of *Pacha* includes where we—the humans, animals, trees, and all of nature—reside. The *Pacha* therefore is a whole with different parts, but a whole nonetheless. This holistic perspective, and the idea that all the parts of the whole are interconnected, make up the vision of Buen Vivir: many different elements live together in unity.

Furthermore, in the *Pacha*, nothing is stagnant. Everything is dynamic, in constant motion, evolving and changing, and time and space move as well, although not in a linear way, but rather in a cyclical way. This constant motion in *Pacha* upends the view that past, present, and future move in a fixed, linear direction; rather, *Pacha* views the past, present, and future as happening in a constant cycle. What one does today has consequences. This appreciation of the whole, the implication that consequences can come back in the next cycle, that all is unified in the whole, supports the message and principle that everything one does in the *Pacha* should be done with respect. In this vision, the *Pacha* is the centre—all have life and all are part of the *Pacha*. This is in complete contrast to the anthropocentric view that humans are at the centre, and that all nature, animals, and living beings therefore exist for humans to exploit.

In times of chaos, it is key to look at the whole, at all the aspects of the systemic crises; it is necessary to focus not only on the economic, environmental, political, social, or some other particular aspect of the crisis, but also to always try to see the entirety of the complex problem we are facing. It is impossible to face and overcome unpredictable situations if we look at only a few aspects of reality. For example, to address the climate crisis we need to look at the root political causes. We must see and act in local realities with respect to their national and global contexts. Chaotic situations can push people to try to isolate themselves or escape from complex reality. But the only way out of the hole is to never forget to see the whole. This is the element of Buen Vivir that most differentiates the ecofeminist, degrowth, or the commons perspectives.

Another core element of Buen Vivir is the principle of multipolarity. As commonly understood, polar opposites cannot co-exist. However, in Buen Vivir, multipolarity is essential. There would be no good if there was no bad. One would not experience happiness if one had not experienced sadness. Yes, they are opposites and contradict, but they also deepen our understanding of the one and the other. In Buen Vivir, the attitude towards this is to appreciate the existence of multipolarity, to learn more about the relationships between opposing things and, more importantly, to learn to be tolerant and accepting of differences and to co-exist in this multipolar world.

In times of chaos, we have to learn to deal with different contradictions at the same time. We cannot wait (or pretend to wait) to deal with productivism or patriarchy only after we have overcome capitalism. All are interrelated. Some feel that we must hide contradictions on the left or in social movements in order to first deal with imperialism. This is against the logic of Buen Vivir. You cannot address some contradictions and ignore others. We must see the new contradictions that are constantly emerging. The only way to address these contradictions is to find new ways of interrelating and co-existing.

Complementing the idea of accepting multipolarity is another critical pillar of Buen Vivir: dynamic equilibrium. Simply put, this is the ever-shifting balance that keeps all the different contradictory parts of the whole in harmony. It recognizes that change is constant, and that movements grow by being flexible and open to improvement, and by changing strategies in the face of new challenges and realities. Tensions and changes may destabilize this equilibrium, but then the search for a new balance starts. Buen Vivir is a constant pursuit for respect for all elements of the *Pacha*, and seeks a balance between humans, nature, and the whole—so as not to go beyond the limits of the planet and for the *Pacha* and its cycles to persist for generations to come.

All these characteristics of Buen Vivir are directly in contradiction to the logic of capitalism. Capitalism needs to keep growing, to keep making profit, to keep acquiring; it is an endless quest for profit. Capitalism may have had advantages in relation to feudalism, but in the current systemic crises it only aggravates the speed towards collapse because it doesn't care about humans or nature.

What must we seek in times of chaos? Balance between the different contradictions. Not all paths bring balance. The false solution of carbon markets and offsets will not balance the economy and the environment, but rather create a new kind of commodification at a new

scale of nature. Capital will flow to markets while there is profit to make and, once the opportunity is over, capitalists will move on to the next business, leaving nature exposed and fully vulnerable. If people only take care of trees because they receive payments for environmental services, then the future of both trees and humanity is doomed. To seek balance with nature we have to recuperate our ancient ways of relating to nature, we have to care for trees because they are trees and we are part of them.

To seek harmony in times of chaos is a very difficult task. Unpredictability is everywhere. Old categories and recipes will not always work as before. For example, democracy has to be reinvented in order to allow participation from nature. It's not enough to defend and recover democracy from an extreme right-wing government that burns the Amazon. We need to transform that democracy in order to save the Amazon. We need to build a democracy of the whole and overcome the current anthropocentric democracy. The challenge is huge. We all want some kind of stability to follow an accomplishment, but in times of chaos, dynamic equilibrium will be more dynamic and complex than ever.

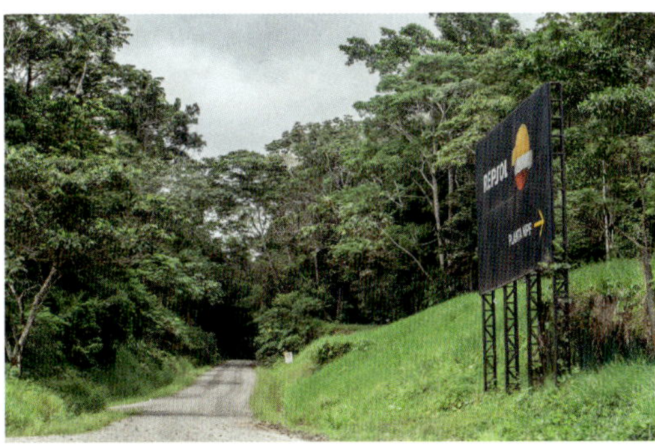

Fig. 1 The oil pumping station within Yasuní National Park

Complementarity is essential to harmony. Not all beings are the same, and that diversity is to be respected. Complementarity seeks to highlight strengths, skills, and talents and, at the same time, find different ways of expressing or manifesting these strengths, skills, and talents. When these tensions come together, we can better learn from one another, produce a harmonious balance, and, again, co-exist, appreciating and contributing to the balance and equilibrium. Capitalism is characterized by competition, not complementarity. The goal is to see who can produce better, faster, more efficiently, and, especially, for the highest profit. The goal of complementarity is to see how we can together find a balance that benefits all parts of the whole.

To seek complementarity in times of chaos is the only way to deal with growing contradictions at all levels: among individuals, communities, cities, rural areas, ecosystems, countries, and continents. Complementarity doesn't mean reciprocal or even relations for all because we are not all on a level playing field. Complementarity means degrowth for some so that others can grow sustainably.

Complementarity takes into account the differences and diversity that exist among all the beings of the whole. Complementarity cannot be achieved by using only one scale or parameter of exchange. Before the arrival of the Spanish, indigenous communities of the Andes found equilibrium through "vertical control of a maximum of ecological levels," which meant that communities cultivated crops in the highlands, in the valleys, and in the *yungas.*[5] The way to deal with climate uncertainty is not to put all the oranges in one basket, but to diversify as much as possible—different crops in different climates. In times of climate chaos, we have to learn from our roots.

A crucial context for Buen Vivir is the hundreds of years of colonization that occurred in the Americas and elsewhere, ostensibly in the search for spices and new land. But it is clear that the conquistadors were mainly interested in extracting precious resources, from gold to silver to other natural resources. In many places that process of colonization was violent; blood was spilled, entire communities were decimated. Furthermore, it was not

We especially need to decolonize ourselves, from old concepts and ideas that lie at the centre of systemic crises. Without decolonizing ourselves we will not be able to deal with structural problems such as inequality, justice, and environmental collapse. Fear and individualism are promoted by the most powerful sectors of society. What we see in this phase of capitalism is a new process of colonization at different levels. The idea of "protecting the economy" is used to justify everything, from violent conflicts, wars, and bunker states/villages to deeper processes of exploitation of humans and nature. Decolonization also has a critical role to play in these crises. It asks every one of us to let go of preconceived notions, unlearn the history written by colonizers, and, most importantly, let our mind, heart, and spirit be free of all the ingrained mantras declaring that capitalism and neoliberalism are the only way, the correct way. Be free of this and you will be able to think new things, be open to new proposals, and let your imagination run wild.

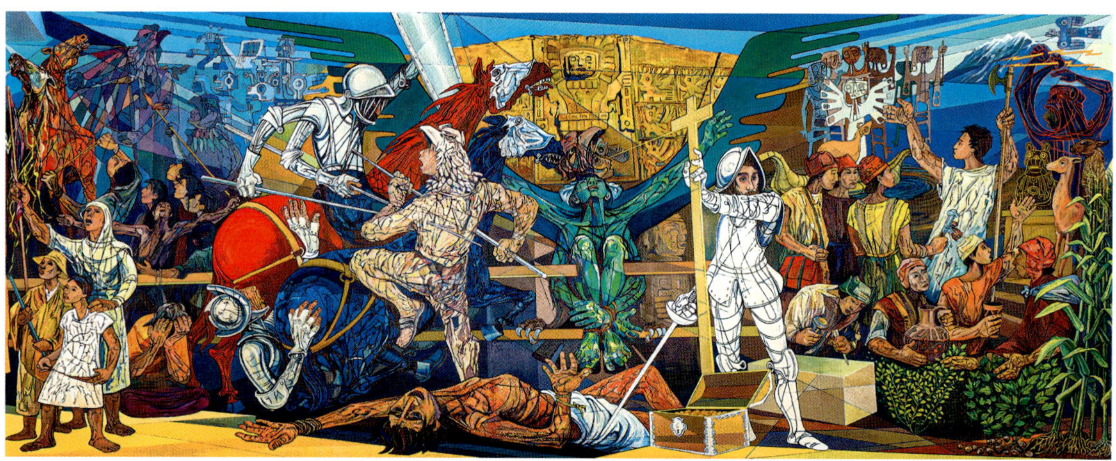

Fig. 2 Mural fragment *Retrato de un Pueblo* by Walter Solón at Universidad Mayor de San Andrés, Bolivia, 1989

enough for the colonizers to take resources and enslave people. Colonization also aimed to control the peoples and places that had been conquered by imposing the language and culture of the colonizers, effectively decimating ancient cultures, languages, rituals, ceremonies, and so many other ancient and rich cultural traditions. Understanding the deep scars left in the hearts of the people helps one understand why decolonization is essential for Buen Vivir. Decolonizing is difficult, it is slow. There is not one thing you can just remove: colonization has rooted itself and ingrained itself deeply in people and communities. It has also ingrained itself in the economy and in spiritual beliefs. The challenge is great, but it is necessary. The peoples may be "free," but their hearts and minds still need to be decolonized. This fight for decolonization is a campaign to reclaim what was once lost and destroyed—peoples' languages, cultures, and, most importantly, economic and political sovereignty.

This decolonization of ourselves is a crucial step for finding linkages and complementarities. And the process of bringing together proposals for systemic alternatives with a freed mindset encourages all of us to find ways to concretize our plans for changing the system. Decolonization, degrowth, ecofeminism, the commons, deglobalization, food sovereignty, and many others are not just fantasies for a utopia, they are a treasure trove of ideas and proposals. But they are not meant to be stagnant: the whole point of trying to bring together these different movements is to create a dynamic where new ideas and proposals continue to be welcome.

As they say, crisis is the mother of all opportunities, and this current crisis of capitalism and neoliberalism is a prime moment for raising awareness of the movements that have made these proposals for systemic alternatives and are helping to make them a reality—a concrete, tangible reality. Do not let the capitalists and bankers go back to business as if the pandemic has not affected millions; from the deaths to the loss of jobs to the loss of homes, there is too much suffering to list. The only way out of these multiple crises is to put forward systemic alternatives and add your own proposals, whether big or small. Small things make ripples that can turn into waves of change.

THE PARADOX OF BUEN VIVIR IN BOLIVIA AND ECUADOR[6]

In a move that was applauded by many, Vivir Bien and Buen Vivir were included in the new constitutions of Ecuador (2008) and Bolivia (2009), respectively. There were slight differences in the way the cosmovision was reflected in each constitution; Ecuador focused on rights while Bolivia focused on the ethics of the paradigm. This achievement was hailed around the world by movements and people who believed in the possibility of changing the system and implementing alternatives such as Vivir Bien.

if the state promotes extractivist policies that destroy forests? And so, as Bolivia had not only continued to extract oil but was also highly dependent on it, the country went into economic crisis when the price of oil collapsed in 2014. Today, both Bolivia and Ecuador are in a deep economic crisis, worsened by the pandemic and their dependence on extractivist principles.

The search for equilibrium between different sectors of the economy and society cannot be achieved without attacking the structural causes of inequality. Redistribution cannot be limited to the reassignment of a fraction of the revenue that is apportioned to economically more powerful sectors. The search for equality between human beings cannot be reduced to welfare programmes while the big landlords, extractive enterprises, and bankers continue to accumulate substantial profits. Buen Vivir is so relevant in times of chaos because it seeks to generate greater resilience in local and national economies facing the ups and downs of the global economy. It is not a question of abandoning exports but rather of

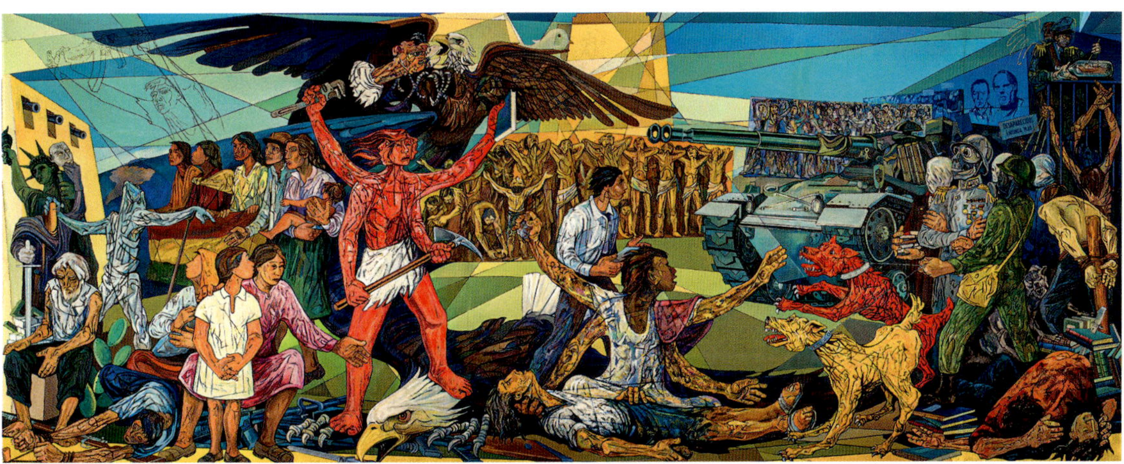

Fig. 3 Mural fragment *Retrato de un Pueblo* by Walter Solón at Universidad Mayor de San Andrés, Bolivia, 1989

However, reality is harsh. Without denying the importance and the major difficulties involved in the drafting and approval of these constitutions, it is obvious that, in their incorporation, Vivir Bien and Buen Vivir lost much of their substance. They were transformed more into symbolic terms for the recognition of Andean indigenous peoples than as points of inflection for the capitalist developmentalist model.

The governments of Rafael Correa and Evo Morales, riding high on enthusiastic support in their countries and abroad, used Buen Vivir as a battle cry. However, when Correa and Morales began to worship economic indicators such as GDP, poverty reduction, international monetary reserves, public investment, infrastructure, and more, this was a sign of things to come. You cannot approach Buen Vivir through economic indicators. Buen Vivir moves beyond old economic policies of extractivism. How can there be harmony with humans and nature

ensuring that the economy does not revolve around the export of a handful of products. The goal is to be more sovereign, strengthening the local human communities and ecosystems of Earth.

Bolivia's pathway to Buen Vivir is linked to agro-ecology, agro-forestry, and food sovereignty in its indigenous communities. Bolivia does not need transgenics, and does not need to feed its population with agro-toxins and glyphosates. It is much better for the planet to be growing local, eating local, and promoting local and community production. The role of the state should not be to create "communitarian" enterprises from above but to empower the networks of production, exchange, credit, traditional knowledge, and innovation at the local level, with the active participation of local actors. Placing local and community production at the centre does not mean abandoning or setting aside state enterprises and public services, which, by their very nature, can best be managed and provided at the state and national level—such as banking, or essential public services like education, healthcare, energy, and telecommunications that benefit from a wider scope. However, such state undertakings and public services should be accompanied by effective mechanisms for citizen participation in order to avoid their bureaucratization and corruption, and to adapt them to the realities of each region.

When it comes to harmony with nature there is a huge chasm in Ecuador and Bolivia between discourse and reality, between law and practice. In the last decade, Bolivia has not shown any real-life examples of respecting the rights of Mother Earth. Provisions like the Mother Earth Ombudsman should be implemented in practice. In Ecuador, the great disappointment was the case of Yasuni. The proposal to leave the oil under Yasuni National Park was a breaking point for the capitalist way of relating to nature. It was a bold move to protect the rainforest and the ancestral homelands of the indigenous peoples. Fast forward to the present, and we see that progress has been in the opposite direction. When developed countries refused to pay the US$3.6 billion in 13 years that Correa demanded in exchange for keeping the oil in the ground, the exploration by extractivist industries began in Yasuni. In 2013, Correa declared the end of the Yasuni protection initiative, with no space for citizens to object. Yasuni is now open to petroleum exploration.

This case shows that the protection of nature cannot be linked to some kind of market mechanism. If rainforests have rights—Ecuador has recognized the rights of nature in its constitution—you cannot guarantee those rights only when there is some kind of monetary payment. The preservation of nature cannot be a bargaining condition. Nature must be protected unconditionally. If there are developed countries or international institutions that support that decision, that is something to encourage, but you cannot violate the rights of nature if there is no money in return.

If we look at Bolivia, where the process of change has been driven from the beginning by influential indigenous communities and social organizations, we can say that, after more than a decade of "progressive" social movements, indigenous communities have been weakened. What happened was something of a paradox. The indigenous communities and social organizations had the power to demand material goods, infrastructure, credits, conditional cash transfers, and services, but the receipt of those goods generated a clientelist logic of patronage. However, after 14 years—since Evo Morales left the government in 2019—indigenous and peasant organizations began to regain autonomy because there is less government control over their social organizations.

The secret of Buen Vivir lies in the strengthening of the community, in boosting its capacity for complementarity with other communities, and in the self-management of its territory. The constitutional recognition of Buen Vivir created the illusion that this could be implemented through a national state-based "development" plan. But the state should not be an organizer and planner of Buen Vivir for society as a whole; instead, it should contribute to the empowerment of the communities and social organizations. More than providing communities and social organizations with material goods, it is necessary to encourage the self-management of territory and to carry out initiatives without waiting for a green light from the state. The experience of "progressive" governments in Ecuador and Bolivia shows that taking power must be paired with emancipation and self-determination from below. Even with such "progressive" governments, persistent colonial structures must be questioned and subverted.

Buen Vivir cannot flourish in a global economy that is capitalist, productivist, extractivist, patriarchal, and anthropocentric. If Buen Vivir is to advance and thrive, other similar processes in other countries must arise to complement it. Buen Vivir must spread to the centres of global power to change the balance of forces. Further integration with decolonization is crucial and cannot be limited to the promotion of agreements between states and governments. Multilateralism has to include civil society as a key actor, not as a three-minute speaker in some global forum. If we want to save the Amazon, we need to go beyond the national borders that obstruct the management of this eco-region that is fundamental to life on the planet. Buen Vivir at first didn't recognize internationalism as one of its components, but now it is abundantly clear that a global scale is essential for its real and plentiful implementation.

1   In this text, we will refer to both Buen Vivir (Ecuador) and Vivir Bien (Bolivia) as Buen Vivir.

2   X. R. Lanata and P. Solón, *¿Acabará el coronavirus con el capitalismo?*, 2020, https://systemicalternatives.org/2020/04/02/reflexiones-sistemicas-acabara-el-coronavirus-con-el-capitalismo (accessed 13 September 2021).

3   More specifically, Buen Vivir developed from the Aymara *suma qamaña* and the Quechua *sumaq kawsay*, which have a more complex set of meanings such as "plentiful life," "sweet life," "harmonious life," "sublime life," "inclusive life," or "to know how to live."

4   P. Solón, Vivir Bien, in *Alternativas Sistémicas* (La Paz: Ediciones Alternativas Sistémicas, 2015), pp. 17–27.

5   J. V. Murra, *Formaciones políticas y económicas del mundo andino* (Lima: Instituto de Estudios Peruanos, 1972), p. 59.

6   P. Solón, *¿Es posible el Vivir Bien?* (La Paz: Ediciones Fundación Solón, 2015).

ROOT AND BRANCH

Close to what was once a Lenape encampment known as Sapokani-can, Washington Square Park and its approximate 270 trees have gone through multiple cycles of appreciation and depreciation over the past 300 years. The formerly enslaved Paolo Dangola, the first non-indigenous settler of what would become Greenwich Village, started a settlement there in 1645, as a buffer zone between the Lenape and the Dutch.[1] With the advent of English rule, the farms along Minetta Creek (now covered over) were expropriated to become summer residences for the new British elite.[2] Over the 18th century, land was subdivided into smaller plots, sometimes bought and sold from afar by heirs living in Britain. After an outbreak of yellow fever in 1797, New York City bought one of these portions for US$4,500, and turned it into a potter's field—a public cemetery for those who could not afford burial—for 600 souls, although it contained 20,000 at its peak, to the dismay of neighbouring wealthy residents. The square we see today was built in 1826. A little over a century later, in the mid-1950s, the community organization Save the West Village, co-chaired by Jane Jacobs, rallied against Robert Moses' plans to build the LOMEX expressway through SoHo, Little Italy, and Washington Square Park. Together with other women activists, including Shirley Hayes and Edith Lyons, Jacobs spearheaded the battle against urban renewal (i.e. slum clearance) in Greenwich Village, and successfully fought to preserve the area for pedestrians. Jacobs criticized the white male planners' definition of a post-war city—self-contained neighbourhoods, super-blocks, rigid plans, and endless acres of grass—as patronizing; she found these views detrimental to the human experience, and argued that value could be found in the widely diverse income, occupational, and cultural groups who were deeply attached to the park.[3] While the expressway was never built, more than 50 years later cars in the area are still a hotly contested issue, not only in light of ongoing air pollution and respiratory health problems. The Covid-19 pandemic has persuaded officials to turn more and more street parking spots into outdoor dining and sitting areas through the city's open restaurants and open streets programmes, first as a temporary measure but now made permanent year-round. The increase in pedestrianization, and the social acceptance of car-free streets, is such that persistent calls for a 25 per cent reduction in car-designated areas by 2025 is no longer unimaginable.

1   A. Osinulu, Re-Conceptualizing New York as an African City, *NYU*, 19 April 2019.

2   E. Kies Folpe, *It Happened on Washington Square* (Baltimore, OH: John Hopkins University Press, 2002), p. 52.

3   J. Jacobs, *The Death and Life of Great American Cities* (New York: Random House, 1961).

LOCATION: Washington Square Park, Manhattan

SPECIMEN: Pin oak (*Quercus palustris*). Branch, 2018

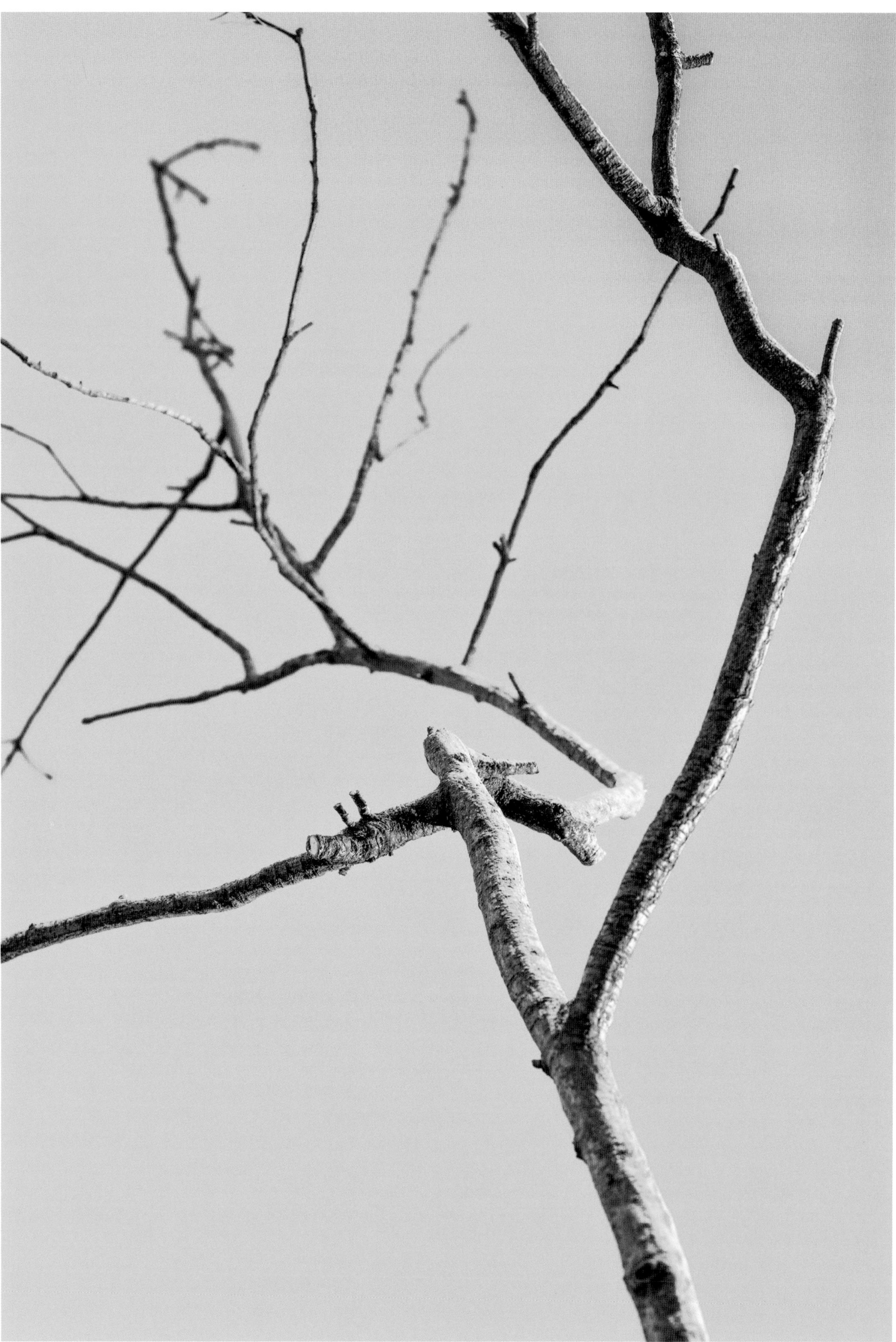

FROM POLLUTION TO DISPLACEMENT

In Sunset Park, numerous factories, a waste treatment plant, contaminated brownfields along the waterfront, and the heavily trafficked Gowanus Expressway are some of the major pollution sources.[1] The United Puerto Rican Organization of Sunset Park (UPROSE), the oldest Latinx grassroots organization in Brooklyn, has been fighting the concentration of polluting facilities in the neighbourhood, which has had a very large ethnic minority population for the last 50 years. This is environmental racism, whereby people of colour are subjected to a disproportionately large number of health and environmental risks in their communities.[2] Alongside some of the highest asthma hospitalization rates in the country, complaints about other respiratory diseases and cancer are ongoing. It is just "too expensive" for the environmental damage in the area to be mitigated. In the meantime, people keep breathing and absorbing volatile, hazardous waste. As well as opposing new waves of waterfront development, fighting to retain jobs in the neighbourhood, and working to keep housing affordable, UPROSE has also challenged the top-down improvement of the area as part of a *displacement economy* based on green gentrification: when underserved neighbourhoods manage to banish pollution, housing prices go up, forcing out long-term residents. The process exacerbates health inequality by ensuring that tenants paying the highest rents have the easiest access to clean air and vibrant public parks. Worse, the most economically disadvantaged groups are sometimes even blamed for "choosing" to live next to toxic sites, where housing is more "affordable."[3] According to Elizabeth Yeampierre, Executive Director of UPROSE and member of the NYC Environmental Justice Alliance, while activists in the environmental justice movement used to organize around pollution, they now primarily focus on housing and displacement.[4] After decades of grassroot struggle, the rapid conversion of brownfields into greenfields often leaves out those who have most suffered from and fought against pollution.

1   J. Sze, *Noxious New York: The Racial Politics of Urban Health and Environmental Justice* (Cambridge, MA: MIT Press, 2007), p. 88.

2   R. Bullard, *Confronting Environmental Racism: Voices from the Grassroots* (Boston, MA: South End Press, 1993), pp. 10–11.

3   L. W. Cole and S R. Foster, *From the Ground Up: Environmental Racism and the Rise of the Environmental Justice Movement* (New York: New York University Press, 2001), pp. 60–61.

4   J. Deaton, The curse of green gentrification, *Cleantechnica*, 25 January 2018, https://nexusmedianews.com/the-curse-of-green-gentrification-936c9b8bf2c3 (accessed 13 September 2021).

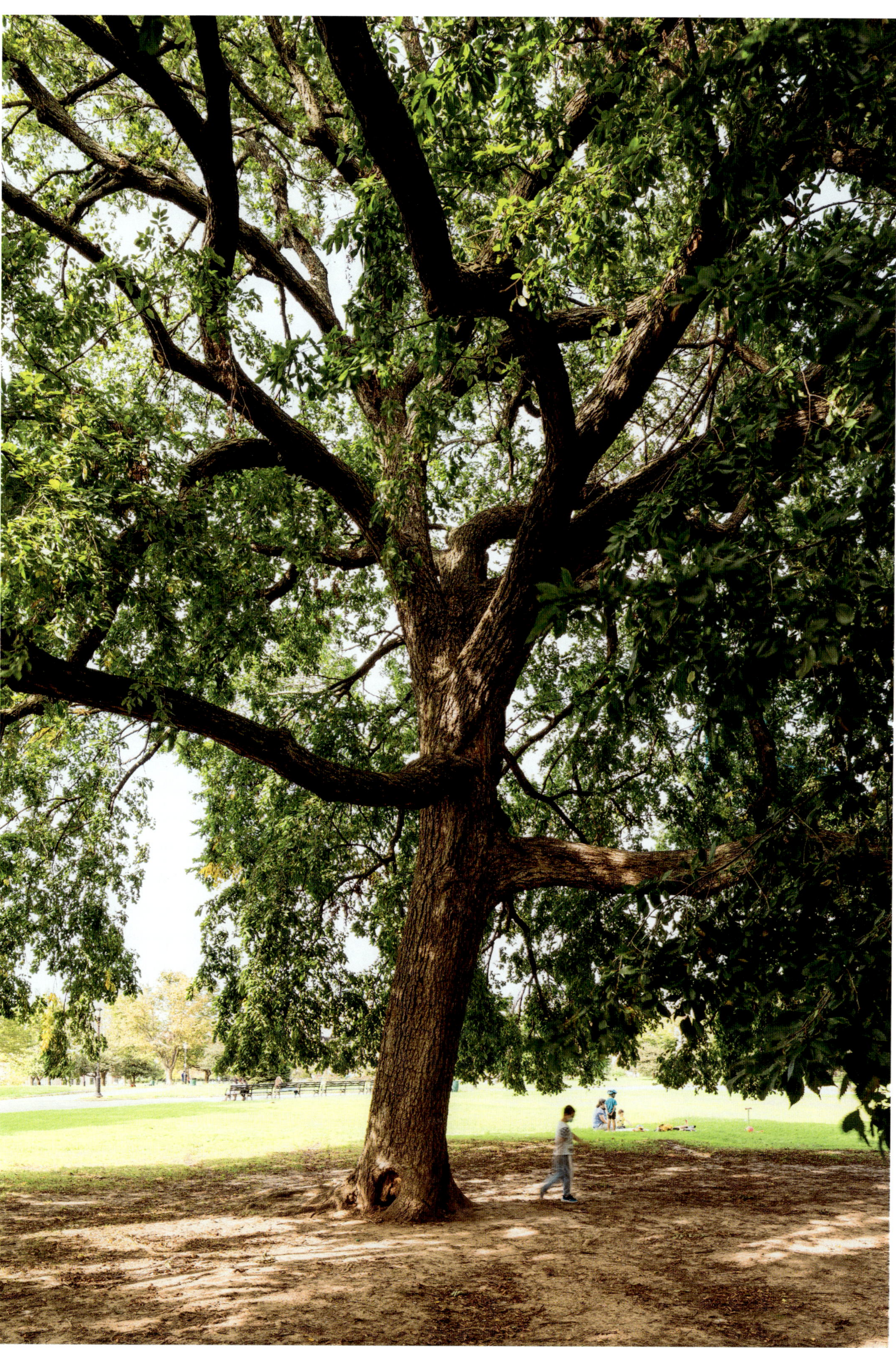

A poem saved the Camperdown Elm in Prospect Park. The tree, which cannot self-reproduce and requires outside assistance in the form of grafting, was first created in the 1830s by the Earl of Camperdown in Dundee, Scotland, when he grafted a mutant branch of a Scots elm onto a typical Scots elm. The resulting Camperdown Elm, from which all trees in this species come, was notably unaffected by widespread Dutch elm disease. One was donated to Prospect Park in 1872, where it suffered years of neglect. A hole in its trunk was patched with concrete, following early 20th-century tree surgery methods. Learning that the tree was in ill health, Pulitzer-winning author Marianne Moore published a poem in the 23 September 1967 issue of *The New Yorker* entitled "The Camperdown Elm." It was Moore's eco-activist poetry that brought financial assistance to this ailing ornamental tree. She later wrote similar poems to help save the Bedford–Stuyvesant magnolia tree (p. 146) and to oppose the felling of trees to make room for police stables in Central Park (the stables were never built).[1] Other poets have also made similar attempts; William Cullen Bryant lobbied for Central Park and Walt Whitman for Fort Greene Park. But, by the time Moore saved the tree, the reputation of the park had begun to deteriorate.[2] Dreamed up to attract the wealthy to Brooklyn in the 1850s, the park went through different periods of glory and decay. By the mid-1970s, Prospect Park was seen by many as a dangerous place to be avoided.[3] It took US$10 million from the city to begin restoration in the 1980s. However, ecological and *social* renewal came hand in hand, making its "real estate borders" grow southward and westward since the 2000s, pricing many existing tenants out of access to these environmental amenities.[4] Even if Prospect Park's Camperdown Elm continues to benefit from the fund established in Moore's will, the question remains whether the elm and its companion trees are equally shared.

1 K. Olson, Marianne Moore's The Camperdown Elm and the revival of Brooklyn's Prospect Park, *Journal of Ecocriticism*, 3(2) (2011): 19.

2 K. Gould and T. Lewis, The environmental injustice of green gentrification: The case of Brooklyn's Prospect Park, *The World in Brooklyn*, 2012: 113–146.

3 D. P. Colley, *Prospect Park: Olmsted & Vaux's Brooklyn Masterpiece* (New York: Princeton Architectural Press, 2013).

4 Colley, *Prospect Park*.

LOCATION: Prospect Park, Brooklyn

SPECIMEN: Camperdown Elm (*Ulmus glabra* "Camperdownii"), Branch, 2018

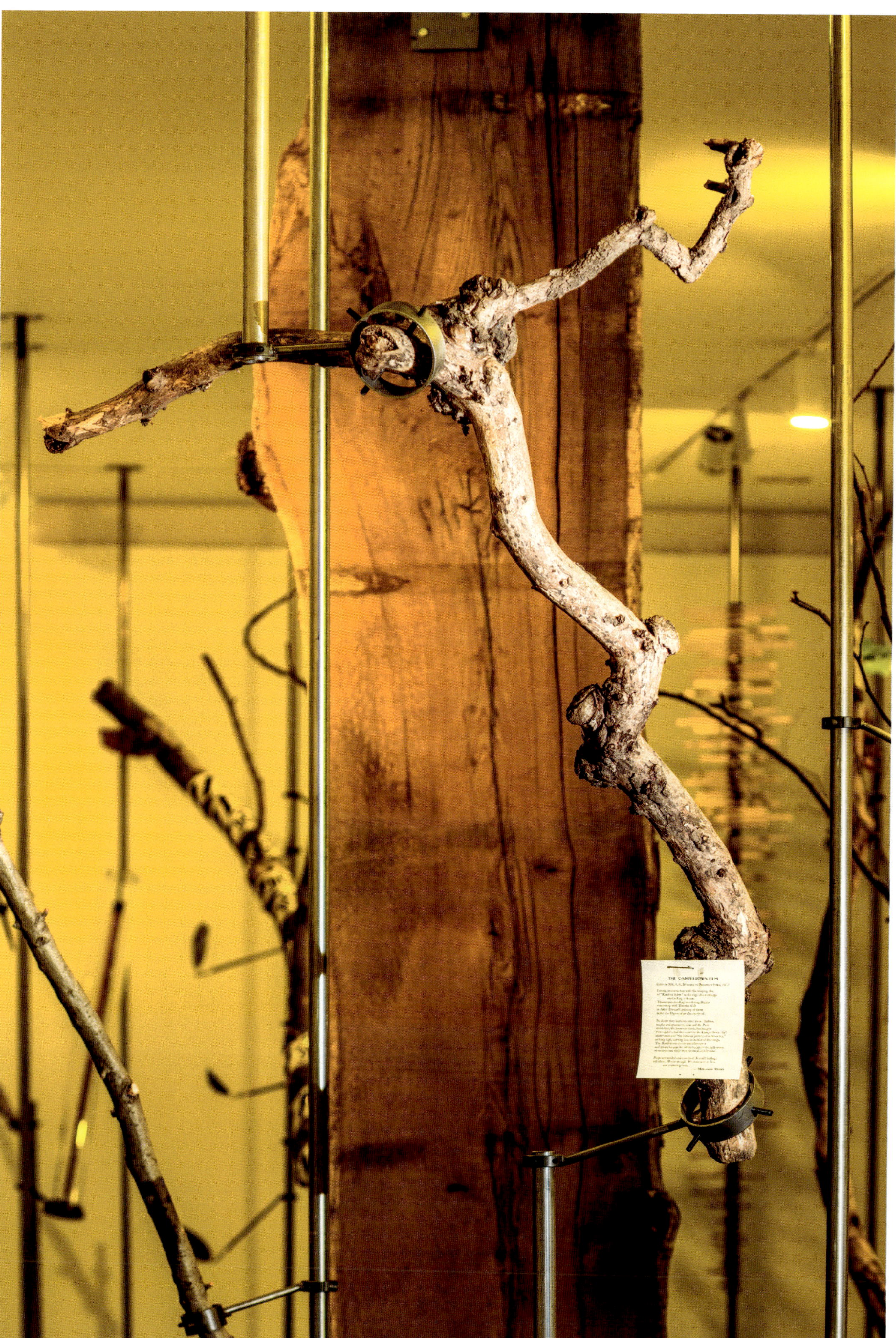
THE CAMPERDOWN ELM

Towards Legal Naturehood

Mari Margil

How do we protect trees in a new way within the city? How do we recognize legal rights of trees within the city of New York? My organization—the Center for Democratic and Environmental Rights (CDER)—has been working with communities across the USA, as well as abroad, to advance a new legal framework for how we protect nature under the law.

Today, we think of nature as a commodity, as an object as opposed to a subject. Nature, under most systems of law around the world, is treated as property or an item of commerce, which means that nature doesn't have standing within the law—for example, if you want to defend the rights of a river, you can't because there are no rights to defend.

Environmental laws permit us to conduct practices that bring known environmental harms. That is why environmental laws have legalized fracking, mountain-top-removal mining, factory farming; practices that bring known environmental harms, that are inherently unsustainable, yet are cloaked within this idea of being environmentally regulated. Therefore, we tend to think it must be okay.

Increasingly, we at the CDER are working with people in groups, civil society, and even governments that are coming to a recognition that after the past 50 years of major environmental laws (in the USA and around the world)—such as the US federal Clean Air Act and the federal Clean Water Act (laws which have been exported to other countries)—things are worse now by almost every leading indicator on the environment.

And we do not have to look too far to see it. We are seeing ecosystems collapse. One of the most noteworthy has been coral reefs, like the Great Barrier Reef off the coast of Queensland, Australia, which are experiencing bleaching and die off. These are ecosystems that provide habitat for millions of species, and they are dying at the hands of humans. We are seeing species extinction occurring today at more than 1,000 times the natural background rates. And, of course, climate change, which is far more accelerated than even the most optimistic scientific models predicted. Today we are in a place of environmental crisis, and yet we're sitting on top of thousands and thousands of pages of environmental laws. People and communities, indigenous tribal nations that we work with, and others are saying, "What went wrong here?" And what went wrong here is that our relationship with the natural world is very much one of commodification.

Environmental laws, therefore, regulate how we can use the natural world as quickly and as fast as possible to build economic power and build economic wealth to support endless growth and development. That is what environmental laws have largely been designed to do.

Once we came to understand that if we continue to work under existing traditional conventional environmental laws we're not going to be able to protect the environment, our work shifted. Today, our work is focused on making a fundamental shift in humankind's relationship with the natural world. That doesn't just mean that we try to recycle more, or we buy hybrid cars, or change out our lightbulbs. Those are all good things, but they don't address the systemic problem that we face, which is that we treat nature as an other. And we're not going to change that unless we make systemic change that's translated into law making; policymaking, which transforms literally how nature is treated under the law, from being rightless property to being rights-bearing, recognized as living entities with legal rights. What we call "rights of nature laws."

In both the USA and the UK, as well as elsewhere, there's a long history of people's movements which have transformed that which is treated as property under the law to become rights-bearing. If we think about the abolitionist movement in the UK, and in the USA, slaves were treated as property under the law. The US Constitution supported that—there were slave codes which regulated how slaves could be used. The abolitionist movement transformed enslaved people from being considered property without legal rights to being rights-bearing individuals. Women were treated as property under the law. If I was born 200 years ago, I would have been the property of my father, or my brother, or my husband. That meant that the rape of a woman was considered a property crime, and therefore the person charged with the crime had to pay damages to the husband of the wife for damage to his property, i.e. the rape. That's how women were treated under the law. We do not talk about that a whole lot. We tend to think of the women's rights movement as a movement for suffrage, but it was for quite a bit more than that. Women had to be transformed in the law from being considered property to being rights-bearing people, and I would argue that with both the abolitionist and the women's rights movements those struggles still continue. That is where nature sits today, nature is treated as property, and so it doesn't have the kind of legal protections that rights afford.

Legal rights are the highest form of legal protection that exist in legal systems everywhere. In 2006, my organization co-founder, Thomas Linzey, assisted a rural community in the US state of Pennsylvania to become the very first place to develop a rights of nature law. This was the first time anywhere, under law, that nature was recognized as having certain legal rights. Since then, more than three dozen communities across the USA in ten different states have established rights of nature laws: laws that declare nature has rights to exist, to thrive, to flourish, to regenerate, to be restored. And that has represented a fundamental transformation, moving from a property to a rights-bearing legal system in which we no longer treat nature as an other and as an object, but, in fact, as a subject of rights. That movement has now gone beyond the USA as well. In September 2008, Ecuador became the very first country in the world to recognize constitutional rights of nature, or what they call *Pachamama*. Bolivia has the Mother Earth law in place now. In Brazil, local communities have established the rights of nature in law. Uganda has established the rights of nature in law, and the Supreme Court of Bangladesh has recognized rights of all rivers. And in India, where no rights of nature laws are in place, a state court has recognized that the Ganga (the river Ganges) has certain legal rights under the law. The court determined that conventional environmental laws were unable to protect this river basin ecosystem, which half a billion people depend on. The court looked outside of India to understand what was taking place in the environmental sphere and applied the rights of nature in India. Since then, the same court has recognized rights of other ecosystems and species as well. In 2018, the Supreme Court of Colombia recognized that the Amazon region in Colombia has certain legal rights that protect it from deforestation and the impacts of climate change.

We are starting to see a movement built to secure the highest legal protections that exist in the law, legal rights for the natural world. Within this context, we wanted to understand what would it look like to bring the rights of nature into the city of New York, with a focus on trees and carbon offsets. This draft law for the city of New York starts off saying: "Whereas we the people of the city of New York recognize that we live at a time of unprecedented species extinction, ecosystem collapse, and global warming, whereas nature, particularly trees and forests are increasingly being used to offset carbon emissions, while humankind fails to take meaningful actions to address global warming pollution. And whereas in this time of environmental crisis, we recognize that to protect nature, we must secure its highest protection through the recognition of legal rights."

It has been drafted as a proposed amendment to the city charter of the city of New York. The actual rights proposed reads like this:

Nature within the city of New York, including ecosystems, natural communities, and species,

possesses rights to exist, thrive, regenerate and naturally evolve; rights to restoration; rights to a healthy, stable climate system; rights to a healthy natural environment free from human caused global warming impacts and emissions; and rights to not be used to offset human caused global warming.

The amendment itself is very carbon-offset-oriented, and very interested in trees and in recognizing nature and trees within the city of New York as having the highest form of legal protection through rights.

But there is still a lot of work to do. There are many who argue that this movement is focused on "giving" nature the same rights as humans, and treating nature as a human, or a legal person. Furthermore, critics argue that if nature has rights, it should also have responsibilities. First, it is absurd to hold nature responsible or consider nature as having obligations or liabilities. Nature performs its natural functions very well when human beings don't interfere with its natural processes. In addition, we tend to forget that we depend on nature, for clean drinking water, clean air, fertile soils where our food grows, species for medicines, a stable climate system, our very lives. The rights of nature movement is focused on protecting the ability of nature to exist in a healthy, robust, resilient way, with which human activity today is interfering and robbing nature of the ability to do. Thus, the movement is not focused on recognizing the same rights for nature as humans possess, rather it is focused on protecting the rights that nature must have protected in order to be healthy, robust, and resilient—something *our* very lives depend upon. This requires a recognition that our current legal systems are not enough to protect nature.

We must recognize that nature possesses legal rights, and establish a means to protect, implement, defend, and enforce these rights, and thus, protect nature. Our current legal system does not recognize nature as a living entity with legal rights; it was never intended to recognize nature's rights, and therefore it cannot contend with it properly. We need to create another legal system, another framework in which nature is treated as a rights/bearing, legal entity, where courts know how to handle these kinds of cases, and where our laws can be interpreted properly. Thus, we need to move beyond where our legal systems are today, towards *legal naturehood*.

The overlapping environmental crises that we face have been brought about by the rise of human interference with the natural world, through industrialization, extraction, and other activities. We have so fundamentally impacted the natural world, *even changing the Earth's atmosphere itself*, that people, communities, first nations and other governments are coming to a shared understanding that the kind of change that is needed must itself be fundamental—making an essential shift in humankind's relationship with the natural world—from one of exploitation, to one of protection. It's time for change.

THE RIGHTS OF TREES NOT
TO BE USED AS CARBON OFFSETS

In his ground-breaking 1972 essay *Should Trees Have Standing? Towards Legal Rights for Natural Objects*, environmental lawyer Christopher D. Stone raises provocative questions about the potential for granting legal rights to natural entities.[1] Since then, the field of international law has shown further interest in rights-based protections for nature. As environmental degradation continues, traditional environmental law is increasingly understood as inadequate for addressing the complexity of environmental crises.[2] In 2006, Tamaqua Borough in Pennsylvania became the first community in the USA to grant nature rights-bearing status. In the USA, the first state constitutional amendment to include rights of nature was proposed in Colorado in 2014. The city of Toledo, Ohio, granted non-human rights to Lake Erie in 2019 (although those rights were later invalidated in the district court); efforts are advancing in Oregon and New Hampshire. In some cases, however, the creation of protected areas and conservation zones is instrumentalized by emissions trading companies to prevent access to forests in order to keep "carbon stocks" intact, thereby displacing indigenous caretakers from their ancestral lands, cosmological relations, and resources essential for survival. This phenomenon of disenfranchisement, which produces "conservation refugees," also happens outside the global South. In cities in the global North, the quantified benefits of the environment impose an obligation on trees to perform as speculative assets in real estate development and environmental mitigation schemes, which has also brought about waves of green gentrification. Is it possible for a tree to own itself and therefore resist financial quantification? Supported by the Community Environmental Legal Defense Fund (CELDF), a draft for a new public ordinance aims to challenge cities to move beyond the extraction of financial services from trees—what trees are able to offset—and instead acknowledge the rights of trees. It takes into account the potential interests of trees as *rights-bearing* entities rather than as a source of profit for humans. Environmental personhood may not be the panacea, but it at least seems to be working as a legal tactic for challenging Western legal systems and their treatment of non-anthropocentric and non-extractivist world views. In parallel, as Mari Margil suggests, we have to keep working on a radically different paradigm, one that does not apply personhood to nature, but pushes us to imagine what "naturehood" may be.

[1]   C. D. Stone, *Should Trees Have Standing? Law Morality, and the Environment* (Oxford: Oxford University Press, 2010).

[2]   Community Environmental Legal Defense Fund (CELDF), *The Rights of Nature: Background*, November 2018 Report.

LOCATION: New York City

SPECIMEN: Ordinance printed on tree-free paper, 2019

PETITION TO AMEND THE NEW YORK CITY CHARTER TO ESTABLISH THE RIGHTS OF TREES

WHEREAS, we the people of the City of New York recognize that we live at a time of unprecedented species extinction, ecosystem collapse, and global warming;

WHEREAS, nature, particularly trees and forests, are increasingly being used to offset carbon emissions, while humankind fails to take meaningful actions to address global warming pollution; and

WHEREAS, in this time of environmental crises, we recognize that to protect nature, we must secure its highest protection through the recognition of legal rights.

THE FOLLOWING IS HEREBY DESIRED AND APPROVED TO AMEND THE NEW YORK CITY CHARTER

Statement of purpose. At all times, and particularly in this time of overlapping environmental crises, it is essential to protect nature with the highest legal protection, which includes taking meaningful action to reduce global warming pollution. Therefore, it is appropriate and necessary to secure legal rights of nature within the city and on city property. The establishment of Chapter 77 of the New York City Charter, and the provisions within it, fulfill this purpose.

The New York City Charter is amended by adding a new Chapter 77, to read as follows:

CHAPTER 77
RIGHTS OF NATURE

Section 3300. Rights of Nature.

(a) *Rights of nature.* Nature within the City of New York or on property owned by the City of New York, including ecosystems, natural communities, and species, possesses rights to exist, thrive, regenerate, and naturally evolve; rights to restoration; rights to a healthy, stable climate system; rights to a healthy natural environment free from human-caused global warming impacts and emissions; and rights to not be used to offset human-caused global warming emissions.

(b) *Rights as self-executing.* All rights secured in this Chapter are inherent, fundamental, and unalienable, and shall be enforceable against both private and public actors without further implementing legislation.

Section 3301. Prohibitions.

(a) *Prohibition on unlawful activities.* It shall be unlawful within the city or on property owned by the city for any public or private entity to engage in activities that would violate, or infringe upon, the rights guaranteed in this Chapter.

(b) *Prohibition on carbon pricing and offsetting.* It shall be unlawful for nature, including trees, within the city or on property owned by the city to be used to establish, maintain, or operate a carbon pricing, taxing, trading, credit, commodification, or other program or system intended to trade, offset, or otherwise compensate for fossil fuel or other polluting emissions that contribute to climate change. In addition, it shall be unlawful for nature, including trees, within the city or on property owned by the city to be used as part of any program or system intended to trade, offset, or otherwise compensate for fossil fuel or other polluting emissions that contribute to climate change.

Section 3302. Enforcement.

(a) *Enforcement by the city.* The city shall take all necessary actions to protect, implement, defend, and enforce the rights and prohibitions of this Chapter.

(b) *Enforcement by nature.* Nature within the city or on property owned by the city may enforce its rights and the prohibitions of this Chapter through an action brought in any appropriate court, in the name of the ecosystem, natural community, or species as the real party in interest.

(c) *Enforcement by residents.* The city, any resident of the city, or group of residents may enforce all of the provisions of this Chapter through an action brought in any appropriate court. In such an action, the city, resident, or group of residents will be entitled to recover all costs of litigation, including, without limitation, expert and attorney's fees.

(d) *Right to intervene.* Nature within the city or on property owned by the city, as well as any resident or group of residents, shall have the right to intervene in any action concerning this Chapter in order to enforce or defend it, and in such an action, other parties to that action shall not be deemed to adequately represent their particularized interests.

(e) *Damages.* Any business entity or government that violates the rights guaranteed by this Chapter shall be liable for any damages to an ecosystem, natural community, or species caused by the violation. Damages shall be measured by the cost of restoring the ecosystem, natural community, or species to its state before the injury, and shall be paid to the city to be used exclusively for the full and complete restoration, recovery, and protection of the ecosystem, natural community or species.

Section 3303. Effective Date.

This Chapter is effective immediately on the date of its enactment.

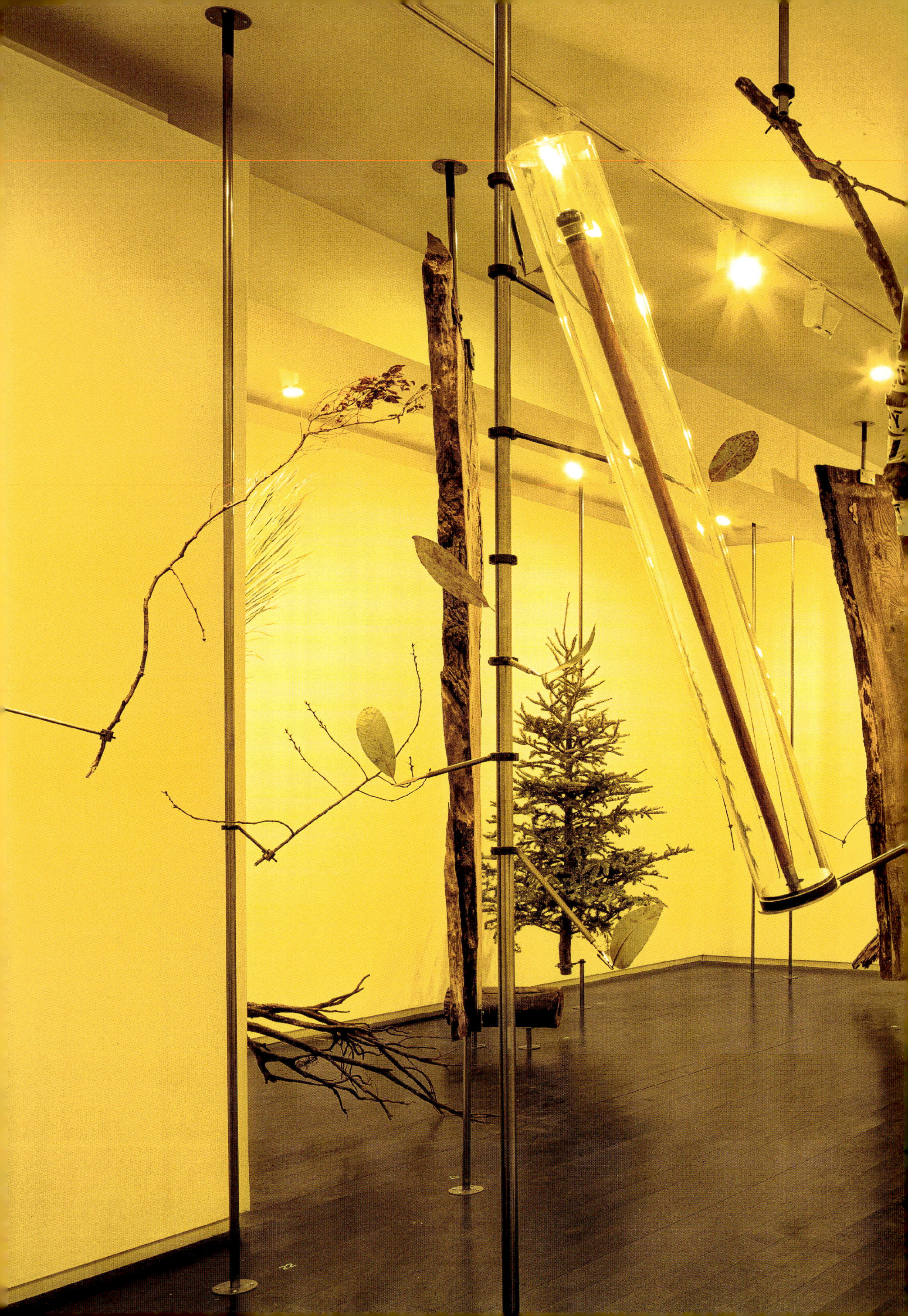

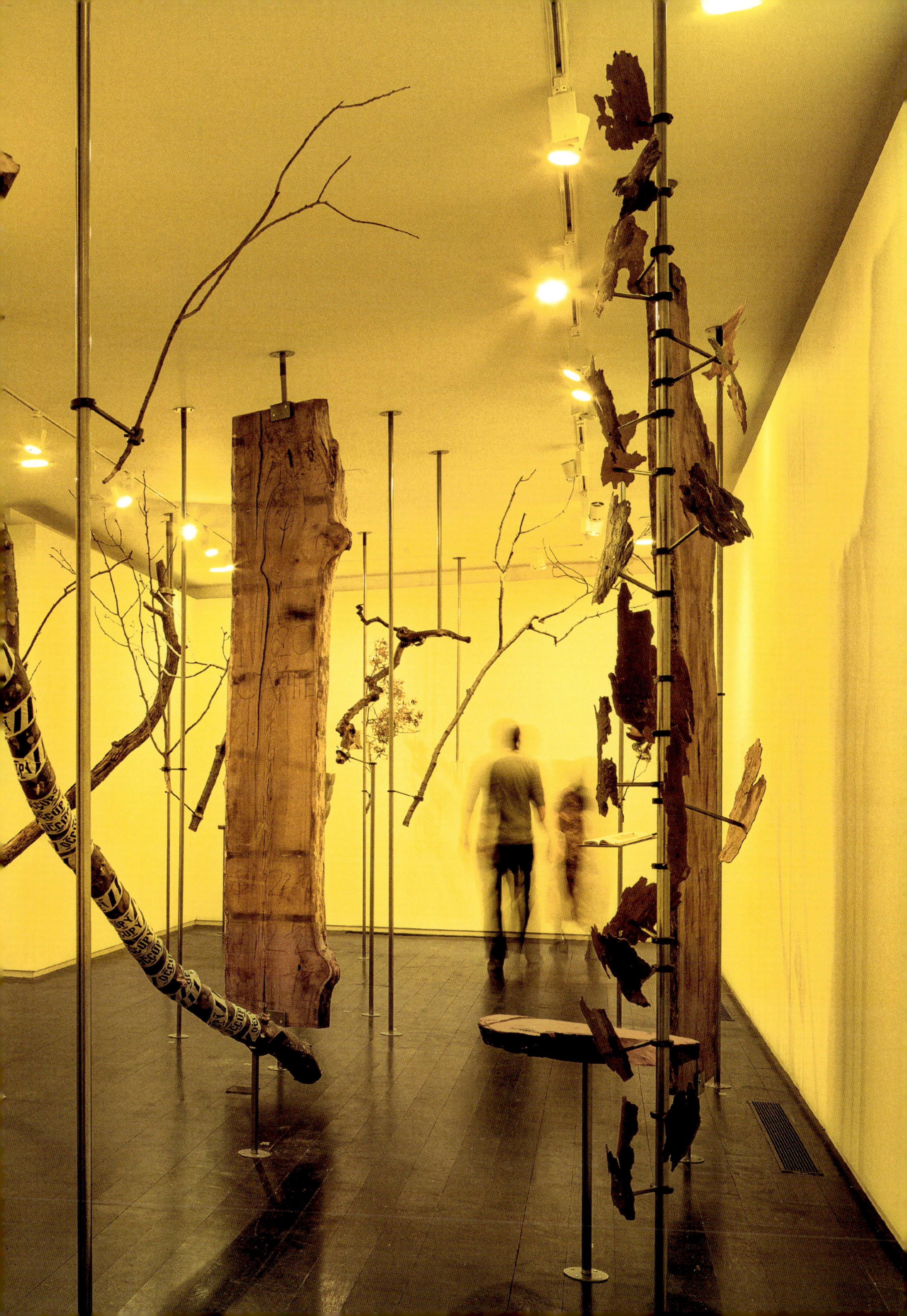

Biographies

NICO ALEXANDROFF is a research architect and designer. His work engages in the entangled relationship between politics, ecology and earth system science. He is currently a PhD candidate at the Royal College of Art researching cosmologies of ice in relation to climate collapse and is interested in how aesthetics can be used as a form of action. He was recently a member of the design-research think-tank at Strelka Institute of Design called 'The Terraforming' and currently teaches a MA Landscape Architecture design studio at UCL.

PENNY ALLAN is the Professor of Landscape Architecture at the University of Technology in Sydney. Her three most recent design research projects—MOVED to Design, Earthquake Cities of the Pacific Rim, and Rae ki te Rae—deal with the relationship between environment, culture, resilience, and design and have all received national awards.

ADENIYI ASIYANBI is the Assistant Professor in Geography at the Department of Community, Culture and Global Studies, I.K. Barber Faculty of Arts and Social Sciences, The University of British Columbia, Okanagan. He researches political ecology at the intersection of forests, climate change, and neoliberalism, focusing on forest-based climate change mitigation and wildfires. Niyi has a PhD in geography from King's College London.

MARTIN BRYANT is a Professor of Landscape Architecture at UTS and a practising landscape architect, architect, and urban designer. His globally significant research has been presented in an urban ecology and resilience policy paper he wrote for the United Nations Habitat III conference in Quito in 2017.

JESSE CONNUCK is an editor and researcher based in London. She is currently working on a PhD in geography at Queen Mary University of London, and was formerly the managing editor of Columbia Books on Architecture and the City. Her writing has been published in *frieze*, *The New Inquiry*, and *Harvard Design Magazine*, among other publications.

COOKING SECTIONS examines the systems that organize the world through food. Using site-responsive installation, performance, and video, they explore the overlapping boundaries between art, architecture, ecology, and geopolitics. Established in London in 2013 by Daniel Fernández Pascual and Alon Schwabe, their practice uses food as a lens and tool to observe landscapes in transformation. They teach a design studio at the Royal College of Art, School of Architecture.

MATTHEW DARMOUR-PAUL is a researcher and designer based in Sydney, Australia. In 2019, he co-founded Feral Partnerships, a collective that focuses on reclaiming architectural knowledge in an age of rapid biodiversity loss and species extinction as spatial practices in the pursuit of multispecies flourishing. Matthew has a BA in architecture from Iowa State University (USA) and holds an MA in architecture from the Royal College of Art (UK).

JAMES EWING is an artist engaged in illustrating architecture, landscapes, and scale models. Influenced by the tradition of architectural drawing, his works reference those of Hugh Ferriss, Ken Adams, and Frank Lloyd Wright. Prints have been exhibited at The Van Alen Institute in New York, Cité de l'Architecture et du Patrimoine in Paris, and The Arthur Ross Architecture Gallery at Columbia University GSAPP, among others.

KRISTEN LYONS is a sociologist with over 20 years' experience in research, teaching, and service that delivers national and international impacts on issues that sit at the intersection of sustainability and development, as well as the future of higher education. Kristen works regularly in Uganda, the Solomon Islands, and Australia, and her work is grounded in a rights-based approach. In practice, this means centring the rights and interests of local communities, including Indigenous peoples, in her approach to research design, collaboration, and impacts and outcomes. Kristen is also a senior research fellow with the Oakland Institute.

MARI MARGIL serves as the Executive Director of the Center for Democratic and Environmental Rights (CDER) and the program manager for the CDER's International Center for the Rights of Nature. Mari previously served as the Associate Director of the Community Environmental Legal Defense Fund (CELDF). In 2008, she served as a consultant to Ecuador's national Constituent Assembly, helping to draft the world's first Rights of Nature constitutional provisions. She is widely viewed as one of the leading global voices for the recognition of legally enforceable rights of ecosystems and nature.

GUILLERMO RUIZ DE TERESA is a curator, editor, and researcher in architecture whose work focuses on the intersection of space, state, and power. Trained as an architect at the Architectural Association and Universidad Iberoamericana, Guillermo received an MA in design studies at Harvard University's Graduate School of Design, and is currently the Stavros Niarchos Foundation PhD Scholar at the Royal College of Art's School of Architecture, where he is also a visiting lecturer.

HANNA RULLMANN is a London-based researcher, filmmaker, and designer, whose practice engages questions of conservation, environmental policy, border landscapes, and legal/political production of natures. She holds an MA from the Centre for Research Architecture at Goldsmiths, University of London, in 2018. She is part of the Border Ecologies Research Network and has worked as a researcher for Airwars and Amnesty. She is a visiting lecturer at the Royal College of Art's School of Architecture.

ISABEL SANDEMAN is an architect with a passion for regenerative design. She graduated from the Royal College of Art in 2017, where her work was shortlisted for the inaugural Architecture Drawing Prize and exhibited at the World Architecture Festival that year. Isabel now works for Feilden Clegg Bradley Studios, and is the co-author of their most recent publication *A Manifesto for Climate Responsive Design*.

HUHANA SMITH (NGĀTI TUKOREHE, NGĀTI RAUKAWA KI TE TONGA) is an artist and academic with wide-ranging experience in Māori visual art and museum practice, exhibition planning and implementation, indigenous knowledge, and science research. She is currently the Head of Whiti o Rehua | School of Art, Toirauwhārangi | College of Creative Arts, at Massey University, Wellington.

PABLO SOLÓN is a Bolivian social and environmental activist, the director of Fundación Solón and former executive director of Focus on the Global South. He joined the struggle against water privatization in Cochabamba (2000) and La Paz (2005), and coordinated the Bolivian movement against the Free Trade Agreement of the Americas (2001–2005). He served as the Bolivian Extraordinary Ambassador for Integration and Trade (2006–2008) and as the Ambassador to the United Nations (2009–2011).

DAVID SSEMWOGERERE is a rural development specialist based in Uganda. David holds an MA in rural development from Makerere University, Kampala, an undergraduate degree in development studies and a diploma in computer science and information technology. He is the founding director of Suubi Education and Community Development Centre, a Ugandan community-based development organization located in Lubanda Village, South Western Uganda.

IRENE SUNWOO is an architectural historian and curator. She is the John H. Bryan Chair and Curator, Architecture and Design, at the Art Institute of Chicago. At Columbia

GSAPP, Irene served as Curator of the Arthur Ross Architecture Gallery and as Director of Exhibitions (2016–2021). As Associate Curator of the inaugural Chicago Architecture Biennial (2015), she helped launch a new global platform for contemporary architecture. She received her PhD from Princeton University School of Architecture.

PAULO TAVARES is an architect, writer, and educator. His work has been featured in various exhibitions and publications worldwide, including *Harvard Design Magazine*, the Oslo Architecture Triennial, the Istanbul Design Biennale, and the São Paulo art Biennial. He is the author of the books *Forest Law* (2014), *Des-Habitat* (2019), and *Memória da terra* (2020), and was co-curator of the 2019 Chicago Architecture Biennial. He currently teaches spatial and visual cultures at the University of Brasília in Brazil and leads the architectural agency autonoma.

ROSA WHITELEY is an architectural researcher and designer based in London. Her work investigates how we have organised the world through toxic flows and how those flows, in turn, organise us. In 2021, Operaciones published Rosa's first book *In the Pink: Lively Architectures of a Death Cloud*. Rosa's work has been presented in Belgium, Germany, China, and the UK. She holds a BA(Hons) in Architecture from Manchester School of Architecture, and an MA in Architecture from the Royal College of Art, London.

Image Credits

Photo James Ewing: 34–35, 39, 41, 51, 53, 57, 67, 75, 77, 79, 81, 83, 85, 91, 93, 95, 97, 103, 105, 107, 109, 117, 119, 121, 127, 131, 133, 145, 149, 151, 159, 161, 163, 167, 168–169
Courtesy of Samuel F. Manning and Wooden Boat Publications: 37
Courtesy of Hanna Rullmann and Faiza Ahmad Khan: 42, 45
Courtesy of Hanna Rullmann: 43, 44
Reproduced under a Creative Commons Attribution-NonCommercial-ShareAlike 4.0 International (CC-BY-NC-SA) licence with the permission of the National Library of Scotland: 43
Courtesy of the Natural History Museum in London: 43
Drents Archief, J.B. Collection, Photo Schröer: 44
Courtesy of the British Ecological Society, *Journal of Ecology*, 17 (1) (1929), 152: 44
Données cartographiques © IGN, Planet Observer: 45
Borough of Manhattan, Department of Parks, Annual Report, 1930: 49
City of New York; Municipal Archives 1910–1919 50-E 14: 55
Courtesy of Nico Alexandroff: 58, 59, 60
Photo James Cheadle / Alamy Stock Photo: 58
Photo by Suzanne Kelly: 59
New York Public Library; General Research Division, extracts from the annual report: 63; Irma and Paul Milstein Division of United States History, Local History and Genealogy: 65 141
Courtesy of Huhana Smith, Penelope Allan and Martin Bryant: 68, 71
Drawing by Martin Bryant: 68
Photo by Penny Allan: 69
Photo by George Leslie courtesy of Adkin Alexander Turnbull Library, Wellington, New Zealand; Photographs of New Zealand geology, geography and the Maori history of Horowhenua. Ref: PA1-f-007-216: 70
Photo by Forest Starr and Kim Starr under a Creative Commons 3.0 (CC 30) licence CC 3.0: 72
Courtesy of Rosa Whiteley: 86, 87, 88
The Scottish Association of Marine Science, NERC INSITE, 2020: 87
Photo by Zephyr Douglas: 99
Courtesy of Isabel Sandeman: 99, 100
Photo by Chester Higgins Jr/*New York Times*/Redux/eyevine: 105
Courtesy of Matthew Darmour-Paul: 123, 124.
The J. Paul Getty Museum, Los Angeles: 129
Photo by Tyko Kihlstedt: 143
Photo by Benjamin Swett: 147
Photo by Joel Enqueri Nequimo: 153
Courtesy of Fundación Solón: 154, 155

Acknowledgements

This book has been produced by the Royal College of Art's School of Architecture with the generous support of the Graham Foundation for Advanced Studies in the Fine Arts.

This research project was part of a 3-year Advanced Design Studio (ADS3) led by Cooking Sections at the Royal College of Art in London, from 2016 to 2019. ADS3 (2016–2019) participants include Shawn Adams, Nico Alexandroff, Umi Baden-Powell, Stacey Barry, Rebecca Bradley, Tatiane Britto, Ibiye Camp, Andrew Copolov, Joel Cunningham, Matthew Darmour-Paul, Matteo De Bellis, Shiqi Deng, Josephine Devaud, Rhiarna Dhaliwal, Samuel Evans, Beth Fisher, Caroline Fok, Tobias Griffiths, Khushboo Gupta, Daniel Hawkins, Harold Keene, Tanya Kramer, Farouk Kwaning, Svitlana Lavrenchuk, Dika Terra Lim, Yujun Liu, Charlotte Moore, Giulia Moretti, Charles Redman, Jonathan Riley, Maria Saeki, Isabel Sandeman, Yuanxu Tang, June Tong, Claudia Walton, Chi-Jen Wang, Rosa Whiteley, Sam Yaghmaei, and Feifei Zhou.

Offsetted was first conceived as a lecture on resilience at Storefront for Art & Architecture, New York, and was then expanded into a lecture-performance for Performa 17, New York, 2017. The project then developed into an exhibition organized by Irene Sunwoo at the Arthur Ross Architecture Gallery of the Graduate School of Architecture Planning and Preservation (GSAPP) at Columbia University. The exhibition, which ran from February to June 2019, was supported by curatorial assistants Daqian Cao, Matthew Darmour-Paul, and Charlotte Grace, as well as the GSAPP exhibition team: Tiffany Lambert, Maria E Perez Benavides, Thomas Chiu, Axelle Dechelette, Oscar DeLeon, Christine Giorgio, Fernanda Gebaili Basile Carlovih, Jenn Kim, Lucy Navarro, and Nika Teper. This publication wouldn't have come to fruition without the incredible work of our editor Jesse Connuck, managing editor Guillermo Ruiz de Teresa, and the design of An Endless Supply. We are also extremely grateful for Adrian Lahoud, the Dean of the School of Architecture, Royal College of Art for his foresight and commitment to this book.

Special thanks are also due to Charles Aubin, Nick Axel, James Ewing, Eva Franch i Gilabert, Daniel Hawkins, Sarah Herda, Beth Hughes, Sam Jacoby, Liz Koslov, Bill Logan, Carlos Mínguez Carrasco, James Pike, and Felicity D. Scott.

Offsetted
Cooking Sections
(Daniel Fernández Pascual & Alon Schwabe)

Contributors: Nico Alexandroff, Penny Allan, Adeniyi Asinyabi, Martin Bryant, Matthew Darmour-Paul, Kristen Lyons, Mari Margil, Hanna Rullmann, Isabel Sandeman, Huhana Smith, Pablo Solón, David Ssemwogerere, Irene Sunwoo, Paulo Tavares, Rosa Whiteley
Editor: Jesse Connuck
Managing Editor: Guillermo Ruiz de Teresa
Copy Editor: Rich Cutler

Design: An Endless Supply
Project Management: Valerie Hortolani, Hatje Cantz
Production: Vinzenz Geppert, Hatje Cantz
Lithography: Repromayer, Reutlingen
Printing and Binding: Graspo CZ, a.s.

Typefaces: Garamond No8 and Lars AES
Paper: GalerieArt Silk 115gsm and Munken Print White 1.5 300gsm
from responsible sources according to FSC standards

Published by Hatje Cantz in cooperation with the Royal College of Art

Hatje Cantz Verlag GmbH
Mommsenstraße 27
10629 Berlin
www.hatjecantz.com
A Ganske Publishing Group Company

This book has been funded with support from the Royal College of Art and the Graham Foundation for Advanced Studies in the Fine Arts.

ISBN 978-3-7757-5199-5

Printed in the Czech Republic